I LOVE you!

KALIE ♥

LIBERTY HYDE BAILEY

LIBERTY HYDE

Bailey

Essential Agrarian *and* Environmental Writings

Edited by

Zachary Michael Jack

Cornell University Press
Ithaca and London

First published 2008 by Cornell University Press

Printed in the United States of America

Library of Congress Cataloging-in-Publication Data
Bailey, L. H. (Liberty Hyde), 1858-1954.
  [Selections. 2008]
  Essential agrarian and environmental writings / Liberty Hyde Bailey ;
edited by Zachary Michael Jack.
    p. cm.
  Includes index.
  ISBN 978-0-8014-4709-9 (cloth : alk. paper)
    1. Agriculture.   2. Nature conservation.   3. Environmentalism.
4. Country life.   I. Jack, Zachary Michael, 1973–   II. Title.   III. Title:
Liberty Hyde Bailey.
  SB63.B3B35 2008
  630—dc22
  2008014063

Cornell University Press strives to use environmentally responsible
suppliers and materials to the fullest extent possible in the publishing
of its books. Such materials include vegetable-based, low-VOC inks
and acid-free papers that are recycled, totally chlorine-free, or partly
composed of nonwood fibers. For further information, visit our
website at www.cornellpress.cornell.edu.

Cloth printing   10 9 8 7 6 5 4 3 2 1

To
Liberty Hyde Bailey,
naturally, and for the holy
earth, always

The sower and the seer each
Down life's unending way
Held fast his single speech
And lived his sep'rate day.

For one man cast his seed
And sped the coupled hours,
He stored his treasured meed
And plucked his garden flow'rs.

And one man stood alone
Where all the world was his,
All things that men have known
And all that was and is.

Alack, all ye that sow
And alack, ye that see,
No longer shall ye go
All sep'rate and unfree:

For one shall make far quests—
The other 'side him fare
And come back from the crests
With star-winds in his hair.

—Liberty Hyde Bailey, "Sower and Seer,"
   from *Wind and Weather* (Scribner, 1916)

Contents

Editor's Preface   xi
  "Sower and Seer": Essential Agrarian and
  Environmental Writings of Liberty Hyde Bailey

Introducing Sower and Seer, Liberty Hyde Bailey   1

I. WORKMANSHIP   39
  "My Father's Hoe" *40*
  "The Honest Day's Work" *44*
  "Nails" *49*
  "From Haying-Time to Radio" *52*
  "Soil" *60*
  "The Daily Fare" *64*

II. CONSCIENCE   77
  "The Separate Soul" *79*
  "The Struggle for Existence: War" *84*
  "The Keeping of the Beautiful Earth" *89*
  "The Habit of Destruction" *92*
  "The Country-life Phase of Conservation" *98*
  "The Middleman Question" *106*

III. EDUCATION   110
  "The Integument-Man" *112*
  "The Meaning of the Nature-study Movement" *115*

Contents

"The Fundamental Question in American
    Country Life" *127*
"The Outlook to Nature" *132*

IV. COMMUNITY   135
    "The Brotherhood Relation" *137*
    "The Neighbor's Access to the Earth" *143*
    "Country and City" *154*
    "The Principle of Enmity" *158*
    "Democracy, What It Is" *162*

V. NATURE   166
    "The Ways to Approach Nature" *168*
    "The Forest" *172*
    "The Spiritual Contact with Nature" *177*
    "The Holy Earth, the Statement" *180*

VI. FARM   188
    "The Democratic Basis in Agriculture" *190*
    "The National Movement" *195*
    "Women's Contribution to the
        Country-life Movement" *203*
    "One Hundred and Twenty-nine Farmers" *208*

VII. POETICS   216
    "What Literature Can Do for Us" *217*
    "The Threatened Literature" *223*
    "The Tones of Industry" *226*

VIII. APPRECIATIONS   228
    "Apple Tree" *229*
    "Wind" *231*
    "Rain" *235*
    "Weed" *239*
    "Peach" *242*

"Horse" *244*
"Evening" *248*
"Morning" *250*

IX. CODA, THE AGRARIAN WAY 254
"Journey's End" *255*

Index 259
About the Editor

Editor's Preface

*Sower and Seer: Essential
Agrarian and Environmental Writings
of Liberty Hyde Bailey*

One hundred years after President Theodore Roosevelt handpicked the foremost agrarian of his era, Liberty Hyde Bailey, to chair a once-in-a-lifetime investigation of rural life known as the Country Life Commission, a Liberty Hyde Bailey resurrection is well underway. As always, it is difficult to account for the precise moment when a historical figure, unbidden, makes a curtain call; factors collude, suggesting a few borrowed words foreign in their intimations: *zeitgeist* or *milieu*. For the literary soul, the resurgent interest in Liberty Hyde Bailey as eco-critic and sage conjures Dickens's ghosts with Bailey as a beneficent visitation, an important haunting—well-timed for our moment of ecological crisis.

In the cold light of day, more logical explanations persist. We attribute a Liberty Hyde Bailey renaissance to a distinct demographic shift, a census-verified "decentralization" repopulating nonmetropolitan areas. We look to predictable one-hundred-year cycles of U.S. history implicit in Mark Twain's witticism "History doesn't repeat itself, but it does rhyme." Digging deeper, we look to the renewal of a biocentric worldview among the current generation of college students, the Millennials, more popularly known as Gen Y, for whom authors Neil Howe and William Strauss (*Millennials Rising: The Next Great Generation*), posit leadership potential rivaling that of the Greatest Generation. Certainly, in the contemporary recommissioning of mothballed collegiate environmental studies majors and minors drawn up in the 1970s, we see still more concrete evidence of Gen Y's Earth-first convictions. Finally, we point to our disastrous dependence on foreign oil and resultant moves toward a bio-economy as good reason for a consensus upgrading of Bailey's environmental stock and cultural currency. High crop prices coupled with a shortage of young farmers means national planners must contend again with Middle America, and especially with Bailey's home region, a broader heartland encompassing the traditional midwestern Corn Belt and reaching as far east as upstate New York. For such a world as this, Liberty Hyde Bailey waits, uncannily well positioned for a comeback.

Former Vice President Al Gore's popular reinvention as a Nobel Prize-winning eco-critic proffering inconvenient climate-change truths intimates a renewed environmental consensus, what Bailey called in 1915 a "New Hold." History shows that we, as a public, choose our leaders based in part on what they pledge to protect. Thus we hired Lincoln to protect our Union; Kennedy to steward our vision; Clinton to safeguard an economic boom. In the next generation, we elect with an eye toward preserving the Earth for our children.

Such a new cultural dawn calls to mind the figure known as the Green Man—a nature motif carved in religious sites and on sacred artifacts found across Europe and as far away as India. Different from the prodigiously rounded fertility figurines of pre-Christendom or the more androgynous Greek representations of the Earth goddess Gaia, the visage of the Green Man sobers more than titillates. The image, called the "foliate mask," confronts us with the face of a wise wild man—imagine, in Shakespearean terms, a mixture of Prospero and Caliban, Theseus and Puck. The ecclesiastical carvings of this natural sage—common from the eleventh century on—suggest the unexpected; namely, the Green Man as a Christian as well as a pagan motif. Of course any iconography arguing woods and wilds as possessed of divine wisdom rather than barely controlled chaos—as imbued with a masculine as well as a feminine principle—challenges conventional, New Age symbology in crucial ways. Liberty Hyde Bailey—botanist, horticulturalist, and agriculturalist; teacher, writer, philosopher, poet, and public servant—is arguably the twentieth century's most rounded embodiment of the Green Man principle.

Liberty Hyde Bailey aside, the last one hundred years have given us few true Green Men of national stature. Two notable exceptions persist—John Muir, with his inimitable combination of environmental advocacy, fieldwork, and ecstatic, arboreal wanderings—and Wendell Berry, whose foundations in salt-of-the-earth farming uniquely credential him as a leading eco-cultural critic. There have been countless others, of course—naturalists, ecologists, scientists, artists, actors, musicians, and politicians—who have argued persuasively for a biocentric worldview; they, too, are Green heroes and heroines. Closer examination, though, shows their power derived largely from a particular profession or discipline, and their rhetoric, however sincerely impassioned, failed to sustain a popular environmental movement. Even fewer of our Green Men and Women have remained culturally relevant across generations, or have had anything more than token attentions paid them by movers and shakers in business and government. Even Aldo Leopold, Bailey's most direct ecospiritual descendant, was almost certainly a greater influence on subsequent generations than on his own. Other contenders for the century's leading agrarians, Iowans Henry A. Wallace and Norman Borlaug, established themselves as civic-minded agriculturalists and humanitarians par excellence, but, measured against the Green Man standard, lacked a sense of wilderness.

As the general introduction that follows makes clear, Liberty Hyde Bailey, uniquely, brings the worlds of nature, agriculture, environment, and education together in a singularly relevant package. The Progressive Era he studied and wrote about echoes, more than any other period in the twentieth century, our own. Like Wendell Berry and Al Gore in our time, Bailey made explicit those threats posed to peace-loving people by finite natural resources, social inequity, environmental degradation, and governmental abuses. His many books examined previously unseen ecologies linking democracy, war, citizenship, community, environment, nature, education, literature, and ethics to a larger national identity. And yet Bailey as cultural critic and political commentator was far from an ideologue, partisan, or zealot. Somehow Bailey, an avowed Democrat and one of the "great country-minded liberals" according to Bailey contemporary and rural sociologist Charles Josiah Galpin, seemed to transcend political boundaries. Bailey, a religious man who saw God everywhere in nature, early and enthusiastically adopted Darwinism. Bailey, the "liberal," was repeatedly asked to run for political office as a member of Teddy Roosevelt's post-presidential party, the Progressives; Bailey, the Democrat, served at the pleasure of then-diehard-Republican Roosevelt on a Country Life Commission whose findings cast a harsh light on the rural civilization of which Bailey was a part. These profoundly productive ambivalences constitute what poet John Keats lauded in Shakespeare as "negative capability"; namely, a temperament that allows "uncertainties, mysteries, doubts, without any irritable reaching after fact and reason." Long vexing to pigeonholing types, Bailey's wonderfully compound nature—careful scientist and exuberant poet, steady husbandman and spirited wilderness advocate, studied professor and giddy nature-study for children advocate—is both the source of his greatness and a factor in his previous neglect by hidebound scholars. Bailey's brand of energetic, environmentally minded interdisciplinarity anticipates the methodology of recent surprise best sellers including those penned by Richard Louv (*Last Child in the Woods*) and Michael Pollan (*The Omnivore's Dilemma*).

As a fourth-generation farmer's son and the product of an Iowa Heritage Farm owned and continuously operated by my family for over 150 years, I am not unfamiliar with the agrarianism of Liberty Hyde Bailey. But it is not, either, second nature. Though I grew up on a farm, I pursued my education in the cities. And though I still call our family farm home, I work in a midwestern city labeled a "technoburg." What I mean to say is this: The agrarianism of Lib Bailey, though I am sympathetic to it, is a challenge to me in this new millennium, and it is a challenge I welcome. Born into a generation said to care not a whit for history, I find it deeply satisfying to reintroduce Bailey to my and to my parents' generation, for whom Wendell Berry often seems the only agrarian hit. Extending the billboard analogy, reading Bailey in preparation for Berry is listening to a scratchy recording of Woody Guthrie before turning, with a newly appreciative ear, to Bob Dylan.

Truth be told, I grew up on an Iowa farm, went to school, graduated college, accepted my first tenure-track teaching job, and founded an agrarian summer school for children without ever having heard of Liberty Hyde Bailey. Dimly, I was aware a star of his magnitude existed, or ought to exist, but I had yet to see it for myself. As a young adult with a rural background, I, like so many others, read Wendell Berry's *The Unsettling of America* and felt therein a shock of recognition, as with a long-lost friend. And while I sensed a deeper impulse, a fountainhead bubbling up somewhere below Berry, my gee-whiz reaction to *The Unsettling* preempted further divining. How grateful I am, now, to have discovered the pure source of much of Berry's thinking—and not just Berry's, mind you, but also Aldo Leopold's, Wes Jackson's, Victor Davis Hanson's, Gene Logsdon's, Barbara Kingsolver's, Linda Hasslestrom's, and the other members of the honor roll of contemporary agrarians, the keepers of the flame.

Any movement or ideology, any *ism* if you will, must have, acknowledge, and hold its own history, gently and knowingly, before it may be fully brought to bear. Toward that good end, *Liberty Hyde Bailey: Essential Agrarian and Environmental Writings,* this first-of-its-kind, contemporary compilation, aims to serve. Bailey's words add heft to an important branch of the agri-environmental family tree at the exact point where agriculturalism and environmentalism, too-often divergent, join to form a sturdy branch.

My great-grandfather's soil conservation classic *The Furrow and Us* (1946) stands alongside Liberty Hyde Bailey's works in the Core Historical Literature of Agriculture at Cornell University. Though I am proud of my great-grandfather, who described himself modestly as an "Iowa dirt farmer" in his book's dust jacket, I mention the connection here not to brag about kin but to suggest deeper connections between contemporary agrarians and environmentalists and oft-forgotten forebears such as Bailey—"grandfathers" begging to be rediscovered. In his essay "From Haying-Time to Radio," Bailey himself wrote:

> Grandparents have peculiar significance in agriculture, for good farming is an affair of more than one lifetime. If one desires a real mark of cleavage between farming and what we are pleased to call business, one will find it here—in the

fact that the land remains generation after generation and that it passes down as men come and go, home and all, carrying the same essential enterprises.... Farming is the only occupation that constantly renews itself: it is a perpetual resurrection.

Liberty Bailey knew his roots as a botanist, naturalist, educator, and agriculturalist went back to Asa Gray, Louis Agassiz, Henry David Thoreau, Jethro Tull, and Charles Darwin, among others. In studying the agrarian and environmental essays of Liberty Hyde Bailey, we do our own long-overdue source work.

After researching my earlier exploration of distinguished farmer-teachers, *Black Earth and Ivory Tower: New American Essays from Farm and Class-room,* and reissuing my great-grandfather's *The Furrow and Us,* I felt my own agrarian roots reinvigorated. My great-grandfather's family, I learned, knew Herbert Hoover's family, having made their farm home less than a mile away from the Hoover house in West Branch, Iowa. My grandfather Edward, an Iowa conservation farmer and seedcorn salesman, knew Henry A. Wallace, the founder of Pioneer Hybrid seedcorn and later vice president and Progressive candidate for president. And Henry A. Wallace's personal hero was none other than Liberty Hyde Bailey, with whom his own grandfather, "Uncle Henry" Wallace, had worked on the prestigious Country Life Commission.

And so we return again to our deepest roots, to springs and fountain-heads; we follow the river to its source.

THE general introduction following offers a thorough biography of Liberty Hyde Bailey accompanied by critical analysis. Its aim is not to indulge histories either revisionist or conventional but, first and foremost, to make a thoughtfully edited digest of Bailey's oeuvre available, richly contexted, to the next generation of scholars and general readers. To that end, typographical errors in the source editions have been corrected where noted and minor changes in punctuation and usage have been made to conform to contemporary style. Stanzas from Bailey's agrarian poems as they appeared in his sole book of verse, *Wind and Weather,* are deployed herein as tone-setting section breaks. Elsewhere, where selections deviate substantively from their presentation in the original volumes, explanatory footnotes have been added.

When the voices of the past begin to speak, our first charge, I think, is to listen.

ZACHARY MICHAEL JACK

Jones County, Iowa

LIBERTY HYDE BAILEY

Introducing Sower and Seer, Liberty Hyde Bailey

Before Wendell Berry and Wes Jackson, before Aldo Leopold and Henry A. Wallace, there was Liberty Hyde Bailey.

In fact, the works of Wallace, Leopold, and Berry, arguably the most influential land-use voices of the twentieth century, all evoke Bailey as a seminal influence. For Vice President Henry A. Wallace, whose grandfather, "Uncle Henry" Wallace, served on the Country Life Commission with Bailey, Bailey was a personal hero. For Wendell Berry, he was a revelation, a symbol of the nature-minded agrarianism Berry himself popularized for the Boomer gen eration. For Aldo Leopold, Bailey offered a model of the scholar-essayist naturalist, so much so, in fact, that the foremost contemporary scholar of environmental history, Roderick Nash, cites Leopold's direct "intellectual debt to Liberty Hyde Bailey."[1] Most recently, in his 2006 release *The Landscape of Reform*, scholar Ben Minteer tell us that Wes Jackson channeled the "Bailey legacy" into his program of sustainable agriculture at The Land Institute. Further, Minteer claims, Bailey's work extends well beyond neoagrarians to echo "across a number of canyons in contemporary environmental thought and practice." Minteer cites Bailey's foundational role in popularizing "ecotheological" writing and environmental ethics while acknowledging his legacy as an impetus for contemporary, secular manifestations of Earth awareness, including the 1992 Rio Summit, the Land Stewardship Project, and the Forest Stewardship Council. Minteer concludes that Bailey's work is "clearly an important historical source for the 'caretaker' ethic in the air today" and declares Bailey's most long-lived book of environmental philosophy, *The Holy Earth,* to be a "classic of the genre."[2]

---

1. Roderick Frazier Nash, *Wilderness and the American Mind,* 4th ed. (New Haven: Yale University Press, 2001), 194.

2. Ben A. Minteer, *The Landscape of Reform: Civic Pragmatism and Environmental Thought in America* (Cambridge, MA: MIT Press, 2006), 46, 49, 50.

In all matters agricultural, environmental, and scientific, Bailey offers an unprecedented resume that includes the chairmanship of Roosevelt's famous Country Life Commission, the editorship of the influential journal *Country Life in America,* and the undisputed, ceremonial "deanship" of disciplines ranging from horticulture, to botany, to agriculture. Ever the virtuoso, Bailey assumed leadership of a dizzying variety of disparate organizations, including presidencies of the American Society of Horticultural Science, the American Association for the Advancement of Science, the Country Life Association, and the Botanical Society of America. Along the way he was decorated with medals from the Royal Irish Academy, the National Institute of Social Science, and the Société Nationale d'Acclimatation de France, among countless others. Scholars and biographers have called him "one of the greatest agricultural leaders...the world has ever known"[3]; a purveyor of a "prophetic ecological worldview"[4]; and "America's best-known plant scientist."[5] In a career spanning more than fifty years, Bailey authored in excess of sixty-five books and edited nearly twice that, a "nearly superhuman rate" of scholarly production.[6] Along the way he popularized nature-study in U.S. classrooms, lobbied successfully for women's rights on and off the farm, and bulwarked Teddy Roosevelt's pioneering conservationism.

In addition to long hours and unrivaled talent, one secret to Bailey's unparalleled productivity as a writer was a two-birds-with-one-stone brand of efficiency. Contemporary researchers have often been surprised to see retooled passages from the author's earlier works; for example, a passage from *What Is Democracy?* (1918) reprinted with minor changes in *The Harvest of the Year to the Tiller of the Soil* (1927). As a lifelong university lecturer working from notes, building on the intentional amplifications such digests made possible was a natural for Bailey, as it was for many agricultural writers of his era, including, most notably, "Uncle Henry" Wallace, whose beloved books for farm boys were often reworkings of his "Sunday School lessons" from *Wallaces' Farmer.* Indeed, partially as a result of such purposeful duplications, Bailey wrote so much of such high quality that he himself lost track of his bibliographic achievements. At the ninetieth birthday party thrown him by Cornell University President Edmund Day, Bailey said with characteristic

---

3. Paul Work, "Liberty Hyde Bailey," *Market Growers Journal,* December 1952, 24.

4. Paul Morgan and Scott J. Peters, "The Foundations of Planetary Agrarianism, Thomas Berry and Liberty Hyde Bailey," *Journal of Agriculture and Environmental Ethics* 19, no. 5 (2006): 461.

5. Alan Carlson, *The New Agrarian Mind: The Movement Toward Decentralist Thought in Twentieth-Century America* (New Brunswick: Transaction Publishers, 2000), 7.

6. Minteer, *Landscape of Reform,* 20.

modesty, "I have written books. I suppose that several hundred have gone through my hands as editor."[7] In 2004, an actual accounting was undertaken by Cornell University in its invaluable electronic exhibit "Liberty Hyde Bailey: A Man for All Seasons," which counts 117 titles edited by Bailey from 1890 to 1940, confirms Bailey's count of 65 books authored single-handedly, and adds 1,300 articles and over 100 papers on pure taxonomy to this remarkable reckoning.[8]

Regrettably, such productivity has partially obscured the full impact of Bailey's legacy, as the sheer volume and breadth of Bailey's writing has daunted some scholars. Citing his dizzying output as a potential explanation for scholarly neglect, two of the most productive Bailey researchers of the new millennium, Paul A. Morgan and Scott J. Peters, lament, "Bailey wrote so much and only a small amount is available to the casual researcher." Moreover, Morgan and Peters add, "Scholarly evaluation has been hampered by the unavailability of much of his writing, and...this has contributed to incomplete and faulty analysis."[9]

This volume, *Liberty Hyde Bailey: Essential Agrarian and Environmental Writings,* amends both deficiencies, separating the wheat from the chaff, appropriately. Here for the first time is a Bailey anthology suitable for the general and scholarly reader alike, offering a comprehensive introduction to Bailey's revolutionary thinking on agriculture, nature, community, and education, among other topics. The selections in this carefully chosen "best-of" have been handpicked from Bailey's nontechnical books, especially the prose works from the seven-volume Background Books series. Diverse selections for this anthology have been made from five of the most important Background volumes: *The Holy Earth* (1915), *Universal Service* (1918), *What Is Democracy?* (1918), *The Seven Stars* (1923), and *The Harvest of the Year to the Tiller of the Soil* (1927). And in deference to Bailey's fine reputation as a poet of the natural world, brief poetic excerpts from a sixth book, the sole volume of verse in the Background series, *Wind and Weather* (1916), are included as section breaks. In these Background books, aimed at nonspecialists, Bailey best articulates the agrarian esprit de corps.

Appropriately, *Liberty Hyde Bailey* also features prose from Bailey's work in the nature-study and the Country Life movements, preserving the organic, whole-Earth consciousness of farm and nature for which Bailey argues so

7. *Words Said About a Birthday: Addresses in Recognition of the Ninetieth Anniversary of the Natal Day of Liberty Hyde Bailey* (Ithaca, 1948).

8. Cornell University Division of Rare Manuscripts, *Liberty Hyde Bailey: A Man for All Seasons.* 2004, http://rmc.library.cornell.edu/bailey/writings/index.html.

9. Morgan and Peters, "Foundations," 452.

persuasively and lyrically in *The Holy Earth*. Additional essays included in this anthology, then, have been selected from *The Nature-Study Idea* (1903), *The Outlook to Nature* (1905), and the *Country-life Movement in the United States* (1911). Rounding out the readings, the brief, opening chapter from Bailey's *The Apple Tree* (1922), a book Bailey biographer Philip Dorf cites as including "some of [Bailey's] most lyrical prose writing"[10] leavens the mix. In sum, ten of Bailey's most influential books are herein represented.

Applying similar logic, Norman Wirzba collected the work of Liberty Hyde Bailey spiritual heir Wendell Berry in *The Art of the Commonplace*, citing Berry's prolific writing—"well over thirty books in the form of poetry, short story, novel and essay"—as necessitating a thoughtful, digestible grouping. The book, a great boon to agrarian scholars and lay readers alike, represents an effort, Wirzba writes, to "return us to the fundamental questions of human existence: 'Who are we? How does our life with others affect this self-understanding? What is a properly human desire? What are the limits and possibilities of communal life? How do we form an authentic culture? What are the conditions of peace and joy.'" That Bailey wrestled with these same questions a century ago argues for a long-view of the agrarian vision. "Agrarianism, in other words," Wirzba continues, "promises a path toward wholeness with the earth, with each other, and with God, a path founded upon an insight into our proper place within the wider universe."[11]

Liberty Hyde Bailey, One Hundred Years Later

Despite a resurgence in interest in agrarianism, Liberty Hyde Bailey is, one hundred years after heading the prestigious Country Life Commission, both overlooked and underappreciated, notwithstanding a flurry of articles in the last decade partially reestablishing his prominence. Morgan and Peters, as noted, offer a full page of analysis of the previous scholarly overlooking of Bailey's work. They identify, among other possible explanations, the unprecedented volume and interdisciplinary tenor of Bailey's writing as a challenge to discipline-bound scholars, scholars who, even if they are willing to undertake the genre- and mind-bending Bailey oeuvre, have difficulty locating it.[12] Though Morgan and Peters overlook it as a factor,

10. Philip Dorf, *Liberty Hyde Bailey: An Informal Biography* (Ithaca: Cornell University Press, 1956), 181.

11. Norman Wirzba, ed. *The Art of the Commonplace: Agrarian Essays of Wendell Berry* (Washington, DC: Counterpoint, 2002), xix, xx, viii.

12. Morgan and Peters, "Foundations," 452.

Bailey's employment at a university for the first twenty-five years of his working life also appears to have undermined, unfairly, his "credentials" as an environmentalist, in particular. In an era when the standard for the naturalist-seer was the rugged, fiercely independent John Muir, an equally progressive visionary on a university payroll seemed something less than bona fide, at least in the popular imagination. In one of the first Country Life analyses undertaken after Bailey's death in 1954, scholar William Bowers posits an anti-intellectual backlash by which the rural public often unfairly scorned "professors, authors, and other intellectuals as 'impractical men' whose statements should be ignored."[13] Of course, no one could dispute Bailey's resume as a plant scientist, agriculturalist, and nature-study advocate, though they could, and did, discount his equally prescient environmentalism vis-à-vis the "Muir standard."

Environmentalist stereotypes aside, Morgan and Peters move closer to the truth of Bailey's underestimation in identifying the uncanny span of his publishing career, 1885 to 1953, the last forty years of which Bailey devoted almost exclusively to groundbreaking botanical studies far away from the U.S. media. Indeed, by his own choice, Bailey, the foremost agrarian of his era, eschewed the limelight after 1913—coincident with his official retirement as Dean of the Cornell Agricultural College—to pursue the life plan he had made as a young man: twenty-five years for training, twenty-five for service, and twenty-five for, as he put it, "doing the things that interested him most."[14] In short, Bailey achieved the highest possible rung in agriculture, horticulture, botany, and nature-study, retired, and never looked back. Like a legendary slugger, it seemed, he hit a homerun and disappeared into the crowds forever. Myths of Bailey's last "at bat" abound. Biographer Dorf writes that one popular, though unsubstantiated, tale of Bailey's swan song recounts Professor Bailey locking the office door on his fifty-fifth birthday, walking out of Cornell University's Roberts Hall, and never coming back.[15]

Bailey's most prescient book, *The Holy Earth,* manifests the singular push and pull Bailey felt: At the same time that he was regarded as the most accomplished figure in early twentieth-century agriculture, he remained one of the industry's strongest critics. *The Holy Earth* embodies such dualities; it neither privileges "environmental concerns nor did it deny economic realities; it merely included them in an integrated mix."[16] *The Holy Earth,*

---

13. William Lavalle Bowers, *The Country Life Movement in America, 1900–1920* (Port Washington, NY: Kennikat Press, 1974), 50.
14. Dorf, *Liberty Hyde Bailey,* 35.
15. Ibid., 159.
16. Morgan and Peters, "Foundations," 460.

which has been reprinted several times and remains in print today, reads eerily like Wendell Berry, even as it predates the classic *The Unsettling of America* by almost a half century. Bailey's prototypical ecological and environmental statements have prompted commentators in the new millennium to classify *The Holy Earth* as "the first manifesto of planetary agrarianism"[17] and a "template for environmental agrarianism."[18] Moreover, *The Holy Earth* merits renewed attention for what scholar Ben Minteer calls its "ecospiritual reflections,"[19] assertions by which Bailey challenges the anthropomorphism—the people-centeredness—of Christendom itself, while, at the same time, codifying a theological reverence for God's creation. Here again, Bailey walks an improbable tightrope, as he had in reconciling evolution with Christian dogma. Minteer stops short of crediting Bailey with coining the twentieth-century "biocentric or life-centered"[20] worldview, though he argues that Bailey's visionary thinking led him "to the doorstep" of such an epiphany. However, the cautious Minteer argues that even a conservative read of Bailey's legacy positions him alongside Muir as "one of the earliest advocates of a nonanthropocentric position in the tradition of American environmental thought."[21]

To assign the revolutionary Bailey a place on the agrarian-environmentalist continuum, then, proves no easy task. Certainly, a new generation of scholars has been right to place him at the very foundation. Because, while Bailey is kin to Wendell Berry, Wes Jackson, Gene Logsdon, and other contemporary farmer-naturalist-environmentalists, Bailey himself is sufficiently original as to appear to have sprung, full-grown, on the early twentieth century. Casting afield for Bailey precedents, one would certainly have to consider Charles Darwin, whose *Origin of the Species* young Bailey read, enraptured, as a Michigan farm boy in the 1860s. Darwin, too, was a visionary, a combination of poet-naturalist-scientist-scholar-adventurer, as Bailey himself would become. Like Bailey, Darwin grew up in a religion-minded household but cultivated a spirit of open theological inquiry requisite to his studies. Darwin, however, the son of a well-to-do society doctor, knew little of farming, especially American farming. Thomas Jefferson, Renaissance man, statesman, educator, and Virginia gentleman planter, offers another compelling Bailey analogue. But Jefferson was not a prolific publisher, authoring just one book in his lifetime, and Bailey eschewed Jefferson's bread-and-butter–politics, ignoring repeated

---

17. Ibid., 450.
18. Ibid., 452.
19. Minteer, *Landscape of Reform*, 42.
20. Ibid., 45.
21. Ibid.

calls that he run for high office. Among other possibilities, it is certain the great Harvard botanist Asa Gray influenced Bailey, as it was Gray who gave Bailey his start as a Harvard lab assistant and showed him the value of studying science directly from, and in, nature. Even so, Gray's influence proved limited, as he disparaged the then-emerging applied science of horticulture, the very discipline that would become Bailey's entrée to international fame. Put simply, Bailey is an American original, full of rich contradiction and unparalleled intellectual range.

The Frontier Years

Born to a pioneering South Haven, Michigan, farm family on March 15, 1858, Liberty Hyde Bailey grew up among the Indians, tradesmen, and plowmen of the then "western" frontier. The industry, dynamism, and localism of the frontier remained with Bailey the rest of his life, as did the profound sense of loss that accompanied the ravages of the unchecked plow and the droves of land-hungry homesteaders. In his address to those gathered in honor of his ninetieth birthday, the usually reserved Bailey spoke of three-hundred Pottawatomie Indians who were allowed to coexist peaceably on his father's farm, and of their hunts for the abundant passenger pigeons that would soon become extinct. Bailey's witness to the ultimate horror of overzealous settlement is revealed in the Edenic tenor of his earliest memories, times when "Animals were in their places in the woods and they were all good. Whatever the human beings might have been in that community...the animals, at least, lived sensible lives."[22] This sense of loss, permeating Bailey's otherwise forward-looking and optimistic work, reverberates in his successor, Wendell Berry, who, in counting his blessings for having been born in the days before widespread, on-the-farm mechanization, recalls in his essay "A Native Hill": "It is strange to think how barely in the nick of time it came to me. If I had been born five years later I would have begun in a different world, and would no doubt have become a different man."[23]

The writing of Liberty Hyde Bailey records for posterity the days before the early and needless divorce of the farmer-rancher and the naturalist, preserving these salad days for twenty-first-century generations in whose collective conscious the farmer typically stands for either enviable simpleton or environmental villain. History confirms the substance of Bailey's nostalgic claims, as in 1893, just six years after Bailey entered college, University of

22. Dorf, *Liberty Hyde Bailey*, 28.
23. Wirzba, *Art of the Commonplace*, 4.

Wisconsin historian Frederick Jackson Turner declared the U.S. frontier all but closed in a speech delivered at the Chicago World's Fair. Three years later, Turner echoed his World's Fair remarks in a school dedication, wondering aloud what would become of his countrymen now that the Wild West had ceased to be wild in men's imaginations and could no longer serve as a "safety valve for social danger, a bank account on which they might continually draw to meet losses."[24] Coincident with Turner's declarations, the era's leading agrarians and preservationists were then rising to prominence in the once "frontier" states of Michigan, Wisconsin, Illinois, and Iowa.

In Bailey's youth, however, the Midwest, as it came to be known, still exhibited frontier traits, existing as a liminal space where the best and worst of the American character were writ large on the U.S. landscape. Bailey, for example, experienced many of the same natural wonders and stern agrarian realities of fellow midwestern naturalist John Muir, who, like Turner, hailed from Wisconsin. Far from any organized libraries, Bailey was a product of a country school, augmenting his studies with what few books and edifying visitors happened to cross his path. Like another agrarian leader of the era, "Uncle Henry" Wallace of Iowa, Bailey's early life in Michigan was touched by tragedy, as young Bailey lost his mother to diphtheria and his eldest brother Dana to scarlet fever before he reached the age of five and was left to do a man's share of farm work alongside his remaining brother, Marcus. Like Muir, whose Wisconsin boyhood is richly detailed in his autobiography *The Story of My Boyhood and Youth,* Bailey exhibited a poetic as well as a practical sense; he was inclined toward philosophical and botanical rumination as much or more than manual labor. Bailey's father, a transplanted New England "Puritan" by his son's account, is reported to have expressed wry doubt about his ability to raise the frail, wandering Liberty Bailey to manhood. But while John Muir would cultivate the life of the self-educated nature savant, Bailey would choose a different route, declaring to his no-nonsense farm father his intentions to attend Michigan Agricultural College, now Michigan State University in East Lansing, where he enrolled in 1877.[25]

At Michigan, Bailey was, as one might expect, precocious, editing the newspaper, *The College Speculum,* excelling in his studies, and earning the acknowledgment of his peers as the top student at the college. Among even his farmed-vested associates, Bailey was better prepared than most for a scientific examination of agriculture, having worked alongside his father

24. Jim Cullen, *The American Dream: A Short History of an Idea That Shaped a Nation* (Oxford: Oxford University Press, 2003), 142.
25. Dorf, *Liberty Hyde Bailey,* 35.

in the Bailey family apple orchards that featured more than 400 trees of every variety.[26] Like a young Theodore Roosevelt, who published a study of Adirondack bird life while still in his teens, the young Bailey was a gifted ornithologist, having become expert on avian activity in the home orchard. Bailey's ornithological paper was reprinted with fanfare in the Pomological Society's Annual Report for 1873, where records from the South Haven society note the election of "Master Liberty Bailey as Ornithologist of this Society."[27] In some ways Bailey's meteoric rise at Michigan Agricultural College (MAC) was, while remarkable, far from anomalous, as other agrarian leaders of the era, including Uncle Henry Wallace and Theodore Roosevelt, enjoyed similar good fortunes and attained comparable accolades at an equally early age. What set Bailey apart was the pace of his advancement as well as the notice it garnered in high places. While other future farm and nature leaders of his generation played at campus newspapers and literary societies, Bailey used his collegiate editorial post as a springboard to national prominence, as his farm-focused editorials in the *Speculum* gained favorable reviews on and off campus. Indeed, Bailey turned to journalism as a means of survival after his junior year at MAC, when an inner-ear ailment causing a chronic and dangerous loss of balance forced him to take a year away from college to convalesce in his brother's home in Springfield, Illinois. There he wrote occasional, country-oriented news and features for the Springfield *Daily Monitor* before returning to MAC for his senior year after successful surgery on his ear.

After a senior year in which he was elected president of the Natural History Society and head of the student government association,[28] Bailey graduated from Michigan Agricultural College, looking to become a professional newspaper man in Springfield. And he nearly accepted a permanent job as city editor on the *Daily Monitor* but for a fateful telegram from Dr. William Beal, Bailey's former professor of botany and horticultural at MAC.[29] The telegram intimated another, finer prospect—a post at Harvard as Asa Gray's lab assistant. At the time, the aging Gray was an internationally renowned botanist directing the Harvard herbarium and botanic gardens. Though the lab assistant job paid substantially less money than the newspaper gig and would delay his goal of being financially "settled" in order to ask for the hand of Annette Smith, all agreed Bailey should assume the post without

26. H. Roy Mosnat, "He Is Your Garden's Best Friend," *Better Homes and Gardens*, October 1930, 68.
27. Dorf, *Liberty Hyde Bailey*, 27.
28. Ibid., 41.
29. Ibid., 44.

delay. In introducing his former pupil, Dr. Beal is reported to have said, "Meet a real genius."[30]

Though Bailey made the sensible decision in opting for an apprenticeship with Gray and a subsequent career in botany, the conundrum did cause him a dark night of the soul, as his later allegorical account, *The Seven Stars*, makes clear. In it, an idealistic young man with a poetic bent and a love for nature waxes philosophic about the changing world around him. The protagonist's muse is a young lady named Winneth, a character likely based on Bailey's real-life future wife, Annette Smith. In the book's final chapter, the young, symbolically named character Questor receives a letter from his beloved encouraging him to "find a real rather than an expedient anchorage."[31] "It is not for me," she writes, "to find the mainspring of your life for you. If it is not real with you, than it will not last."[32] With arrangements made for his trip to Cambridge, Massachusetts, Bailey asked for Smith's hand, and they married in Pine Lake, Michigan, in June of 1883, a few short days before embarking on their trip east to Harvard.

Annette's guiding counsel was once again evident when, nearing the end of his appointed term at the Harvard herbarium, Bailey parted ways with the great scientist Gray to accept a professorial position in an as-yet-unknown field, horticulture—the science or art of growing fruits, vegetables, flowers, or ornamental plants—at Bailey's alma mater, Michigan Agricultural College. Gray and others considered horticulture beneath botany, as it was not, they claimed, a "real" science—positioned, as it was, somewhere between the manual labor of the farmer-gardener and the experimental, laboratory-based work of the scientist. Bailey biographer Dorf reports that, upon learning of his assistant's new appointment, Gray himself demanded of his young charge, "What do *you* know about horticulture?"[33] A sterner rebuke came from established botanist-educator John Merle Coulter, who warned Bailey that his acceptance of the job at Michigan would mean that he would "never be heard from again."[34] Here once more the fates of the century's two foremost agrarians, Liberty Hyde Bailey and Wendell Berry, exhibit an almost eerie resonance, as Berry recounts, in his essay "A Native Hill," a strikingly analogous encounter with an elder faculty member at New York University. As Berry makes his intentions to return home to Kentucky clear to his mentor, he comes face to face with the older man's bias, a belief "long

---

30. Mosnat, "He Is Your Garden's Best Friend," 68.
31. Liberty Hyde Bailey, *The Seven Stars* (New York: Macmillan, 1928), 158.
32. Ibid., 159.
33. Dorf, *Liberty Hyde Bailey*, 51.
34. Ibid., 48.

honored among American intellectuals and artists and writers, that a [home] could be returned to only at the price of intellectual death; cut off from the cultural springs of the metropolis, the American countryside is Circe and Mammon."[35]

Bailey, always the farmer's son, followed his heart to Michigan and set to work developing the MAC horticultural program as a one-man department. True to his upbringing, he began in the College's apple orchard, where he carried on experiments in grafting, pruning, feeding, tilling, and spraying that proved sufficiently successful as to compel publication in he *Speculum* of the following notice to students: "Now boys don't go over into that orchard; if you do have occasion to go, however, don't steal any apples; but if you do steal apples, do not under any circumstances steal green ones."[36] In 1885, junior professor Bailey was tested by the American Pomological Society and certified "excellent" in his field, earning the Marshall P. Wilder Bronze Medal for his berries, nuts, and other fruits.[37] His teaching methods also proved remarkable, further distinguishing him from his lab-coated mentors and prefiguring the hands-on, extension-minded pedagogy that would become the norm at land-grant agricultural universities thereafter. Bailey, for instance, both lectured about berries and joined his students in picking them, according to the *Speculum*.[38] At Lansing, Bailey quickly became a popular teacher precisely because, when he could not take his students out into the woods or fields, he brought nature and agriculture to his horticultural disciples in the form of field specimens. He was also not afraid to read poetry to them, serving notice to all his young protégés that horticulture was an art as well as a science. To understand living things, he argued, required both imagination and rational analysis.

The newness of the agricultural college, of applied agricultural science, and of horticulture, in particular, made Bailey's first years as a professor at his alma mater heady ones, as he found an eager audience for his research not only among his students but among readers. By the end of his first year teaching at Lansing, Bailey had published his first book with Houghton Mifflin, *Talks Afield: About Plants and the Science of Plants* (1885). While primarily a technical manual, Dorf's analysis of the book points to Bailey's citation of Shakespeare as an early sign of a distinctive literary as well as scientific predilection. Bailey's second book, *Field Notes on Apple Culture*, published the following year, was dedicated to his father, "the results of whose

35. Wirzba, *Art of the Commonplace*, 6.
36. Dorf, *Liberty Hyde Bailey*, 52.
37. Ibid., 55.
38. Ibid., 53.

teachings are embodied in these pages." Unfortunately, the frenetic pace of Bailey's scholarly and pedagogical achievement meant that his upkeep of the campus grounds, then a common charge for faculty at agricultural colleges, was less than impressive. Of a young professor's aesthetic inattentions, Dorf quotes a sympathetic MAC President Willis as saying, "Bailey's genius lies in other fields. You don't hitch a race-horse to the plow."[39]

As in any field in its infancy, the possibilities in horticulture seemed limitless. Bailey taught, and his students learned, with confidence that horticultural skills would be in demand. It surprised no one, then, when Bailey himself got a call from the "big leagues" in the form of a job offer from Cornell University to head their horticulture department. Not only had Bailey published two books in his first two years at the College, he had succeeded in convincing the State Board to build the first campus horticultural building in the country, while concurrently earning his Master of Science degree. In explanation of the academic thrust of his efforts, Bailey proclaimed, "Horticulture the art is old; horticulture the science is new." Among the administration at MAC it was viewed as inevitable that Professor Bailey would once again head east to exist at the nexus of the then-emerging fields of rural sociology, agriculture, horticulture, and nature-study. Cornell University proved a logical post, as Bailey had completed a winter-vacation stint as a visiting lecturer there in the waning days of 1887. Not long into the spring semester, Cornell president Charles Kendall Adams called on Bailey in Lansing with an attractive offer—$3,000 a year in salary, complete control over the horticulture department, and an expenses-paid trip to Europe where the new hire would begin collecting specimens for the herbarium. At MAC, the loss of a favorite professor, and a native Michigan son at that, was a difficult pill to swallow, though the *Speculum* put the best face on it, summarizing, "While his going is a decided loss to this college, it is a loss of which the college may justly be proud and reflects a great credit upon Professor Bailey."[40]

At Cornell, Professor Bailey could build a program of his own design, from the ground up. He joined just one other professor in applied agriculture, Isaac Phillips Roberts, likewise a farm boy, though lacking Bailey's academic credentials. The gruff Roberts, who lacked an advanced degree and who joked that he matriculated at "Brush College" in upstate New York, found an invaluable teammate in Bailey, as he discovered his junior colleague to be unusually persuasive, and gladly ceded to him the job of fund-raising and trustee-lobbying.

39. Dorf, *Liberty Hyde Bailey*, 56, 60.
40. Ibid., 59, 63.

Bailey at Cornell

Early on in his days at Cornell, Bailey proved himself a writer as well as a scholar; indeed, his prodigious output showed the two roles, teacher and scholar, to be inseparable. From 1889 to 1896, Bailey authored the majority of the bulletins issued by the Cornell University Experiment Station. Resolved to take advantage of the popularity of farm and garden books, he was then "possessed" with the idea that he needed to write books in a way that would appeal to a large and diverse readership. His informed, straightforward style—at once impressionistic and scientific—was, according to biographer Dorf, "worthy of rank with the best of Burroughs, Muir, and Emerson." While the early works were brought out by Bailey's colleagues at the Rural Publishing Company, a subsidiary of the *Rural New-Yorker* journal, they were not distributed on a national scale, which prompted Bailey to move on to Macmillan. Macmillan would, by word of its president, George P. Brett, publish anything Bailey wrote as fast as he could write it, so great was their faith in both the burgeoning market and Bailey's place in it. Within five years of Macmillan's carte blanche, Bailey had delivered eleven books, most on gardening and agriculture and some, including *Plant Breeding* (1895), *Survival of the Unlike* (1896), and *Sketch of the Evolution of Our Native Fruits* (1898), on plant genetics and evolution. Reviewers, if not somewhat incredulous at the scholarly outpouring, nonetheless gave positive reviews. One of these reviewers, Charles R. Barnes, vice president of the American Association for the Advancement of Science and a professor of botany at the University of Chicago, enlisted an appropriately botanical metaphor in writing, "Professor Bailey is a living disproof of the doctrine that over-productiveness is at the expense of the quality of the fruit."

Beyond the acquisition of necessities, Bailey spent the royalties from his aggressive publishing program on two loves—agricultural books and, more important, a summer lakefront retreat north of Ithaca. The summer home, which Bailey would dub Bailiwick, allowed Liberty, his wife Annette, and their two daughters, Sara and Ethel Zoe, to leave town seasonally for environs more like Bailey's native farm and woods. At home in Ithaca during the academic year, the Bailey clan lived in a house they built on the Cornell campus, a place Bailey named Garden Home in homage to the specimens he transplanted there from his boyhood stomping grounds near South Haven, Michigan. The garden itself visually represented Bailey's growing advocacy of nature-study, which he argued could fill a spiritual void for a country increasingly urban. Dorf reports that when visitors to Garden Home remarked on the straightness of the owner's garden rows, Bailey would intimate that he had sewed them on his knees, an appropriate posture, given the holiness of the endeavor.[41] As a garden and nature-study guru, Bailey was a natural, empowering amateur and would-be green thumbs to try and err, to experiment, to plant their hearts' desire. "I know poets who do not write poetry,"[42] Bailey wrote, suggesting by analogy that it was indeed possible to be a born gardener who had not yet uncovered his deepest talents. Money was not the key to a good garden, he maintained, nor necessarily was order, but love and enthusiasm. And for those who didn't have room for a garden, Bailey recommended a flowerpot or, failing that, a simple stroll through a park. In any case, he recommended nature as a cure for "melancholies."[43] It was the nurturing of life that proved wholly instructive, metaphysically indispensable. "One never knows a plant until one grows it and cares for it from first to last in all its vicissitudes," he maintained.[44] And though Bailey's garden and horticulture writings were often directed at the urbanite and suburbanite, he also recommended botanical beautification for the stoic farmer, for whom he suggested ornamental flowers should be as important as a cash crop.

While Bailey advocated an anything-goes love of gardening, his desire to protect his readers from outdoor fads and trends led him to develop definite opinions on the most egregious landscape and nature-study gimmicks. In 1903, when naturalist John Burroughs published his inflammatory essay "Real and Sham Natural History" in the *Atlantic Monthly*, the balloon of popular nature writing was burst, as Burroughs and nature writer Dallas Lore Sharp spoke out against "nature fakers" then writing sensationalist or sentimental accounts in popular periodicals. Bailey, considered by many Burroughs's heir apparent, maintained a similar cynicism about what Sharp had criticized as "unnatural natural history."[45] Writing in 1908, Sharp grudgingly acknowledged a "fad just now to adopt abandoned farms, to attend parlor lectures on birds, and to possess a how-to-know library."[46] Bailey, gatekeeper in the worlds of horticulture and agriculture, registered similar alarm. He did, not, for example, endorse rock gardens, in part for their lack of vegetation. Similarly, he did not like effortful abstractions of "landscape art" of the kind typified by painted rocks and sculpted trees; he deemed nature's own beauty sufficient. He particularly disliked decorative fences, which, in disagreement with the classic Robert Frost poem, he found to be unnecessarily dividing.

41. Ibid., 74–78, 80–82.
42. Mosnat, "He Is Your Garden's Best Friend," 68.
43. Dorf, *Liberty Hyde Bailey*, 82.
44. Ibid.
45. Dallas Lore Sharp, *The Lay of the Land* (Boston: Houghton Mifflin, 1908), 118.
46. Ibid.

Echoing others of the era who believed schoolyards should inculcate true nature appreciation, Bailey wrote that America's schools, so crucial in forming a child's character, should carefully avoid such landscape transgressions. In understaffed urban schools or one-room country schoolhouses, Bailey suggested the children themselves should be enlisted in the cleaning, planning, preparing, and planting of greenery. In editing a new edition of his mentor Asa Gray's classic text *Field, Forest, and Garden Botany* (1895), which Bailey had eagerly read as a young man in Michigan, he took up the mantra of naturalist Louis Agassiz, who famously claimed "Study nature— not books." Bailey's books devoted to nature-study, including *The Nature- Study Idea* (1903) and *The Outlook to Nature* (1905) reflect his commitment to raising children with an appreciation for the natural world. Resisting educational hardliners who decried nature-study as so much whimsical dabbling at the expense of requisite theoretical science, rote, and drill, Bailey, in sympathy with youth, declared, "Nature-study is not a science. It is not knowledge. It is not facts. It is spirit. It is concerned with the child's outlook on the world."[47] More to the point, Bailey wrote, "If it were possible for every person to own a tree and to care for it, the good results would be beyond estimation."[48] Confirming Isaac Phillips Roberts's regard for him as a man of purpose, Bailey put his nature-study principles into action, forming the American Nature-Study Society (ANSS) in 1908, and serving as its first president. The ANSS, the oldest environmental organization in America, also underwrote the *Nature-Study Review Journal,* which helped to further the nature-study gospel.

Such strong and, at the time, radical prescriptions concerning nature and community seemed only to increase the public's demand for Bailey's consultations. In the last few years before the turn of the century, a young Professor Bailey accepted countless invitations to speak on all matters of land-use. His job title at Cornell, "Professor of Practical and Experimental Horticulture," encompassed pomology, floriculture, crops, and landscape gardening,[49] making him the horticultural equivalent of the family doctor. When communities came calling with a malady, it was not atypical for Bailey to offer holistic advice on everything from the necessity of public paths to community recreation centers. Already, Bailey's efforts across the U.S. landscape, inclusive of town and country, were being noticed, as the Royal Horticultural Society of London awarded him an honorary medal

47. Liberty Hyde Bailey, *The Nature-Study Idea* (New York: Doubleday, 1905), 5.
48. Cornell University Division of Rare Manuscripts, http://rmc.library.cornell.edu/bailey/ naturestudy/naturestudy_1.html.
49. Dorf, *Liberty Hyde Bailey,* 89.

in recognition of his efforts to advance the cause of horticulture. With his editing of the exhaustive, four-volume *Cyclopedia of American Horticulture* (1900–1902), Bailey further solidified his reputation as the premier expert in all matters horticultural. The book, for which Bailey served as principal contributor as well as editor, was greeted with effusive reviews from, among others, the *New York Daily Tribune,* which called it a "monumental performance" that would "probably never be superseded."[50]

In country matters, Bailey's star was also rising, as, with the success of the *Cyclopedia of American Horticulture,* a title that quickly became the gold standard, he began work on a four-volume companion *Cyclopedia of American Agriculture* (1907–1909), which he would complete less than five years later. As an encyclopedist, Bailey was unrivaled. Writing in 1930, some thirty years after its initial publication, H. Roy Mosnat called the *Cyclopedia of American Horticulture,* "truly the standard work on that extensive subject" and "the cornerstone of the horticultural library."[51] At the time of Mosnat's writing, "this monumental work" had already gone through "edition after edition."[52] As late as 1952, when Paul Work profiled Bailey for the *Market Grower's Journal,* the *Cyclopedia* and Bailey's *Manual of Cultivated Plants* were praised as "prodigious" labors, and Bailey's book *Hortus* (1930), Work maintained, remained "the standard reference."[53] That Bailey would undertake two definitive cyclopedias in separate disciplines within the same decade was just one measure of his unprecedented scholarly reach. During the same period, Bailey also undertook the editing of what quickly became the first-class magazine of rural life, *Country Life in America.* Here as before, he both edited the magazine and served as a principal contributor. And, though Bailey used the upstairs of the carriage house at his new, on-campus Ithaca home, Sage Place, as the "headquarters" of the periodical, he made it a point to get out and survey conditions on the ground. In one series of articles for *Country Life in America,* Bailey traveled to farms in every region of the country, documenting for his readers how the differing personalities of the owners, coupled with the particular demands of each region and crop, made farming far more diverse than urban dwellers might imagine.

Significantly, Bailey's growing reputation as the foremost authority on rural life came at a time when America was undergoing a back-to-the-land craze that promised to reverse an earlier cityward migration. In academe the

50. *New York Daily Tribune,* 1900, quoted in Dorf, *Liberty Hyde Bailey,* 119.
51. Mosnat, "He Is Your Garden's Best Friend," 40.
52. Ibid.
53. Work, "Liberty Hyde Bailey," 24.

popularity of the country in general, and the farm in particular, was implicit in the establishment of agricultural programs of study such as the one run by Professors Roberts and Bailey at Cornell Agricultural College. Indeed, while Bailey had originally arrived at Cornell to find one colleague, one building, and a handful of students, by 1896 Cornell had already moved to establish an official College of Agriculture within the larger University. By 1904, Bailey had been appointed dean of the College and had succeeded in lobbying the New York legislature to fund his program as well as to declare it the official State College of Agriculture. By 1907, when the back-to-the-land craze peaked with country-loving Teddy Roosevelt occupying the nation's highest office, the U.S. hinterlands themselves become a natural obsession, a canvas for the nation's utopian aims. Though he listened to Country Life movement schemes that ranged from moving the unemployed to resettle the nation's once-abandoned farmhouses to housing delinquents in farm-based reformatories, Dean Bailey consistently urged caution. As a farmer's son, he knew that taking up the plow was different than mere garden idling. Thus, while some observers expected Bailey to cheerlead a countryward movement with the unbridled enthusiasm with which he championed nature-study, they found, instead, a carefully qualified endorsement. If the city man wanted to become a farmer, Bailey said, let him first serve as a hired man or apprentice on an actual working farm. In the same way, he advised, homebuyers should regard with trepidation sales pitches made by realtors, then as now, advertising the "little farm well-tilled"[54] as escape. As an alternative to the neophyte purchasing a farm based on propaganda alone, Bailey suggested a summer home—the kind of middle ground between home and away he himself had found at his retreat along the shores of New York's Lake Cayuga. For Bailey, the pressing question was not how to make more farmers, or swell the population in the country, but how to keep the best family farmers on the land. Here, the city dweller with agrarian sympathies could be useful in buying the farmer's products directly, in paying the farmer a fair price, and in privileging the quality workmanship of the farmer-craftsman. In his attempt to educate the consumer rather than flood the country with would-be ruralites, Bailey proved he had the farmer's best interests at heart. For the society as a whole to be healthy, he reiterated, it had to take care of its farmers, which meant farmers first had to obtain a standard of living comparable to that of a city denizen.

To the cause of farm women Liberty Bailey was particularly empathetic because he realized, as did other rural policymakers of his day, that necessity

54. Dorf, *Liberty Hyde Bailey*, 146.

dictated the farmer and the farmer's wife work as a unit. At Cornell, Dean Bailey moved quickly to appoint Cornell's first women professors, beginning with nature-study pioneer Anna Botsford Comstock in 1899 and Martha Van Renssler and Flora Rose in 1911. And though these appointments strengthened the Department of Home Economics as a division within the College of Agriculture, Bailey made it clear that women were not to feel confined there. In a Cornell Reading Course Bulletin from 1913, Bailey declared, "I would not limit the entrance of women into any courses of the College of Agriculture; on the contrary I want all courses open to them freely and on equal terms with men."[55] Bailey's sympathies for women at home on the farm were based on a careful, compassionate gathering of feedback under the auspices of the College's Farmer's Reading Course. In one notable letter dated 1901 and addressed "To the Farmer's Wife," Bailey opens by saying "In all the vocations of life, there are none in which success depends so much on the wife as in farming."[56] In the very next paragraph, Bailey urges the farmer's wife to "talk back" so that he and his colleagues could get a handle on the most vexing issues facing often voiceless farm women. He concluded with a reminder that return postage would be paid by the State on behalf of the College of Agriculture. Indeed, Bailey got more than he bargained for, as 2,000 women responded with their assessment of domestic life on the farm.[57] Elsewhere in his extension writings, Bailey mobilized women's efforts for the betterment of rural life in general. On the subject of sanitation and running water in the country, for instance, Bailey played the role of provocateur, advising country girls to decline all proposals from suitors who failed to promise them running water and a usable kitchen once married.[58] In section six of the *Report of the Country Life Commission*, entitled "Women's Work on the Farm," Bailey lodged emphatic claims on behalf of the nation's farm women, arguing that "the relief to farm women must come through a general elevation of country living" and that, as it was, the "burden of...hardships falls more heavily on the farmer's wife than on the farmer himself."[59] Bailey's interest in retaining all that was best in country life for the entire farm family while ameliorating rural shortcomings via scientific study earned him the presidency of the Association of American Agricultural Colleges and Experiment Stations in 1906.

55. Cornell University Division of Rare Manuscripts, http://rmc.library.cornell.edu/bailey/womeneducation/index.html.

56. Cornell University Division of Rare Manuscripts, http://rmc.library.cornell.edu/bailey/womeneducation/womeneducation_1.html.

57. Ibid.

58. Dorf, *Liberty Hyde Bailey,* 149.

59. *Report of the Country Life Commission and Special Message from the President of the United States* (Spokane, WA: Chamber of Commerce, 1911), 44.

Agricultural experiment stations, established with the farmer in mind, also served as a vehicle for exchange between key farm and environmental players in government and higher education. It was inevitable, then, that two of the leading agrarians and conservationists of the early twentieth century, Teddy Roosevelt and Liberty Hyde Bailey, would meet. Roosevelt had been on the bill with Bailey in the 1907 meeting of the Association of American Agricultural Colleges and Experiment Stations and had been impressed with Bailey's moving and poetic speech about the haunting prospects facing family farmers. In particular, Roosevelt admired Dean Bailey's refusal to point fingers. "The remedy," Bailey had asserted, "is not complaint or recrimination, but an earnest and patient effort to undo the wrong."[60] In President Roosevelt, Bailey had found a logical supporter. Roosevelt was a native New Yorker and one-time Badlands rancher enamored of the strenuous life hard hewn from the land, a Jeffersonian in his support of the farmer as foundational man, and a tireless, charismatic mover of men. Moreover, Roosevelt, as a Progressive, believed that education and science could improve the quality of life for all Americans, particularly for the hard-pressed and marginal—fitting descriptors for farmers who had weathered recent economic downturns to remain on the land.

Bailey's speech was still on Roosevelt's mind the following year when he formally invited Dean Bailey to serve as chairman of a proposed Country Life Commission. Bailey feared this chairmanship, if agreed to, would entangle Cornell University in national politics, particularly with an election year approaching. Roosevelt, sensing Bailey's hesitation, made his pitch in person in Washington, D.C., where Bailey agreed to serve on one condition: that his former student, now president of Massachusetts Agricultural College, Kenyon Butterfield, likewise be appointed. For Roosevelt, who later admitted that he would likely have abandoned the idea of a commission without Bailey at the helm,[61] a Butterfield was well worth a Bailey. The investigative body was quickly assembled with what Country Life scholar William Bowers calls "an impressive group of academicians, journalists, public servants, and practical organizers."[62] Gifford Pinchot, Roosevelt's chief forester within the U.S. Department of Agriculture (USDA) and the nation's foremost utilitarian conservationist, represented government interests. Journalists "Uncle Henry" Wallace of *Wallaces' Farmer,* Walter Hines Page of *World's Work,* and William A. Beard of the *Great West Magazine*

60. Andrew Denny Rodgers III, *Liberty Hyde Bailey: A Story of American Plant Sciences,* facsimile ed. (1949; repr., New York: Hafner Publishing, 1965), 354.

61. Dorf, *Liberty Hyde Bailey,* 153.

62. Bowers, *Country Life Movement,* 25.

joined Georgian Charles S. Barrett, president of the Farmer's Cooperative and Educational Union of America, in rounding out the exemplary, and controversial, commission.

The Country Life Commission

Put simply, the Country Life Commission made Liberty Hyde Bailey, already a touchstone in agricultural and horticultural circles, a household name in halls of Congress, in the White House, and, via periodicals, in middle-class homes. Based on a study of press coverage during the period, pioneering Country Life Commission scholar Clayton Ellsworth puts the Commission's high profile in perspective, claiming that Commissioners received "about the same amount of favorable space as a big league baseball team on a barnstorming tour."[63] "Despite Theodore Roosevelt's national leadership," William Bowers declares in his definitive study *The Country Life Movement in America, 1900–1920,* "the personality of Liberty Hyde Bailey looms largest in the history of the country life movement during the opening decades of the twentieth century."[64] The Commission, charged in August 1908 with the "reporting upon existing social, economic, and education conditions in the country, the means available for remedying deficiencies, and the best methods to use to organize a permanent investigation"[65] mobilized Bailey's uniquely comprehensive vision. The methodology of the Commission drew heavily on Bailey's existing Cornell University Farmers' Reading Course and agricultural extension playbook, as Chairman Bailey began work by sending out detailed questionnaires or "circulars" to over half a million farm families.[66] The process, both exhausting and painstaking, was uniquely Bailey, who habitually turned to the quasi-scientific questionnaire as the best way to ascertain real conditions on the ground. As many farmers could not take the time to complete a lengthy survey or otherwise lacked reliable rural delivery, Commissioners organized listening posts and town hall meetings. The tension between these two distinct methods of data gathering—the staid survey on one hand, the unpredictable town hall meeting on the other—revealed the tensions in Bailey and in Progressivism itself, which desired to be of the people at the same time it hoped to educate and correct popular misconception and malpractice. The surveys, according to

---

63. Clayton S. Ellsworth, "Theodore Roosevelt's Country Life Commission," *Agricultural History* 34, no. 4 (1960): 164.
64. Bowers, *Country Life Movement,* 45.
65. Ibid., 25.
66. Ellsworth, "Theodore Roosevelt's Country Life Commission," 163.

Bowers, counterpointed the intrinsic subjectivity of the Commission in giving the appearance, at least, of reform based on "scientific appraisal."[67]

Conversely, the town hall meetings, lending to the proceedings the flavor of old-time Populist politics, put the scientific model in its place. The gatherings themselves, often contentious, resembled political debates and rallies as much as fact-finding symposiums. Many of the farmers and ranchers present were seeing Bailey and the other commissioners for the first time and were tempted to view them as outsiders, especially as the overwhelming majority of the leaders of the Country Life movement were college-educated men from "comfortable, economically secure stations in life."[68] Here the presence of the wealthy yet decidedly homespun Commissioner "Uncle Henry" Wallace helped smooth ruffled feathers, as Wallace's kindly face and down-home words were well-trusted in Middle America by virtue of his phenomenally popular periodical *Wallaces' Farmer*. Wallace and Bailey, whom history reveals as the foremost agrarians of their era, complemented each other nicely, with Bailey able to intuit the farmers' moods, which sometimes tended toward open revolt, and Wallace able to defuse their anger with his inimitable combination of lay preaching and storytelling. Within the Commission, differences also emerged, and here again, Bailey, principal writer of the report, negotiated opposing views. Wallace, a former Presbyterian minister, wanted any criticism of the country church and its methods eliminated from the final report, though Bailey, himself a religious man but also a thoroughgoing scientist, eventually convinced the majority of the Commission that even the church must be subject to scrutiny.[69] In the introduction to the report, Bailey expressed the Commission's charge as "nothing more or less than the gradual rebuilding of a new agriculture and a new rural life."[70]

Despite the ambitiousness of their objectives and the national reach of their efforts, the Bailey-orchestrated Commission report would ultimately be derailed by politics, as partisan Congressmen in January of 1909 had already begun jockeying to replace Theodore Roosevelt. The publishing of the report, opponents reasoned, could do nothing but further the cause of Teddy's anointed successor, William Taft, among rural voters,[71] while simultaneously allowing Roosevelt eleventh-hour grandstanding as a rural savior. Eventually, in 1911, the suppressed report was published by the Spokane,

67. Bowers, *Country Life Movement*, 25.
68. Ibid., 33.
69. Dorf, *Liberty Hyde Bailey*, 152.
70. *Report of the Country Life Commission*, 16.
71. Ellsworth, "Theodore Roosevelt's Country Life Commission," 162.

Washington, Chamber of Commerce under the title *Report of the Commission on Country Life and Special Message from the President of the United States*. In it, Roosevelt's introductory letter anticipates a congressional audience hostile to the idea of even meager appropriations for the productive, albeit unilaterally appointed Commission: "The only recommendation I submit," Roosevelt wrote in his prefatory "Special Message from the President of the United States," "is that an appropriation of $25,000 be provided to enable the Commission to digest the material it has collected, and to collect and to digest much more that is within its reach, and thus complete its work."[72] This, he argued "would enable the Commission to gather in the harvest of suggestion which is resulting from the discussion it has stirred up." Indeed, at Roosevelt's request and much to Wallace's chagrin, the Commissioners had served without governmental pay for their extraordinary efforts, which included thirty hearings in all but twelve states and a more than 150-page report produced in just five months. "It is hard," scholar Clayton Ellsworth reflects, "to recall a commission which did so much in such a short period of time as did this pioneering one." Despite the plea, Roosevelt did not receive the requested appropriation. In fact, further indignities awaited the hard-pressed Commission, as many of the farmer questionnaires, according to Ellsworth, fell into the "hostile hands" at the USDA and were "destroyed before they could be published." While a percentage did reach the Census Bureau for tabulation, and still others survive in Bailey Hortorium at Cornell, answers to the most vital question on the circular, "What, in your judgment, is the most important single thing to be done for the betterment of the country life?" have since been lost.[73]

In spite of its unavoidable omissions, agricultural historians now regard the *Report of the Commission on Country Life* as one of the most important documents of twentieth-century American agriculture. Bowers calls it "the great galvanizing event in the history of the rural reform movement,"[74] while Ellsworth considers it the "central charter of farm people in their democratic quest for their just share of the material and spiritual things in life."[75] Hindsight reveals it to be one of the most controversial reports in agricultural history—a report that has became a double-edged sword for the legacy of the jack-of-all-trades Bailey. In lending his star to the Commission, Bailey had become, like it or not, associated with a political ideology he did not wholly support. Like an accomplished actor unfairly typecast, the moniker "Chair"

72. *Report of the Country Life Commission*, 8.
73. Ellsworth, "Theodore Roosevelt's Country Life Commission," 163, 164, 168.
74. Bowers, *Country Life Movement*, 24.
75. Ellsworth, "Theodore Roosevelt's Country Life Commission," 156.

of the Roosevelt Commission on Country Life would follow Bailey ever after, linking him, for better and for worse, to Progressive politics and to the do-gooding, efficiency-minded "technocrats"[76] of the Roosevelt era. In effect, Bailey had fallen into a political trap no one intended for him, but which he had nonetheless good reason to fear. Galvanized by his support of his friend Teddy Roosevelt and his abiding interest in the welfare of the U.S. farmer, Bailey's science and his heart did not always agree. Still and all, the Commission's report drew widespread praise, especially from farm women, many of whom wrote to Roosevelt to thank him. In an extant letter in the Bailey Hortorium dated September 5, 1908, Mrs. H. B. Rose gushed, "It must have been divine inspiration that caused you to understand the loneliness of a farmer's life." In general, Ellsworth concludes, "the purpose, methods, and personnel of the Commission appealed strongly to the American people," and the "agriculture press, with a few exceptions, blessed the venture." In an analysis largely overlooked by contemporary scholars, Ellsworth argues criticism for the Commission as an "election trick" or a "paternalistic act" originated almost exclusively in the urban press.[77] The differing views of the Commission in the eyes of ruralite and urbanite, historically validate the need for the Commission in the first place and explain Bailey's fated chairmanship, as Bailey's writings were unique at the time in their consistent call for greater understanding between city and country.

Among Bailey's legacies as inscribed in the Commission report, his pro-education stance has had the most long-lasting effect on rural America. In his 1911 book, *The Country-Life Movement in the United States*, he reiterated his belief that "in the future only the well-informed and efficient-thinking man can succeed" and further that "by the very nature of the progress we are making, the college man must go to the farm."[78] While the Commission report conceded a growing prosperity in the country, it faulted the public school system for "ineffective farming, lack of ideals, and the drift to town"[79] and recommended that the agricultural colleges amend these deficiencies via more intentional, widespread outreach.

A result of Bailey's prescriptions was the Smith-Lever Extension Act of 1914, which formalized cooperation between agricultural universities and the U.S. Department of Agriculture toward the end of more and better agricultural extension throughout the fifty states. However, even the Smith-Lever Act, envisioned as an unequivocal boon to food producers, has, according

76. Morgan and Peters, "Foundations," 451.
77. Ellsworth, "Theodore Roosevelt's Country Life Commission," 164.
78. Carlson, *New Agrarian Mind*, 17.
79. *Report of the Country Life Commission*, 51.

to contemporary farm writers Gene Logsdon and Wendell Berry, run tragically amuck. Both Berry and Logsdon point to the Smith-Lever Act, and the agricultural extension paradigm it insinuated, as the beginning of corporate agriculture and the decline of the family farm. In his chapter entitled "The Failure of Agricultural Education" Logsdon lambastes land-grant education as a "mystifying world of self-aggrandizing noneducation"[80] used to "promote a prosperous oligarchy of wealthy absentee landowners, megafarms, and international agribusiness firms as indispensable to a global, centralized, urban power structure."[81] Berry puts it more bluntly in his classic *The Unsettling of America*, where he decries land-grant university education where "self-interest, laziness, and lack of conviction augment the general confusion about what an education is or ought to be."[82] Though Bailey's own land-grant university, Cornell, was an emphatic exception to this latter-day criticism, the legacy of the Commission's "mainstream associations,"[83] write Morgan and Peters, has adversely, and unfairly, impacted Bailey's record as a visionary agrarian.

Though by this time he owned his own farm, directed Cornell's agricultural experiment station, and spoke routinely to farmer's groups throughout the land, Bailey's association with the Country Life Commission temporarily compromised, for some, his reputation as a man of the people. Though the Commission's report was largely a reflection of consensus opinions heard at farmers' and ranchers' listening posts, Bailey's name on a government-initiated report, some food producers maintained, belied his status as urbanite—one of the legions of college-educated men in ties then canvassing the country preaching the gospel of efficiency and environmental responsibility. Indeed, 1908 editorial cartoons in urban newspapers such as the *New York Evening Post* and *New York Times,* among others, showed Commissioners "wearing plug hats and Prince Albert coats going out in the country to milk the farmer's cows."[84] Indeed, Bailey and his mostly country-born colleagues found themselves scapegoated by metropolitan journalists. Bailey's citified reputation, unearned, is further codified in David B. Danbom's important book *The Resisted Revolution*, where Bailey is labeled "the most popular and vocal representative of urban agrarianism,"[85] a distinction that

80. Gene Logsdon, *At Nature's Pace: Farming and the American Dream* (New York: Pantheon, 1994), 60.

81. Ibid., 61.

82. Wendell Berry, *The Unsettling of America,* 2nd ed. (San Francisco: Sierra Club Books, 1997), 148.

83. Morgan and Peters, "Foundations," 450.

84. Ellsworth, "Theodore Roosevelt's Country Life Commission," 164.

85. David B. Danbom, *The Resisted Revolution: Urban America and the Industrialization of Agriculture, 1900–1930* (Ames: Iowa State University Press, 1979), 26.

further conflates Bailey's academic and governmental audience (urban) with his native ideology (rural) and his experiment station constituency (rural). Conversely, William Bowers, writing just five years before Danbom, views Bailey's conclusions as evidence not of surreptitious urban leanings but of an old-fashioned subscription to the Jeffersonian "agrarian myth"[86] of farmer superiority. At heart a Jeffersonian, Bailey believed that farmers are God's chosen people and the most virtuous and indispensable citizens in peace and in war. Ultimately, vis-à-vis his service on the Country Life Commission and his subsequent labeling by future generations of scholars, Bailey was, in farmer parlance, "damned if he did and damned if he didn't." If he had refused to serve on the Commission, he would have forgone a once-in-a-lifetime opportunity to improve the rural life he cared for passionately. If he executed his fact-finding Commission work successfully, he would inevitably find and publicize deficiencies in a lifestyle he viewed as endangered. To fully understand history's ambivalent view of the Country Life Commission is to recall that Bailey served reluctantly, only at the request of the President, and in spite of what he knew would be a personally detrimental political reckoning. By analogy, contemporary readers might understand Bailey's trepidation by way of the hot-potato chairmanship of the 9–11 Commission or the much-anticipated, much-maligned report of the Iraq Study Group headed by James Baker.

Politics, the very concern that nearly prevented Bailey from accepting the chairmanship of the Country Life Commission, dogged him well into his sabbatical year of 1909–1910, which he spent in Europe. When Bailey returned in July 1910, he called on ex-President Roosevelt, who was then fomenting a Progressive Party from his office at the *Outlook* magazine. According to Bailey biographer Philip Dorf, the *New York Times* reported at length on the Bailey-Roosevelt tête-à-tête on matters of conservation and rural life, commenting that a "revitalized" spirit of rural and environmental awareness was in the offing and, further, that the spirit had been "snuffed out...by a hostile Congress after the Colonel's [Roosevelt's] departure from the White House."[87] The visit also fueled rumors that Bailey, at Roosevelt's urging, was about to launch a campaign for congressional or gubernatorial office, a rumor that Bailey quickly denied. These refusals of high office would soon become part of the Bailey mythos and of his standard biography. Writing in the October 1930 *Better Homes and Gardens*, Mosnat declares, "Three presidents of the United States would have been glad to have this same boy

---

86. Bowers, *Country Life Movement*, 35.
87. *New York Times*, July 13, 1910, quoted in Dorf, *Liberty Hyde Bailey*, 155.

[Bailey] as secretary of agriculture, and several times he was considered for governor of New York State, but this never came to pass because Dr. Bailey has no taste for practical politics."[88]

Adding to the public office speculation at the time was Bailey's ongoing, and open, disagreement with the Cornell University Board of Trustees over more proposed home-rule or "self-government"[89] within the larger university for the flagship College of Agriculture. Word of the rift was reported in the *Cornell Countryman,* where editors hoped there might be a vote of confidence in Dean Bailey as such "an emphatic expression of our desire to have him remain with us that he will be unable to resist it."[90] So great was the on-campus debate that Roosevelt himself stepped in. Under the pretext of a visit to Cornell to survey land for possible government reclamation, Roosevelt addressed the Cornell student body, arguing that it would be a "calamity, not only to the state, but to the nation"[91] if Bailey were to step down as dean.

While Bailey would remain at Cornell for another two years, the final straw proved, ironically, to be Roosevelt's nomination for president by the Progressive Party in 1913, which further fueled media speculation that Bailey would likewise represent the upstart party for governor of New York. As the 1912–1913 academic year wore on, Bailey continued to foreshadow his retirement and the beginning of the "third phase" of his life—a period in which he intended to move from professional service to personal passions. According to biographer Dorf, Bailey said he wanted "out of the harness"[92] at a New York City dinner put on by the Cornell Club. Bailey was only fifty-five, but if he hoped to spend what he calculated would be the last quarter of his life for high-energy travel and botanical fieldwork, he needed to make haste. The resignation, when it arrived in the spring, was made effective July 31, 1913—the end of the academic year.

In every way, Liberty Hyde Bailey had left Cornell University better than he had found it, having built new facilities; secured future funding; and infused nature-study, agricultural extension, and experiment station work in the Cornell curriculum. Calling the Dean Bailey years "an era almost without parallel in the history of higher education" biographer Dorf describes the transformation of the once-ragtag agricultural college: "In one short decade, through the ability and drive of one man, a small agricultural college operating as a department of a university had been converted into a front-rank,

88. Mosnat, "He Is Your Garden's Best Friend," 68.
89. Rodgers, *Liberty Hyde Bailey,* 382.
90. Dorf, *Liberty Hyde Bailey,* 156.
91. Rodgers, *Liberty Hyde Bailey,* 384.
92. Dorf, *Liberty Hyde Bailey,* 159.

state-financed institution enjoying a national reputation."[93] The facts speak for themselves; during his tenure Bailey almost single-handedly increased enrollment in the agricultural college from 100 to nearly 1,400 and increased state appropriations from a paltry $35,000 at the beginning of his tenure to a whopping half million dollars by its close.[94]

Liberty Hyde Bailey's Last Quarter-Century

Liberty Hyde Bailey had long admired the transcendentalists—men who lived deliberately and on their own terms. Such separate souls, Bailey explained, are "liberated personalities, rare and prophetic."[95] Mosnat, among other popular journalists of the time, made the transcendentalist comparison explicit, dubbing Bailey a "successor"[96] to the three great American naturalists—Emerson, Thoreau, and Burroughs—and the apostle of "a philosophy that has been so rare since Carlyle and Emerson ceased to be heard." Truth be told, Bailey's interaction with nature in the last quarter of his life would be different than the meditative poetics of the transcendentalists, as it more closely resembled John Muir's ecstatic, botanical wanderings. Even so, the Bailey–Muir comparison has its limitations: Bailey was an academician by profession, a trained scientist with a poetic bent, while Muir was the opposite, a born poet mostly self-taught applied science. Certainly, Bailey's retirement from "organized" agriculture at the collegiate level allowed him to craft his own, more intentional image. Not long after he left Cornell, descriptions of Bailey in the popular press evolved to highlight his hybrid interests. In a short profile, Mosnat ascribes a number of appellations, from "garden philosopher"[97] to philosopher-poet. By 1951, as the end of Bailey's three decades of groundbreaking botanical fieldwork drew to a close, descriptions of his virtuoso abilities grew still more expansive. In his March 1951 profile, Carol Aronovici captures Bailey's complex bailiwick as "explorer, innovator, teacher and administrator, philosopher and poet"[98] and as "[a] Jeffersonian grafted with scientific experience and Vermont individualism." Later sobriquets add ecologist and environmentalist. Uniquely, the eclectic nature of his genius means that Bailey has meant something different to each passing generation.

93. Ibid., 160.
94. Ibid., 161.
95. Liberty Hyde Bailey, *The Holy Earth* (New York: Scribner, 1915), 135.
96. Mosnat, "He Is Your Garden's Best Friend," 40.
97. Ibid.
98. Carol Aronovici, "Liberty H. Bailey," *The Survey*, March 1951, 123.

As Bailey's claim to fame broadened beyond his initial quartet of academic disciplines—horticulture, botany, agriculture, and nature-study—he also enlarged the scope and breadth of his publishing efforts via a series called the "Background Books." In his retirement, Bailey the scholar began to court general audiences with what he called his "budget of opinions" expressed in nontechnical books.[99] Dorf extols the Jeffersonesque range of cultural criticism offered by the Background Books, which warned the American public of thoughtless consumerism, blind allegiance, adulterated foods, unreasonable appetites, commercial morality, and needless medical prescriptions—in short, a nascent agrarian manifesto. Each of these trespasses Bailey decried for their unnaturalness and their estrangement from common-sense, grounded values. Such indulgences and shortcuts as these, Bailey counseled, would alienate citizens from the spirit of fellowship and brotherhood he advances in the wartime Background Books *Universal Service* (1918) and *What Is Democracy?* (1918).

Such unapologetic truth telling did not make the Background Books best sellers, though Dorf notes that reviewers lauded them as "the utterances of a true seer," and "inspiring and truthfully poetic."[100] The *Brooklyn Eagle* lauded *Universal Service* for a "philosophy that is broad enough to take in all of humanity and sweeping enough to efface from the earth the 'horror of militarism.'"[101] Amplifying many of the same themes, *What Is Democracy?* was praised by the *New York Tribune* as "a luminous little volume" written by an "enlightened agriculturalist."[102] The Background Books, according to Morgan and Peters, "seemed to sense that the most important work was changing the worldview" to show humans' responsibility to the environment and to one another. The treatises, encompassing poetry, philosophy, and allegory, fundamentally combine a "civic emphasis"[103] and a "pluralism of environmental values"[104] to represent Bailey's democratic convictions. Taken as a whole, Minteer argues, the books of the period "should be viewed against a larger social and political backdrop in which the adoption of reverence for the earth was seen as producing both good farmers and good citizens."[105] In discussing the intersection of environment, science, literature, government, philosophy, and current events, Bailey was once again in the vanguard as

99. Dorf, *Liberty Hyde Bailey*, 190.
100. Ibid., 193.
101. Cornell University Division of Rare Manuscripts, http://rmc.library.cornell.edu/bailey/writings/writings_6.html.
102. Ibid.
103. Morgan and Peters, "Foundations," 46.
104. Ibid., 48.
105. Minteer, *Landscape of Reform*, 49.

one of the first scientists of the twentieth century to write effectively for an audience of both specialists and nonspecialists. Prefiguring the advent of later writers such as E. O. Wilson and Stephen Hawking, Bailey had a gift for expressing complex, frequently interdisciplinary notions in accessible language. While critics regarded the Background Books as evidence of his revolutionary thinking, Bailey himself eschewed the label *radical*. Instead, he said, he stood for "the conservation of native values."[106]

The first of the Background Books, *The Holy Earth* (1915), would become the most concise distillation of Bailey's revolutionary agri-ecological thought, and the epic story of the book's creation only contributed to its visionary essence. As the story goes, Bailey booked a trip in the summer of 1914 to New Zealand, where he was to deliver a series of lectures at the government's invitation. The long sea voyage proved the perfect milieu for a book that had been brewing in him for some time, a book that would not be exclusively agricultural or environmental but would be informed by both, a book that would lay the foundations of what scholars would later call "planetary agrarianism." At its base, the book was an expression of conservationist views expressed by Gifford Pinchot and others in the Roosevelt administration, but with an important difference. While Pinchot's utilitarian conservationism stood for a self-centered "equal opportunity for every American citizen to get his fair share of benefit from these resources, both now and hereafter,"[107] *The Holy Earth* faulted the citizen-consumer for exactly this rapaciousness in going after their "fair share" and exhorted them to a higher moral calling in dealing with Mother Earth. Moreover, *The Holy Earth* turned on its head the biblical maxim that man, in his superiority to beasts, was destined to steward. Not so, Bailey wrote, citing the excesses of the industrial revolution. While traditional nature books viewed nature through a distinctly human lens, *The Holy Earth* reversed that equation, considering humankind's telling ecologies—its habits of work and play, consuming and providing, family and society. If nature was a series of interconnected processes, human life must be bound by the same natural laws. Human action and inaction, Bailey argued, were essentially moral or immoral to the extent they accommodated ecologies or denied them. Written in the years prior to U.S. entry into World War I, the book manages to express gathering evils even as it articulates unshakeable optimism. War and peace along with tyranny and democracy figure prominently in the narrative as emblems of humankind's worst and best. In Bailey's brand of "planetary agrarianism," it made sense that a world run by men steering the Earth headlong into war was a world whose

106. Ibid., 191.
107. Gifford Pinchot, *The Fight for Conservation* (New York: Doubleday, 1910), 79.

benevolence could not be trusted. The visionary manifesto that is *The Holy Earth,* written haphazardly on whatever scraps of paper Bailey could find as his ship steamed through equatorial heat, expressed its author's deep-seated beliefs—"that a righteous use of vast resources of the earth must be founded on religious and ethical values."[108] Published by Charles Scribner and Sons, the first run of the alarmist *The Holy Earth* sold less than two thousand copies despite positive reviews from critics who found in its mixed-genre approach "a touch of philosophy, something of sentiment, much of beauty, and an abundance of common sense."[109] While some of Bailey's technical works had gone through as many as twenty-two editions by the late 1920s[110] and accounted for the vast majority of Bailey's nearly one million books sold,[111] *The Holy Earth* realized a conspicuously quiet birth before enjoying a latter-day resurgence during World War II.

The international travel that fueled the Background Books' circumspection—travels first to New Zealand and then to remote China—had, for Bailey, both practical and existential value. Practically, the trips enabled the collection of valuable botanical specimens as Europe trended toward war. Spiritually, they represented the release of Bailey's wanderlust built up during the relatively staid Cornell years as well as a playing out of an abiding desire to see how the rest of the world worked—particularly how it farmed and how it "faithed." Bailey returned home when the United States entered the War; though he was now a citizen of the world and a student of its religions, he was, above all, a patriot. Bailey's midlife patriotism surprised those who knew him at Michigan Agricultural College, which he had threatened to leave when he learned military drill was requisite. In fact, it was young Bailey's resistance to war that, ironically, put him on the path to greatness in horticulture in the first place. His Quaker mentor at MAC, Dr. Beal intervened and arranged for him to collect plant samples for the College laboratory in lieu of otherwise required military exercises. While others in agriculture insisted on pacifism and isolationism at any cost, including Bailey's good friend Uncle Henry Wallace, Bailey had grown more pragmatic in his advancing years. His love of democracy and belief in service caused him to declare, "It is the obligation of every able-bodied man to be his own soldier, when soldiering is necessary."[112] Cynics and pundits treated Bailey's

---

108. Dorf, *Liberty Hyde Bailey,* 167.

109. Cornell University Division of Rare Manuscripts, http://rmc.library.cornell.edu/bailey/writings/writings_6.html

110. Mosnat, "He Is Your Garden's Best Friend," 40.

111. Cornell University Division of Rare Manuscripts, http://rmc.library.cornell.edu/bailey/writings/writings_6.html.

112. Dorf, *Liberty Hyde Bailey,* 175.

apparent change of heart, without evidence, as a harbinger of political ambitions. The February 9, 1918, *New York Times,* for example, reported that the Democratic nomination for governor of the state of New York should "definitely...go to Dr. Liberty Hyde Bailey, former Dean of the Cornell College of Agriculture." Likewise when, not long afterward, Bailey spoke at the convention of the New York Federation of Agriculture, the *Times* labeled him a "possible Democratic candidate for Governor this Fall." Not to be outdone, the *Sun* lauded Bailey as a "leader in...the improvement of country life" and "one of the foremost workers in America."[113] "His fame," the *Sun* continued, "is by no means confined to any one State or sphere."

As if to disprove those who accused him of ulterior motives, Bailey set sail again for far-off lands as soon as the War ended. This time he headed for the island of Trinidad in the Caribbean, where a new botanical passion took root: palms. While *Rubus* (principally blackberries and raspberries) and *Carex* (sedges) had been the objects of his lifelong horticultural affections, the palm promised greater drama and more travel. Still, as the allures of the palm began to obsess him, the lure of his childhood haunts and habits pulled him homeward. Biographers describe Bailey's winter in Trinidad as both stimulating and lonely, as he missed the northern climes of New York and Michigan, especially their pastures and woodlands. When he returned to the States in 1922, his nostalgia blossomed into *The Apple Tree,* a book-length ode to the very same crop he and his father had long-ago grown in Michigan as members of the Pomological Society. By the early 1920s Bailey's botanical version of the American Dream had come full circle, as he had assumed the national presidency of the American Pomological Society he had first joined as a teenager.

In his pursuit of palms, begun in earnest in the 1920s, Bailey was every bit as passionate as in his other advocacies. Like the swashbuckling Victorian horticultural expeditionists, Bailey was willing to go anywhere, do anything, to return with a promising specimen or picture thereof. Though well into his sixties when the palm obsession overtook him, Bailey thought nothing of bushwhacking his way into remote jungles with a camera, saw, ax, or pruning shears and would do so for the next thirty years.[114] A pioneer in the use of the camera in botanical fieldwork, Bailey viewed an acceptable photo as crucial to the understanding of any rare or exotic species in the field—so much so he insisted on developing his own photos near or on-site, knowing that a return trip might be impossible. Thanks to his rhapsodic and exacting fieldwork, Bailey became a kind of pioneering adventurer cum

---

113. *New York Times,* February 19, 1918, quoted in Dorf, *Liberty Hyde Bailey,* 175.
114. Ibid., 184.

scientist cum documentarian, pursuing his science as an independent agent rather than a salaried man. Undertaking his studies expressly as a "private person" allowed him to redress earlier laments penned in *Outlook to Nature,* where he had defined an institutional man as one who "depends on some one else" and whose opinions are "controlled."[115]

Bailey's brand of field science—informed by poetry and philosophy—won him the respect of many of his laboratory-based colleagues, resulting in his election as the president of the Association for the Advancement of Science in 1926. The *New York Times,* sympathetic to Bailey throughout, approved of the Association's choice for a replacement for the outgoing physicist Michael Pupin. In praising both Pupin and Bailey, the *Times* cited the wisdom that "a poet should tent along with the scientist out on the verges of the known. . . . Sometimes though rarely the scientist is himself a poet."[116] In part due to his decidedly global outlook, Bailey's star was now international. In 1927 alone, for example, he received the National Institute of Social Sciences gold medal, the Grande Médaille from the Société Nationale d'Acclimatation de France, and a medal from the Royal Irish Academy in Dublin.[117]

As Bailey reached the pinnacle of several related yet disparate fields, the roundness of his intellect made him less partisan than in early years, his "years of service" as he called them, when disciplinary ties are strong. Bailey's return to field science renewed his objectivity and his fierce independence. Aided by a deepening critical distance, Bailey rebuked both agriculturalists and scientists, when needed. In the 1920s and 1930s, especially, the "critic and sage" moniker proffered by Bailey biographer Dorf seemed especially apt. In fact, some devotees of agriculture and conservation, two of Bailey's earliest and most enduring passions, viewed his increasing distance as tantamount to abandonment. Others paid their respects to Bailey as a fountainhead of the sustainable and permanent agricultural movements, leaving him to his well-earned retirement. In 1930 a young agrarian named Russell Lord described the agrarian living legend with a hint of disappointment as "serenely unperturbed as to agricultural organization or organization of any kind."[118] Such insinuations, understandable in light of Bailey's great potential as an elder statesman, were largely unfounded; in 1931, a year after he was accused of being organizationally inactive, Bailey served as president of the American Country Life Association and led the first National Conference on Rural

115. Liberty Hyde Bailey, *Outlook to Nature* (New York: Macmillan, 1905).
116. Editorial, *New York Times,* January 2, 1926, quoted in Dorf, *Liberty Hyde Bailey,* 187.
117. Ibid., 188.
118. Ibid., 197.

Government. Clearly, the inheritors of the Bailey tradition, including Lord himself, had come to view Bailey as a forefather and wanted more from him as the sustainable agriculture movement came of age in the 1930s. It is clear, however, that Bailey did not regard himself as irreplaceable, acknowledging that movements would continue and even prosper without him, a case he had made emphatically earlier in his career when supporters at Cornell claimed the university would be ruined in the event of his premature departure.

In truth, Bailey had not abandoned agriculture in any sense of the word, as his studies of the palm were intimately tied to its global potential for food and fiber. Here he could make a groundbreaking contribution, as he had already in agriculture, horticulture, conservation, and nature-study. No single definitive work had been published on the palm, while thousands of varieties worldwide awaited classification and cataloging. Meanwhile, the number of species in Bailey's personal herbarium in Ithaca, which he would donate to Cornell University, continued to grow, with more than 125,000 by the mid-1930s.[119] Back on campus in Ithaca, and indeed wherever Bailey went, he was viewed increasingly as a national wonder, a living legend. Nowhere was the interest in Bailey greater than at Cornell, where campus publications regularly tracked his adventures with something approaching awe. Bailey would become for Cornell faculty, staff, and students what the fictional professor Indiana Jones would become for his archaeology students: a jaw-dropping wonder. In 1937, writers at the *Cornell Countryman* reported he had celebrated his seventy-ninth birthday in Port-au-Prince Haiti, of all far-flung places, where he was reported to be "hale and hearty" and "travel[ing] alone with the guidance of natives."[120] The fascination with the preternaturally gifted and copiously decorated Bailey also increasingly led reporters to Bailey's door in search of comments on his accumulating honorary degrees and awards, ranging from the Gold Medal of the Garden Club of America to the Distinguished Service Award of the American Association of Nurserymen. So diverse were Bailey's achievements that the question facing the grantors of his many honorary doctorates was what field to issue them in. Dorf reports that, by the 1930s, Bailey had added the ceremonial titles "dean of American horticulturalists"[121] and "dean of American botanists" to his extant reputation as the "dean of American agrarians."

Bailey's pursuit of palms in South and Central America and the Caribbean continued against the backdrop of great personal loss: His daughter Sara died in 1935, and, as a result, he and his wife took Sara's orphaned

119. Ibid., 202.
120. Ibid., 203.
121. Rodgers, *Liberty Hyde Bailey,* 479.

children into their home in Ithaca. Just three years later, Bailey and his surviving daughter Ethel Zoe experienced still more tragedy, as Bailey lost to illness his wife of fifty-five years, Annette, who he described as "the most wonderful woman in all the world."[122] Despite opening up a new chapter in his life devoted to world travel, genial ambassadorship, and the pursuit of the palm, other events in his life were coming full circle. In the aftermath of his wife's death, Liberty Hyde Bailey Memorial Park was dedicated in his hometown of South Haven, Michigan, though he was unable to attend. In 1942, Bailey returned to East Lansing, Michigan, for his sixtieth college class reunion, where friends reported he wandered among sand dunes refamiliarizing himself with the plants of his youth.[123] Among the reporters present, Russell Lord best captured the poignancy of Bailey's homecoming, observing, "They weather well, these old American agriculturalists."[124] Indeed, Bailey's popularity in the early 1940s was much more than ceremonial. World War II precipitated the resurgence of Bailey's *The Holy Earth*, prompting a request from the Christian Rural Fellowship for rights to reprint the book at twenty-five cents apiece for maximum dissemination. Indeed, some five thousand copies of *The Holy Earth* were reprinted in the early to mid-1940s,[125] an impressive figure for a book already more than twenty-five years old and offered for sale in a wartime economy.

By 1948, when Bailey celebrated his ninetieth birthday, even *Time* magazine took note, explaining why Cornell University would have to wait to roll out the red carpet: "The birthday boy was nowhere found. Liberty Hyde Bailey, when last heard from, was somewhere in the West Indies wandering through jungles in search of rare plant and palms."[126] When Bailey did return in late April, more than a month after his birthday, a banquet of some two hundred guests had been organized for him, the proceedings of which were published in a small keepsake volume, *Words Said About A Birthday: Addresses in Recognition of the Ninetieth Anniversary of the Natal Day of Liberty Hyde Bailey* (1948). Because Bailey rarely talked about his personal life, the significance of the evening was more than ceremonial, as the birthday boy, waxing nostalgic, offered an unusually personal account for future biographers. The evening itself unfolded as part tribute, part roast, and part honorary address. In his

122. Dorf, *Liberty Hyde Bailey*, 205.
123. Ibid., 213.
124. Ibid.
125. Ibid., 214.
126. Ibid., 228.

speech, Bailey addressed the inaccuracies of his mythos while begetting new mysteries—no, he had no special recipe for long life beyond a genetic predisposition to longevity—yes, the number of his book-length publications, rumored to be in the hundreds, had been exaggerated; by his own count he had authored roughly sixty-five, though he could not say how many he had edited. He was, he admitted, nearly finished with another, a new version of the more than one-thousand-page tome *Manual of Cultivated Plants*. And there were other books he had abandoned, he informed a shocked audience, including a long-ago unpublished novel he "burned vividly," as it was "the best book he had ever written."[127] He had, too, he said, once torched a book of scholarship in sympathy with a young horticultural scholar who had lamented that Bailey always seemed to publish before anyone else had a chance. Concluding his discussion about his prodigious publishing history, Bailey told his dinner guests that his real "magnum opus" on palms had yet to be written. Most in attendance realized that to complete his research Bailey intended to travel for the first time to Africa, to the Congo and to Nigeria specifically.

Sadly, the trip planned for early January of 1950 never came to pass. On December 28, immediately after buying one-way tickets to African destinations such as Dakar and Leopoldville, Bailey, headed for his bank, was bumped by a hasty pedestrian on Wall Street, fell down a series of steps, and broke a bone in his thigh, below the hip.[128] His trip to the hospital was reported by the *New York Times*, which indicated he was "fairly comfortable"[129] in the moments before he underwent surgery to insert temporary screws. After surgery Bailey demanded he be released. The trip to Africa, he insisted, was still on.

As his doctors had predicted, Bailey's recovery would be slow and would prohibit a trip halfway around the world. As the realization dawned on Bailey, he turned to working on unfinished horticultural manuscripts, though his motivation flagged. He would live for four more difficult years, occasionally entertaining guests at his Sage Place home in Ithaca, though his visitors noted with sadness that he could not always recall their names.[130]

Liberty Hyde Bailey died on Christmas night in 1954 at the age of ninety-seven, prompting those who loved him best to attempt the impossible: memorialize his astounding accomplishments. The following year, G. H. M. Lawrence,

---

127. *Words Said About a Birthday*, 32.
128. Dorf, *Liberty Hyde Bailey*, 234.
129. *New York Times*, December 30, 1949, quoted in Dorf, *Liberty Hyde Bailey*, 234.
130. Ibid., 236.

who succeeded Bailey as director of the Liberty Hyde Bailey Hortorium, wrote in *Nature:*

> Most great men can be classified by the profession or field of activity whereby they achieved their greatness; not so with Liberty Hyde Bailey, for his greatness is due to his manifold contributions produced almost concurrently in many fields. To some persons, his renown is as a botanist, explorer, and horticulturist; to others as an educator, administrator and rural sociologist; to a third group as an editor, lecturer, and writer; while still a fourth group knows him best as a poet, philosopher, and counselor.[131]

From the late 1940s to the mid-1950s, two full-length Bailey biographies were published and countless posthumous honors followed, including the naming of a men's dormitory at his alma mater, Michigan State University, in 1956. In the years that followed, the Bailey name would be commemorated throughout the United States at sites tied closely to his life's work, including the Liberty Hyde Bailey Hortorium at Cornell University, the Liberty Hyde Bailey High School in East Lansing, Bailey Hall at Morrisville State College in Morrisville, New York, and the Liberty Hyde Bailey Palm Glade at the Fairchild Tropical Garden, Coconut Grove, Florida. More recently, Michigan State University paid tribute to its accomplished alumnus in 1997, establishing the Liberty Hyde Bailey Scholars Program to prepare undergraduates for "lifetime contributions as stewards of the biosphere."[132]

The breadth and depth of Bailey's teachings made an especially lasting impression on his students, many of whom would resurface in Bailey's last decade to sing his praises. Writing for the *Survey* in March 1951, former student Carol Aronovici paid homage to a virtuoso professor he described as "scientist, explorer, encyclopedist, poet, humanist."[133] "I have yet to meet anyone," Aronovici marveled, some half century after meeting Bailey on the Cornell University campus, "who could project his knowledge and vision into so many forms of endeavor and achieve his ends with such sturdy realism, such balanced serenity."[134] Jared Van Wagenen Jr., Cornell class of 1891, similarly remarked, on the occasion of Bailey's ninetieth birthday celebration, "A few students were born too soon and many others born too late; but I was born in the very nick of time so that in my student years I was

131. G. H. M. Lawrence, *Nature* (1955), quoted in Diane M. Doberneck, "The Life of Liberty Hyde Bailey: A Brief Biography," http://www.bsp.msu.edu/Background/BaileyBio.cfm.
132. Diane M. Doberneck, "The Life of Liberty Hyde Bailey: A Brief Biography," http://www.bsp.msu.edu/Background/BaileyBio.cfm.
133. Aronovici, "Liberty H. Bailey," 128.
134. Ibid., 123.

privileged to sit under two great Master-teachers: [Isaac Phillips] Roberts and Bailey."[135]

Bailey's last major public appearance, as it turned out, proved to be the ninetieth birthday party he had done his best to avoid. In retrospect, the dinner organized by Cornell President Edmund Day in honor of "a great and good man" allowed its reluctant honoree to organize his affairs and reiterate his life's philosophy. His remarks from that evening serve as fitting self-appraisal of an ecstatically productive life. Bailey closed:

> It is a marvelous planet on which we ride. It is a great privilege to live thereon, to partake in the journey, and to experience its goodness. We may cooperate rather than rebel. We should try to find the meanings rather than to be satisfied only with the spectacles. My life has been a continuous fulfillment of dreams.[136]

135. Jared Van Wagenen Jr., quoted in *Words Said About a Birthday,* 13.
136. Liberty Hyde Bailey, quoted in *Words Said About a Birthday,* 36.

I WORKMANSHIP

Some hands go to the manicure
To primp and polish and shine
Some hands go to the velvet lure
And some to the jewel shrine;
But these are the hands that hold the plow
The self-same hands as of old and now—
They are the hands that court'sy and perk
But these are the hands that do the work.

—From "Hands," *Wind and Weather* (New York: Scribner, 1916)

Workmanship infuses the six quintessentially agrarian essays that follow: "My Father's Hoe," "The Honest Day's Work," "Nails," "From Haying-Time to Radio," "The Soil," and "The Daily Fare." Reminiscent of the essays of John Burroughs and Henry David Thoreau in both sentiment and subject, Bailey's work is more autobiographical here than elsewhere, as he strongly ties his agrarianism and liberal-minded theology to his life story. In each piece, Bailey considers "handiness" and "handiwork," paying tribute to the "gentle art of doing things yourself." Implicit throughout is the notion that these "gentle arts" are "lost arts," affording Bailey, the scientist, moments of unabashed nostalgia for bygone days when the worthiness of an enterprise was not measured in terms of cold, hard cash. Bailey's yeoman sympathies cause him to question progress, scientific and otherwise, where progress, so-called, increases our helplessness or trends us toward profligacy. Throughout these pages, Bailey remains an optimist rather than a disgruntled Luddite and often, particularly when conjuring a long-ago boyhood, hints at a wry understanding of his own, nonscientific sentimentalities. "The Honest Day's Work," for example, elegizes the days before the time clock, the public works crew, and the overzealous labor union— regrettable fixtures in public life as Bailey sees them. By way of contrast, the author presents the independent, painstaking work of the plowman as an ever rarer, ever more valuable commodity. "The Daily Fare" likewise seeks the authentic, offering a contemporary-sounding critique of our food's artificiality and our habit of absent-minded consumption. Sounding uncannily like Wendell Berry, the author laments, "And so we all live mechanically, from shop to table, without contact, and irreverently."

My Father's Hoe

Either side the clock in my workroom hangs a weapon.[1]

On one side is a fearsome musket that one of my ancestors is said to have captured in the War of the American Revolution. On the stock is crudely punctured the legend, "Samuel Mash, 1777." The bayonet and its leather sheath are still in place; I shudder to think what horrible traffic that blade may have executed. There is also the bullet-case, made of a block of wood into which two dozen holes are bored for the balls, three-fourths-inch wide and nearly three inches deep, enclosed in a crude leather case with a flap over the top and a pocket on the front. The old flintlock and the priming-pan are yet in condition and the flint itself is in place. Empty of its contents and lacking the ramrod, this gun weighs eight and one-half pounds. It is four feet eleven inches long from muzzle to butt; it should have sent its bullet straight.

It was a hardy man that wielded this laborious firearm, in frontier days of crude equipment and of long journeys by sinking roads. Not many men could it have dispatched, for it must be loaded again by the muzzle after every single discharge; the loose powder was poured in, proper wads were inserted, the great homemade bullet placed, and all rammed home with the rod; the flint was adjusted; the pan was primed; and the weapon was ready for destruction, if it did not get wet or misfire. But this weapon, and others like it, did their work well and we in the later day enjoy the fruits of their conquests; yet it has not taught us to abolish weapons for human slaughter. I like to think that the old gun hangs on my wall as a silent monitor of yet better days.

The other side the clock hangs my father's hoe. No other object is so closely wrought into my memories; my father left it hanging in the shed

1. From *The Harvest of the Year to the Tiller of the Soil* (New York: Macmillan, 1927), 135–142.

before the summons overtook him to leave the farm forever, and I brought it home with me that I might know it every working day.

There is not merely a hoe. It is a symbol of a man's life. One of my persistent memories is the sound of that hoe in the early morning when the lids of sleep were so slowly slowly opening, and I knew that he was in the garden and all was well. *Clish, clish, clish* in an even rhythmic easy subdued cadence the hoe moved up and down the rows, never chopping, never hacking, never faltering, for my father was a hoe-man as another man might be a welder or a wheelwright, taking pride in the skill of his handiwork. Very smooth and even the ground was left, with a thin loose surface such as in the later sophisticated days we came to know as the earth mulch. Six-foot-one he stood, and yet he scarcely stooped; with his right hand he grasped the handle near its end and always in the same way, with the thumb lengthwise on the wood, the four fingers clasped underneath, and the end of the stock not projecting from the back of the hand. Four inches from the end, a hollow has been worn by the ball of the thumb, and underneath are furrows where the fingers grasped.

When the job was finished, the hoe was cleaned and hung in its own place; no one else ever touched it. There was no proscription on it, but we would not think to use his hoe any more than to wear his shoes or his hat.

For how many years he used that hoe I do not know, but my memory does not go back to the time when it was not a part of him. In his later years, he felt that the old hoe was becoming too much worn and the handle too weak, so he hung it away and purchased another. This other hoe, much worn away, is also preserved, but it is relatively a modern affair and of a different breed.

Wonderful execution the old hoe has wrought. It would be difficult to estimate how many millions of young weeds have succumbed to it; the big weeds were pulled by hand, but the little growths fell beneath its steady, even march. It was a maxim with us that no weed should go to seed on the farm. And the hoe performed the acme of good and thorough surface tillage; this was its major contribution. The implement shows its service; the blade is worn to a thin plate with evenly rounded ends, three inches wide and six inches long; the handle at the shank is worn down to half its strength, and the furrows are deeply cut by grit and storm and time along the grain of the ashen wood.

It must have been good material in that handle and thimble and blade. He told me that it was one of the first hoes made at the State Prison at Jackson. He came into Michigan from the Green Mountains in 1841. The farm on which I was born was taken from the wilderness about 1855, and long before that he had purchased a farm elsewhere. Recently I applied to the warden of the Michigan State Prison for information about the beginnings of the hoe-making there. He sent me an interesting report by one of the prisoners, who has been interested in the history of the institution; and from this I learn that contracts for hoe-making there were begun as early as 1848.

My father's hoe goes back, therefore, to the beginnings of an industry, and it is a witness of all the modern developments in manufacture and in agriculture. It spans one of the significant turning points in history, when manufacture succeeded handicraft and when farming emerged from a simple separate occupation to a commanding part in the discussions of men.

Yet, even so, a hoe is for personal and not for corporate use. I doubt whether we breed hoe-men any more. Now and then I see an old man who can use a hoe with purpose and skill and with a feeling of good workmanship, but for the most part we disdain these simplicities and pride ourselves on grander things. Thereby do we miss some of the essentials and deprive ourselves of many simple means of self-expression. When I see someone using a hoe I do not catch the feeling of pride in the implement or satisfaction in the deft handling of it, quite aside from its gross usefulness in opening the ground and covering the seed.

I remember that I looked forward with pleasure to hoeing the corn, a labor that now arouses surprise. For one thing, it was escape from harder labors; and the long rows of corn invited me, with the burrows of moles and mice, the yellowbirds that nested in trees in the growing summer, and the runnels that heavy rains had cut. The odors of the corn and the ground were wholesome and pleasant. Quickly the growing corn had made a forest since planting time, and when it became head-high to a boy and the tassels were in the tops, the field became a hiding-place for many wild creatures and there were mysteries in the shadowed depths; we went straight into these mysteries when we hoed the corn for the last time in the season, and every fence corner at the end of the rows was another world of interest. Father took one row and I another alongside, and patiently we went back and forth across the field, laying the pigweeds and thistles along the spaces, straightening up the lopped and broken stalks. The rows looked thankful when we had done with them. There was not much conversation; there did not need to be; there was interest all along the route; we were part of the silence of nature; but the few words I heard were full of meaning and they sank deep.

Often I am tempted to contrast these two old implements, the gun and the hoe, and to estimate their values. I reflect that the gun does not express a man's life, but is a weapon to be used on occasion, and for this one the occasion was indeed dire and heroic. Its conquests ended, it was hung away and was brought out only for display. But the hoe was a companion throughout a man's productive lifetime. It was never on parade. It did its work stead-fastly and well, and no one paused to give it notice. It made no mourners. It helped to make the land better, the crops better, and the man better, and it entered into the life of a boy. If the first requisite of social service is that a man shall do his own work well, then the old hoe has been verily an imple-ment of human welfare and there need be no apology for hanging it along-side the heirloom firelock.

Now that we are so eagerly aware of all our troubles, the hoe recalls another time; and as I look back on those cornfield days I am aware that I never heard a complaint about farming from my father. We did not think of it that way. We were farmers; it was ours to make the farm worthwhile and to be satisfied. We did not compare our lot with that of others. We went about our farming as the days came, the program being determined by the weather and the seasons. Nor do I recall laments about the weather: it will come out right in the end, we shall follow the Lord's will—this was the attitude.

Perhaps these practices and outlooks cannot develop the most skillful or productive farming, but farming was not then a competitive business. There were years of "glut," but we had not heard about "surplus." We needed little and were never in want. We had not learned to substitute machines for men. We knew nothing about "efficiency," and cost-accounting was not even in the penumbra of dreams. The men of that stripe and generation would have resented the idea that farming can be measured by money; it was too good for that.

All this is very crude and far away; but the old hoe still hangs by the clock as the days are ticked off one by one, and I am glad that it led me through the rows of corn.

The Honest Day's Work

Yesterday for some time I observed eight working men engaged in removing parts of a structure and loading the pieces on a freight car.[2] At no time were more than two of the men making any pretension of working at once, most of the time they were all visiting or watching passers-by, and in the whole period the eight men did not accomplish what one good honest man should have performed. I wondered whether they had sufficient exercise to keep them in good health. They apparently were concerned about their "rights"; if the employer had rights they were undiscoverable.

We know the integrity and effectiveness of the body of workmen; yet any reader who has formed a habit of observing men on day work and public work will recognize my account. Day men usually work in gangs, frequently too many of them to allow any one to labor effectively, and the whole process is likely to be mechanical, impersonal, often shiftless and pervaded with the highly developed skill of putting in the time and reducing the time to the minimum and of beginning to quit well in advance of the quitting time. The process of securing labor has become involved, tied up, and the labor is not rendered in a sufficient spirit of service. About the only free labor yet remaining to us is the month labor on the farm, even though it may be difficult to secure and be comprised largely of ineffective remainders.

Over against all this is the importance of setting men at work singly and for themselves; this can be accomplished only when they own their property or have some real personal share in the production. The gang-spirit of labor runs into the politics of the group and constitutes the norm. If we are to have self-acting men, they must be removed from close control, in labor as well as elsewhere. If it is necessary that any great proportion of the laboring men shall be controlled, then is it equally important that other

2. From *The Holy Earth* (New York: Scribner, 1915), 66–69; 70–74. The first paragraph of "The Honest Day's Work" has been omitted for clarity.

men in sufficient numbers shall constitute the requisite counterbalance and corrective. It is doubtful whether any kind of profit sharing in closely controlled industries can ever be as effective in training responsible men for a democracy, other things being equal, as an occupation or series of occupations in which the worker is responsible for his own results rather than to an overseer, although the profit sharing may for the time being develop the greater technical efficiency.

The influence of ownership on the performance of the man is often well illustrated when the farm laborer or tenant becomes the proprietor. Some of my readers will have had experience in the difficult and doubtful process of trying to "run a farm" at long range by means of ordinary hired help: the residence is uninhabitable; the tools are old and out of date, and some of them cannot be found; the well water is not good; the poultry is of the wrong breed, and the hens will not sit; the horses are not adapted to the work; the wagons must be painted and the harnesses replaced; the absolutely essential supplies are interminable; there must be more day labor. Now let this hired man come into the ownership of the farm: presto! The house can be repaired at almost no cost; the tools are good for some years yet; the harnesses can easily be mended; the absolutely essential supplies dwindle exceedingly; and the outside labor reduces itself to minor terms.

Work with machinery, in factories, may proceed more rapidly because the operator must keep up with the machine; and there are also definite standards or measures of performance. Yet even here it is not to be expected that the work will be much more than time-service. In fact, the very movement among labor is greatly to emphasize time-service, and often quite independently of justice. There must necessarily be a reaction from this attitude if we are to hope for the best human product.

The best human product results from the bearing of responsibility; in a controlled labor body the responsibility is shifted to the organization or to the boss. Assuredly the consolidating of labor is much to be desired if it is for the common benefit and for protection, and if it leaves the laborer free with his own product. Every person has the inalienable right to express himself, so long as it does not violate similar rights of his fellows, and to put forth his best production; if a man can best express himself in manual labor, no organization should suppress him or deny him that privilege. It is a sad case, and a denial of fundamental liberties, if a man is not allowed to work or to produce as much as he desires. Good development does not come from repression.

Society recognizes its obligation to the laboring man of whatever kind and the necessity of safeguarding him both in his own interest and because he stands at the very foundations; the laboring man bears an obligation to respond liberally with service and goodwill.

I. WORKMANSHIP

Is it desirable to have an important part of the labor of a people founded on ownership? Is it worthwhile to have an example in a large class of the population of manual work that is free-spirited, and not dominated by class interest and time-service? Is it essential to social progress that a day's work shall be full measure?

ONE of the interesting phenomena of human association is the arising of a certain standard or norm of moral action within the various groups that compose it.[3] These standards may not be inherently righteous, but they become so thoroughly established as to be enacted into law or even to be more powerful than law. So is it, as we have seen, with the idea of inalienable rights in natural property that may be held even out of all proportion to any proper use that the owners may be able to make of it; and so is it with the idea of inviolable natural privileges to those who control facilities that depend on public patronage for their commercial success. The man himself may hold one kind of personal morals, but the group of which he is a part may hold a very different kind. It is our problem, in dealing with the resources of the earth, to develop in the group the highest expression of duty that is to be found in individuals.

The restraint of the group, or the correction of the group action, is applied from the outside in the form of public opinion and in attack by other groups. The correction does not often arise from within. The establishing of many kinds of public service bodies illustrates this fact. It is the check of society on group selfishness.

These remarks apply to the man who stands at the foundation of society, next the earth, as well as to others, although he has not organized to propagate the action of his class. The spoliation of land, the insufficient regard for it, the trifling with it, is much more than an economic deficiency. Society will demand either through the pressure of public opinion, or by regularized action, that the producing power of the land shall be safeguarded and increased, as I have indicated in a earlier part of the discussion. It will be better if it comes as the result of education, and thereby develops the voluntary feeling of obligation and responsibility. At the same time, it is equally the responsibility of every other person to make it possible for the farmer to prosecute his business under expression of the highest standards.

There is just now abroad amongst us a teaching to the effect that the farmer cannot afford to put much additional effort into his crop production, inasmuch as the profit in an acre may not depend on the increase in yield,

3. The first sentence under the original subhead (here omitted) "The group reaction," p. 70. The extra return preceding the original subhead is here preserved as a section break.

and therefore he does not carry on obligation to augment his acre-yields. This is a weakening philosophy.

Undoubtedly there is a point beyond which he may not go with profit in the effort to secure a heavy yield, for it may cost him too much to produce the maximum; so it may not be profitable for a transportation company to maintain the highest possible speed. With this economic question I have nothing to do; but it is the farmer's moral responsibility to society to increase his production, and the stimulation reacts powerfully upon himself. It is a man's natural responsibility to do his best: it is specially important that the man at the bottom put forth his best efforts. To increase his yields is one of the ways in which he expresses himself as a man and applies his knowledge. This incentive taken away, agriculture loses one of its best endeavors, the occupation remains stationary or even deteriorates, and society loses a moral support at the very point where it is most needed.

If the economic conditions are such that the farmer cannot afford to increase his production, then the remedy is to be found without rather than by the repression of the producer. We are expending vast effort to educate the farmer in the ways of better production, but we do not make it possible for him to apply this education to the best advantage.

The real farmer, the one whom we so much delight to honor, has a strong moral regard for his land, for his animals, and his crops. These are established men, with highly developed obligations, feeling their responsibility to the farm on which they live. No nation can long persist that does not have this kind of citizenry in the background.

I have spoken of one phase of the group, as suggested in the attitude of the farmer. It may be interesting to recall, again, the fact that the purpose of farming is changing. The farmer is now adopting the outlook and the moral conduct of commerce. His business is no longer to produce the supplies for his family and to share the small overplus with society. He grows or makes a certain line of produce that he sells for cash, and then he purchases his other supplies in the general market. The days of homespun are gone. The farmer is as much a buyer as a seller. Commercial methods and standards are invading the remotest communities. This will have far-reaching results. Perhaps a fundamental shift in the moral basis of the agricultural occupations is slowly underway.

The measuring of farming in terms of yields and incomes introduces a dangerous standard. It is commonly assumed that state monies for agriculture education may be used only for "practical"—that is, for dollars-and-cents—results, and the emphasis is widely placed very exclusively on more alfalfa, more corn, more hogs, more fruit, on the two-blades-of-grass morals; and yet the highest good that can accrue to a state for the expenditure of its money is the raising up of a population less responsive to cash than to some other stimuli. The good physical support is indeed essential, but it is only the beginning of a process. I am conscious of a peculiar hardness in some of the agriculture enterprise, with little real uplook; I hope that we may soon pass this cruder phase.

Undoubtedly we are in the beginning of an epoch in rural affairs. We are at a formative period. We begin to consider the rural problem increasingly in terms of social groups. The attitudes that these groups assume, the way in which they react to their problems, will be determined in the broader aspects for some time to come by the character of the young leadership that is now taking the field.

Nails

"Pull out the nails before you come in."
"But they can be bought at the store cheaper than I can pull them."
"You have nothing else to do, and the store is far away."

The significance of this situation did not come to me then.[4] Probably I had been told by some wise person that a boy's time was worth money and that nails and such trifles are cheaper than hours; and, besides, the old stick and the big rusty nails probably did not look any too attractive to a hungry boy.

A boy's time—has it only a cash value? Is that not the time when habits of frugality, industry, obedience, and self-help should be formed, and can these results be stated in any kind of bookkeeping? There are hours or minutes when time has no recognizable accounting value; it is better to employ them in effort that may not meet the needs of strict "efficiency" than to let them go to waste or the mind to lie fallow. And the store, that was not my problem, for it was far away; my problem was the nails in a splintery hemlock scantling.

But on the whole I liked to pull nails. It was almost like play. Moreover, it saved me from weeding onions or cleaning out the cistern. These were "cut nails," with the four sharp angles and real heads, not the shiny improved kind that buckle in the middle. I think they did not hold so tight as the modern nail and were therefore better adapted to boys. They came out bent and crooked; some of the big spikes had to be hammered through the scantling and then driven back again for a better hold. Most of them had to be straightened; this was real sport, to put them on the end of the big tree trunk block standing by the barn door and to hammer them into shape; it was like making something; a boy could immediately see the result of his work; and how perfectly they would drive afterwards! I remember that when I had nails to drive I always

4. From *The Harvest of the Year to the Tiller of the Soil*, 191–195.

chose the rusty ones or those that had been straightened, and I fear this pernicious habit has remained in some degree to the present year of efficiency. Perhaps there was a sense of ownership about it, for new nails were all alike and anybody could have them; in these days I suppose we would call this perversity by the big name "self-determination."

But I had not really intended to write about nails when I started this article. The title of an article or a lecture is one thing, the subject is quite another matter. I meant to pay my respects to the gentle art of doing things yourself.

The hinge is broken on the henhouse door: fix it. The hoe needs a new handle; the strap is broken; the lock is out of order; the barn door is off the track; the saw is dull; the fencepost has rotted off; the gate is sagging; the clevis is bent and out of shape; a tooth is missing from the hay rake; the plow handle is loose; the crosscut saw is rusty; the pump will not work; the eavetrough needs painting; the pipe to the watertank is stopped; a shingle is off the barn roof; a stanchion is rickety: do it yourself.

There are no servants to wait on you, no one to hire. There are no "regulations" about it, no one to consult for permission or regularity, no indirection. The little set of simple tools is a great consolation. Its employment to make things for oneself is good recreation. The hand tools were one of the wonders of my younger years. Many of them are now rare and some of them are obsolete. Last year I went to a hardware store to purchase an inch-and-a-half auger; I thought one would look well in my shop. The young man behind the counter wanted to know what I meant, how I spelled it, had never heard of such a tool. I asked him how folks bored big holes any more, and he replied that they did not bore them, they took them to town to be bored.

To be apt with hands and tools is to be "handy." The handiness means something when the work is real, and not make-believe; it has both interest and educational value. In all the range of human occupation, I know of none that properly calls for so many kinds of hand-cleverness with simple elemental tools as farming. Of course there is evidence enough of the lack of any kind of hand skill not to say of plain indifference to appearances and to upkeep; but awkwardness and slovenliness are not a part of anything. Nothing is more suggestive than the old tools even if past their usefulness; with them go the boxes of nails and screws and nuts and bolts and washers probably all mixed as to sizes and kinds; they stand along the plate four and one-half feet above the floor near the window in the south end of the horse barn; there is a bench the other side the window, with a big and little hammer, brace and bit, jack-plane, scythe-stone—you know the rest if you have been there, and the spider webs.

But I am not dealing here with memories except as I may state my theme. I hope farm tools and shops are better and cleaner than in the past, that the satisfaction of good workmanship is growing, and that persons take pride in their ability to turn their hands to many kinds of action. It is a real problem how to train the hands and to produce something worthwhile at the same time, and to make the training count toward life. It should be a necessity to try to eliminate go-betweens and indirectness in the usual needs and affairs, to wait on oneself, to enjoy the independence of it, not to depend on others. With the increasing complexity of houses and machines and the minute subdivision of labor, we are forced more and more into the hands of experts and specialists, and there is danger that we become more helpless and indirect.

I think the pulling of nails meant more than simply saving the cost of new ones. If we pulled more nails, in a metaphorical sense, we should have less facility in calling on someone else.

From Haying-Time to Radio

"Haying-time" in that day, fifty years and more ago in what was then called "The West," was a momentous event.[5] Dates were reckoned from it. With house-cleaning in early spring and sheep-shearing later on and hog-killing in the autumn, it was one of the epochs of the year. It was interesting to see the great fleece come off the sheep and to watch the thin, wraith-like animal that was hidden within it take strangely to the field and try to make itself at home again, but there was no event in the work of the year that seemed to change things so completely as haying.

In those early days I was not heavy enough to take much part in the mowing, and there were men in the neighborhood (we had no communities then) who were adept with the scythe; but I carried water for the men and the inevitable lunches in the mid-forenoon and mid-afternoon and I was stout enough for the hand rake and the cocking of the hay; and the change that came over the field was very real as I watched the grass fall evenly hour after hour under the advancing *swish-swish* of the scythes around and around the fields, and even the whetting of the long blades as the mower stood the snath on its end added punctuation to the transformation of the scene.

Since May the meadow had been forbidden territory. Every track through the timothy would show. We might skirt the edges of the field, along the rail fence; we might go up the little brook that started from the upturned stump in the farther corner of the field; but we could not be tempted into the grassy wilderness, not even by meadowlarks and bobolinks or the silent bells of wild lilies. Yet we knew there must be strange things in the depths of the grass. The mowing would disclose it all; and eagerly we would watch the mowers as they closed in on the last square of grass in the middle of the field, an operation known as "catching the rabbit." Like the odor of new-plowed

5. From *The Harvest of the Year to the Tiller of the Soil* (New York: Macmillan, 1927), 25–41.

land in spring, the fragrance of new-mown hay and wilting weeds was itself worth waiting for, even for a year and a day. When the grass was down we had a new landscape. Again we could go to the old stump, we could climb on the stone pile now grown full of raspberries, and the brooklet once more dominated the scene. We would not go around by the road any more, but "cut across" the meadow.

It was like a holiday when the first mowing machine came to that part of the country. It came in from York State—and that of itself was an event—and my father was proud to have the neighbors look it over; and I doubt not that much engineering wisdom was dispensed by the visitors. We took much pride in the machine although it was a lumbering invention as compared with the patterns of the present day; but somehow the meadow began to lose its interest to me. We spent much time in fall and early spring cleaning the fields of stumps and stones and stubs, and in leveling the uneven surfaces; this of itself made the meadow much too respectable for wandering boys. Moreover, the machine could not talk but only whiz and burr and get tangled up in the long weeds and balk against a snag; and I never became civilized enough to enjoy turning grindstone to sharpen that endless cutter-bar, and the holder of it seemed to delight in putting his whole weight on it.

But my chief indictment against the mowing machine was the fact that haying-time was no longer an epoch in the year. In the former time haying lasted three weeks; men came to the house to stay and they had stories to tell and experiences to relate, and they had new ways of doing things; now the wheel rake had come with the mowing machine and haying was only a mechanical labor and it was all over in less than a week. It was only the loading of the hay from the cock or windrow and the hauling to the barn and the "mowing away" in the bay that made haying a human event and a separate season; and now even this event is taken away from us by the hay-loading machine and the power fork.

While we did not realize it then, the advent of the wonderful mowing machine marked the beginnings of a significant change in our farming; and what was true for us was equally true for everyone else as machines and new ideas began their fateful entrance into the farming regions. These changes have been of two diverse kinds—those affecting farming practice, and those altering the sentiment of the farming people.

Not in years but in effect those days are long ago. My father was reared in the "golden age of homespun," now made real for us by Horace Bushnell and Jared Van Wagenen, and I was brought up with his recollections; and I myself saw the last fading years of that epoch and even then every good farm was in some sense a factory, and the village blacksmith, harness-maker, wagon-maker, shoemaker, cooper, tanner and miller were realities, and the sawmills were doing their best to use up the timber.

It is not necessary to recount the innovations in farming practice now represented in such matters as wire fencing, sulky plows, tractors, bagged fertilizers, separators, milk tests, milking machines, feeding rations, dehorned cattle, disease prevention, spraying, incubators, seed tests and seed selection, hard roads, motor cars, gas stations, central heating, market reports, hail insurance, daily newspaper, rural delivery of mail, reapers, radio, and a thousand other items so common that we do not know we have them.

These many innovations increase desires and deepen the daily life, let alone the great influence exerted by colleges of agriculture and experiment stations, the periodical and book press, and the free advice from everybody. We remember the pride of the farm boy in a snappy horse and buggy with which he could drive to town; then came the flair for the bicycle; then the automobile; and I do not know what it will be tomorrow. We are advised that the farm needs new machines; the residence must be newly furnished, and with electric lights and waterworks, a piano, talking-machine and radio, the kitchen must be sanitary, the diet must be varied and caloried and vitamined. The clothing must be as fashionable as in the town; the health regulations for the children must be adopted; the physical scale of living must be as good as that for any other range of people. The youth must join the clubs and go to college.

All this costs money, and in more than geometrical ratio. Yet the productivity of the land is capable of only limited increase. The selling price of the produce may rise, but the buying prices of manufactured supplies rise in at least equal ratio. The producing power of the land cannot extend in proportion to the coveted increase in scale of living; and the farmer finds himself dealing with nature and living against a natural market, whereas many of those with whom he deals or at least whom he emulates live in artificial conditions and increase their income by arbitrary mass action through organization and understandings rather than by the merit or skill or necessity of the service or the labor; and the increased cost of products arising from such unnatural control are charged back on the farmer and other consumers. The very statement of the case shows the money disadvantage under which the farmer works.

It is not alone in the field labor that changes have come. The hand manufacture has gone out of the household, and the farmer now buys in the market what once was his own production. As long as the old home was in the family, I looked for the candle molds when I returned to it; I recalled the melted tallow, and I had helped to "try it out" after the sheep were killed;

54

I remember wicking the molds and pouring in the melted fat; and of course I could not forget the eagerness to see the product taken out the next day or the attractiveness of the long white glistening candles with the handsomely tapered end and the modest protruding wick. I can yet hear the creak of the cheese press and the strain of the wooden frame as the weight was applied. I remember the skimmer with which the cream was taken off the pans of milk on the pantry shelves, an implement now forgotten. I know the back-ache in the old dash churn and recall with grief how the birds sang and the band played in the streets just when churning-day was on in the cellar; the wooden butter bowl and the ladle completed the process. I can hear the matronly hum of the spinning wheel and the thud of the loom. I recall how we tanned hides and made soap. In the wood-fire days, when we were burning up the forests and putting them into buildings, the lye barrel was always standing under the tree by the grindstone, and in the soap-making season we caught the scalding lixivium as it dripped from the hardwood ashes; this enterprise was an essential part of a good farm home. The first sewing machine I saw was set on the windowsill and was turned by a crank; we knew it was only for the rich. Some things we unmade; I remember the first watch I saw and the curiosity to know what was inside it; and for years when I went home I found some of the wheels of it still resting in the button box. In those days inventions and machines were not commonplace.

On all these many little manufactures we now pay a profit to someone else, and the farm must produce the income to enable us to do it. It does not occur to us, when we puzzle ourselves over the farming situation, that the farm is now loaded with a thousand expenditures that were not required in former days.

We are not to stay innovations. They stimulate new life and make for effectiveness. But there is danger in them in the fact that they may awaken an insatiable desire for mere novelty and for baubles, that have no relation to life and that are not earned by the requestor. Parents become so desirous of granting every wish that children grow up with little sense of values, with the mind so blinded by trifles and toys that realities may have no meaning. All this imposes a heavy tax on resources, far above anything known fifty years ago, and I sometimes fear that there may be no real benefit in making them. This has particular significance to the conduct of those who live with natural values and are not able to increase daily income by an organized attack on society or by campaigns of alluring advertising.

YET, with all the mutations that have come over farming and country life, the changes have not been revolutionary. The problem of production from the land, which is farming, is the same as ever even though modified and ameliorated by a thousand new practices and inventions. As far as anything is stationary, farming is the one occupation that exhibits it. Then it follows that major readjustments in other affairs, in the revolutions of transportation and commerce and in business advantages, tend to react unfavorably on the farmer's position. As he is the bottom man, living on the native soil, he cannot take it out on someone else; he cannot greatly change his personal status by means of prepared drives; he stands his ground as long as he can and then quits, and in the process he may deplete or abuse the land and leave society that much the poorer.

It is only the good farms well farmed that can support all these extra necessities and the luxuries. This means that infertile lands should not be tilled until the need for them is far greater than at present, and it is doubtful how far it will ever pay us to go in an effort to remake them.

Added to the natural difficulties of the situation are the inequalities of sumptuary legislation. We naturally reprehend blocs and class legislation and hope it will not be necessary for farming to make its headway by such means; yet we are to remember that in the United States we have been more or less governed by blocs for any number of years although we have not known the high tariff forces for manufacturers, labor drives, and other mass movements, under that designation. If vast changes have come about in methods and in organized effectiveness it is to be expected that they must come equally in basic legislation. Adjustments need to be made horizontally and throughout. Wholly aside from the specific effects of high tariff and similar legislation—and both sides of the question can be abundantly supported by citations—we are to remember the moral effect on the sentiments of the people of any trade legislation instituted by a particular caste for its benefit. There is danger even in the presumption of class benefit that is raised by such legislation. The discriminatory nature of tariff legislation in the United States is itself a greater damage than the specific favors granted to industries and groups. And the situation is all the more obnoxious from the fact that to this day the subject is obfuscated by partisan propaganda on both sides, and the long effort to "take the tariff out of politics" has not succeeded.

My argument here is not particularly to expound any movement, for probably we have movements too many, but to express the essential difficulty in which the farmer finds himself by being a farmer, and to call attention to the fact that society as an organism has a direct concern in the situation not only in the narrow question of the cost of food supplies but in the broad requisite to safeguard the men and women who keep the earth for the good of all of us and who constitute the only real social background. The great changes in farming and in rural life, while eventuating highly to the good of the farmer, nevertheless tend to accentuate the essential difficulty of the agricultural profession and make the situation a national concern.

My own suggestion for radical modification of our political or legislative action in respect to the farmer has been made many times in recent years; I shall repeat it in due time in this little book [*The Harvest of the Year to the Tiller of the Soil*], for it is only a sentence; it seems singularly inept to most persons and therefore there is no need of haste in presenting it. In parenthesis it may be observed that it is a pity that we are obliged to associate legislation with partisan politics as if the two were of the same breed; it ought to be possible to enact legislation on a logical and scientific basis, and when we can do this we may consider ourselves to have arrived at civic mastery.

FREQUENTLY I am asked whether farmers of this day are really as well off as fifty and more years ago. This question cannot be answered, for much depends on the yardstick whereby we measure; nor is it safe to rely on situations that live now only in the sacred mists of memory. Yet some things are plain. We have largely changed our valuations of life. We have passed the time when men naturally lived the life of the common lot and have entered the day of accounting the incomes; every public or semipublic record of income, whether for purpose of efficiency or taxation, affixes the fiscal standard and stimulates competition or even rivalry in financial rating. We even have the assurance to place statistical values on human beings. The desire for gain becomes so dominant as to beget discontent. The bare analyses of agricultural returns, continually repeated without reassuring counsel, tend to develop this habit of mind. It would seem as if we set out laboriously to breed dissatisfactions.

If I am disturbed by the troubles of the present day, I like to go back to the agricultural literature of fifty to one hundred years and more ago, when the art of retailing woes was less developed than with us, and read "observations on cattle, sheep and hogs," about blind drains, "the plough," pasture grounds and fencing, spring grains and early potatoes, the poultry yard, the honey bee, family salt, and specially the farm surveys and reckonings. Men then, in North America, were nearer the pioneer stage, when great tasks were to be accomplished that needed muscle and fortitude. In at least the situations I knew there was wholesome common effort and neighborhood spirit that we now try vainly to produce by means of organizers and applied pressures; the forms of expression were crude, to be sure, we had little or no bank account, but there was nothing like the current discontent. We relied wholly on our own efforts, which is an essential to success. Of course I would not go back to the old days, even if I could; undoubtedly we are evolving a new type of farmer; yet I find myself thinking that the spirits of the grandfathers and grandmothers have something to tell us when we are ready to hear. I am wondering now and then whether we have not cast off our moorings before we have named the port to which we have set sail.

Grandparents have peculiar significance in agriculture, for good farming is an affair of more than one lifetime. If one desires a real mark of cleavage between farming and what we are pleased to call business, one will find it here—in the fact that the land remains generation after generation and that it passes down as men come and go, home and all, carrying the same essential enterprises and its accumulated impulsion even from century to century. Farming is the only occupation that constantly renews itself: it is a perpetual resurrection.

Family continuity should be strong in agriculture. A man does not learn his land and his climate and the possibilities of his place in much less than a working lifetime. When a man takes a farm, he settles. The roving peripatetic tillers of the soil are really not farmers; they do not identify themselves with a piece of land. The man who takes the farm from his father has a strong start, if the farm is a good one and has been well kept.

The number of grandfather farms in a community has real importance. Of course there are many farms not good enough to be passed to grandsons. There are many other reasons and conditions making it impracticable or impossible for farms to remain in the family. The present pressures on farming are driving people from the poor and crabbed lands and the inaccessible places even as they are forcing out the persons not adapted to the occupation; at present this movement from the land is especially strong and we may expect it to continue until adjustment has become more or less complete.

All the more impressive, therefore, are the true grandfather farms. There is great pride in any business that has continued for one hundred years, and records are made of such accomplishments. Will not someone begin a study of grandfather farms, noting those that have passed down in direct line for three generations and more as actual workable properties that make the support and the life of all these occupants? The changes have been many since the whetstone days of my boyhood. The whole reaction in the fabric of rural life has come within this period. I have been vastly stimulated by the observation of it and know that the present days are preferable to the past. If I have no illusions as to the agricultural situation neither do I harbor any despair. I still look for wholesome changes, and I see every reason for encouragement even in the face of maladjustments. These maladjustments are largely monetary. But there are other rewards than the money income although one would hardly be aware of them from current discussions, which, in the language of the day, are set in terms of business. One would think that the achievements of civilization are to be expressed in tonnage.

These other rewards cannot be taken away by commercial and legislative movements, although, to be sure, one must have an untroubled mind to enjoy them to the best; yet if one is sensitive to what, on an earlier page, I have called the psychic income, one is able to surmount and overcome much that is discouraging. We are led to think that the farmer's value to society is in his turnover, in the food and fiber that he can produce cheaply, but his major contribution is in the psychic or spiritual realm, and on his attainment in this range will his ultimate destiny as a person depend.

FIFTY eventful years have passed. In that period we have come from conditions relatively ancient to prospects that baffle the imagination. We are in a prophetic time, our eyes to the future. The riches of life have multiplied, and the good things we may have for little effort are numberless. We may take our choice from the multitudes; we surfeit ourselves and fail of satisfaction if we try to take them all. If we give up the old we may still retain a pleasant memory of it and restrain ourselves to moderation in the present. In the midst of it all we should be able to develop a gentle philosophy of life. The haying-time of those days has gone forever, and I no longer want the scythe as a major agricultural instrument; nor do I need all the contrivances of the present day.

Soil

They would have us believe that mechanical power will be so abundantly distributed and so pleasantly adjusted that the farmer may keep his hands in his pockets and not even drive a horse; for all the tillage will be accomplished by oversight rather than by labor.[6] It is said by others that in some remote future we may cease entirely to till the soil in the current sense and raise food and other supplies from improved kinds of trees and shrubs that require planting only once in a generation or two and no attention of tillage in the meantime. It is said, also, that we shall raise plants in water of lakes and swamps and thus escape the tillage. Others, again, will have us cease eating and take our food in doses from a test tube or other chemical contrivance or in capsules; and still others will practice some kind of subtlety with sunshine and nitrogen and derive our manna from the atmosphere.

It is surprising to what painful theories men will consign themselves in the hope of escaping labor; and it is the more amazing when the labor is altogether so satisfying as the tilling of the land. There may be an overplus of anything, but I never knew a farmer or a gardener who did not like to work in the soil; or if there is such a one, then he is not a farmer or a gardener. To break the land is the first rousing ambition of spring. Seedbags and corncribs and bins of potatoes all wait for spring and the planting: that is their destiny; or if some of the number fall to the merciless hap of the cook then is their misfortune complete and hopeless. For tillage is not alone the opening and the stirring of the soil: it is the beginning and the nurture of new generations. It is a mighty power the soil-tiller holds, from bare earth or in place of vagabondish weeds to produce cotton and sugar cane and chrysanthemums.

Yet the manual tillage is itself an entertainment. One feels that things are let loose when the land is plowed and dragged. Slumbering powers are

6. From *The Harvest of the Year to the Tiller of the Soil* (New York: Macmillan, 1927), 127–134.

awakened. Rains are invited. The night and the morning contribute to the process. The sun enters in. The air invades the pores. The multitudes of mighty living things so small we cannot see them are somehow vivified and set to work.

Beside all this, it is a sensation to hear the break and crackle of the furrow, to catch the loosened odor that comes out of the ground, to see the stubble and weeds fall under, to feel the exhalation of buried moisture newly released. It is all a pleasant contrast from hard and particularly from newly swept pavements, from barn floors, and fences and roofs and all the things that men proudly contrive. We get back, even if for a short time, to men in olden time, to prairies, to forests newly cleared. We are out by brooks and nesting birds, and windy bloom, and soaring hawks, and horizons bounding real landscapes. What if there were no brooks and nesting birds, no windblown bloom and soaring wings, no horizons resting on the hills? Ah well! and well!

Very likely it is true that we shall find new sources of energy and of food; this is to be expected, and this is probably the answer in part to those who foresee starvation ahead of us; but in our time, at least, we may safely count on tilling the soil; and even if beyond our present dreams we find the new sources, we shall probably need the soil in the bargain to satisfy the desires if not the actual needs of the race; and perhaps, also, men will be recompensed for tilling the soil in the very joy of tilling it, seeing that men must always have occupation; and in these natural kinds of occupation we shall ever find new satisfactions as knowledge accumulates and as appreciation grows, for the discovery of the nature of the soil is not yet complete.

A soil becomes personal to a man. The longer he works it the more it means to him and the greater should be its response. It never grows old to him. Memories become imbedded in it, and it expresses the generations of men. There is a flair for new land, and yet it is on the old soils that a permanent agriculture must rest.

IN my youth we knew that we knew all about the soil, or as much as farmers need to know. It was then, under the teaching of Liebig and the early explorers, a reservoir of chemicals. Then came the great subject of "soil physics," and a new conception of the soil was placed before us. We began to talk about the soil particle, and structure and texture. Then came the biology of it, with the discovery and apprehension of the micro-organic life therein, and we visioned a living soil. Now we are uncovering the complex subject of colloid matter in the soil. Acidity and alkalinity have become realities in practice. Probably in no field of knowledge touching farming has there been such a wealth of new information to stimulate interest in such a common subject. There are professorships in soils; it was only a score of years ago that the word began to find itself in such titles; and in 1927 the United States has had the privilege of entertaining an International Congress of Soil Science. "Soils" has come to be a department of knowledge.

In these days of tractors and gang-plows and all the curious implements, we little realize how recent is the idea of soil tillage by any other means than human muscle. It is only two centuries ago that Jethro Tull began to develop his "Horse-hoeing husbandry" and to explain the reasons for tillage; and even in my youth the application of other power to the land was not within our dreams. Yet in spite of all this advancement, and partly because of it, tillage becomes ever more significant, and the man cannot separate himself from the soil.

The practice of tillage is no longer the mere stirring of the soil, for the careful tiller must know what he is doing. The fertilizing of land is not now merely a process in subtraction and addition. Drainage has new reasons. If the hoe-man and the plowman are alive to the new knowledge they will find recuperation for the spirit; and St. Paul wrote to Timothy that "the husbandman that laboureth must be the first partaker of the fruits." It is not to be supposed that we are even yet in sight of the end of it. The next generation may have a very different conception of the supply of soil nitrogen and of fertility in general. The inexorable subject of soil exhaustion even now takes on a changing form of discussion, although the necessity of safeguarding fertility is as much a moral and social problem as ever. There are reasons for supposing that we shall discover electrical phenomena of great importance in relation to soil fertility.

As far as authoritative science is concerned, tillage takes on constantly a new significance; and thereby it is elevated above drudgery into the realm of rational procedure. The importance of tillage as an operation in the affairs of men is ahead of us rather than behind us.

We shall welcome every new method and source of food supply. Some day we may utilize the ponds and swamps without necessarily draining and tilling them: with others, I have long recommended it. We shall have synthetic foods, but the importance of them to the major problems of existence is yet at least visionary. But we shall also keep the plow and the harrow in condition, and the cultivator and hoe, and shall find increasing use for them and more joy in applying them. With the increase of learning, we find the common objects and the usual relations to have unsuspected meanings; the riches of life are constantly and repeatedly augmented.

Thin like the skin of an apple, the soil layer of the earth has been formed through countless ages of weathering and disintegration and the accumulation of organic remains. The history of the planet is recorded in it. Whatever may be at the center of the Earth, we know that this thin exterior supports the life of the planet, and it is the arena on which the drama of civilization is acted. The plants and animals cease to live and their remains go back to the earth from which they came—to the soil beneath and the air above, expressing the union of the physical elements of life. All we know of life and death and bold activity are conditioned on the ground and to it we ourselves return, to the dust of the scripture, a word without special connotation and that suggests the universality of the process.

Only once have the King James translators rendered a term into the agricultural word "soil," wherein was planted the vine of Ezekiel's riddle, "that it might bring forth branches, and that it might bear fruit, that it might be a goodly vine." To us the word suggests fertility, yields, occupations, industries, the foothold of all things. It suggests many tools of strength and great simplicity, not less artistic because so common. The staff, the wheel, the easel, and many other tools and contrivances appear in artistic interpretations; if good line and proportion, simplicity, direct adaptation to use, appropriate materials, are elements of art, then the hoe, the rake, and the modern plow are abundantly qualified. It would be much loss to the imaginative inheritance of men if the sense of tillage tools were eliminated.

We admire all work that is well executed. It may be a bridge spanning a river, a monument, a smooth-running machine, a well-woven fabric. I trust we are quick also to admire a well-prepared field ready for the seeding: the boundaries are definite and clean; the contours are pleasing; the colors exist nowhere else; the plowing is straight and uniform; the surface preparation leaves a finish suggesting good intention and prosperity; the area is abundant with promise; and if you yourself fitted the field you have a memory of weather, of clouds adrift, of birds and perhaps of little quadrupeds, insects, cattle on greensward, distant barns, dusty wind, tools with no superfluities, the sound of good tilth, little runnels for the rain, stones and perhaps of rock, roots seeking food, trees and blossoms, last year's dead leaves, earthy odors, and of satisfaction in an honest useful day's work.

The Daily Fare

It was more than three centuries ago that native Thomas Tusser, musician, chorister, and farmer, gave to the world his incomparable *Five Hundred Points of Good Husbandry*.[7] He covered the farm year and the farm work as completely as Virgil had covered it more than fifteen centuries before; and he left us sketches of the countryside of his day, and the ways of the good plain folk, and quaint bits of philosophy and counsel. He celebrated the Christmas festival with much conviction, and in the homely way of the home folks, deriving his satisfaction from the things that the land produces. His sketches are wholesome reading in these days of foods transported from the ends of the earth, and compounded by impersonal devices and condensed into packages that go into every house alike.

Thomas Tusser would celebrate with "things handsome to have, as they ought to be had." His board would not be scant of provisions, for he seems not to have advised the simple life in the way of things good to eat; but he chose good raw materials, and we can imagine that the "good husband and huswife" gave these materials their best compliments and prepared them with diligence and skill. Not once does he suggest that these materials be secured from the market, or that any imported labor be employed in the preparation of them.

> Good bread and good drink, a good fire in the hall, Brawn, pudding, and souse, and good mustard withal.

Here is the whole philosophy of the contented festival: the fruit of one's labor, the common genuine materials, and the cheer of the family fireside. The day is to be given over to the spirit of the celebration; every common

---

7. From *The Holy Earth* (New York: Scribner, 1915), 90–102; 103–114. For concision, this excerpt begins with the third paragraph of the subheading "The daily fare."

object will glow with a new consecration, and everything will be good—even the mustard will be good withal. What a contempt old Tusser would have had for all the imported and fabricated condiments and trivialities that now come to our tables in packages suggestive of medicines and drugs! And how ridiculously would they have stood themselves beside the brawn, pudding, and souse! A few plain accessories, every one stout and genuine, and in good quantity, must accompany the substantialities that one takes with a free hand directly from the land that he manages.

It surprises us that he had such a bountiful list from which to draw, and yet the kinds are not more than might be secured from any good land property, if one set about securing them:

> Beef, mutton, and pork, shred pies of the best,
> Pig, veal, goose, and capon, and turkey well drest,
> Cheese, apples, and nuts, joly carols to hear,
> As then in the country, is counted good cheer.

In these days we should draw less heavily on the meats, for in the three centuries we have gained greatly in the vegetable foods. Tusser did not have the potato. But nevertheless, these materials are on the very bone of the land. They grow up with the year and out of the conditions, and they have all the days in them, the sunshine, the rain, the dew of morning, the wind, the cold foggy nights, and the work of laborious hands. Every one of them means something to the person who raises them, and there is no impersonality in them. John's father drained the land when yet he was a boy; the hedges were set; long ago the place was laid out in its rotations; the old trees in the fields are a part of it; every stall in the stables and every window-seat in the old house memories; and John has grown up with these memories, and with these fields and with the footpaths that lead out over brooks and amongst the herds of cattle. It is a part of his religion to keep the land well; and these supplies at Christmas time are taken with a deep reverence for the goodness that is in them, and with a pride in having produced them.

And Thomas Tusser, good husbandman, rejoiced that these bounties cost no cash:

> What cost to good husband, is any of this?
> Good household provision only it is.
> Of other the like, I do leave out a many
> That costeth a husbandman never a penny.

To farm well; to provide well; to produce it oneself; to be independent of trade, so far as this is possible in the furnishing of the table—these are good elements in living. And in this day we are rapidly losing all this; many persons already have lost it; many have never known the satisfaction of it. Most of us must live from the box and the bottle and the tin can; we are even feeding our cattle from the factory and the bag. The farmer now raises a few prime products to sell, and then he buys his foods in the markets under label and tag; and he knows not who produced the materials, and he soon comes not to care. No thought of the seasons, and of the men and women who labored, of the place, of the kind of soil, of the special contribution of the native earth, come with the trademark or the brand. And so we all live mechanically, from shop to table, without contact, and irreverently.

May we not once in the year remember the earth in the food that we eat? May we not in some way, even though we live in town, so organize our Christmas festival that the thought of the goodness of the land and its bounty shall be a conscious part of our celebration? May we not for once reduce to the very minimum the supply of manufactured and sophisticated things, and come somewhere near, at least in spirit, to a "Christmas husbandly fare?"

Yet, Thomas Tusser would not confine his husbandly fare to the Christmas time. In another poem, he gives us "The farmer's daily diet," in which the sturdy products are still much the same, secured and prepared by those who partake. All this may be little applicable literally on our present living, and yet I think it is easily possible, as certainly it is very desirable, to develop a new attitude toward the table fare, avoiding much unnecessary and insignificant household labor and lending an attitude of good morality to the daily sustenance.

Much of our eating and feasting is a vicious waste of time, and also of human energy that might be put to good uses. One can scarcely conceive how such indirect and uncomfortable and expensive methods could have come into use. Perhaps they originated with persons of quality in an aristocratic society, when an abundance of servants must be trained to serve and when distinctions in eating were a part of the distinction in rank. But to have introduced these laborious and unintelligent methods into hotels, where persons tarry for comfort and into homes that do not need to maintain an extrinsic appearance, is a vain and ludicrous imitation. The numbers of courses, with more service than food, that one often meets at the table d'hôte of the frequented hotels abroad, are most exasperating to one who values time and has a serious purpose in travel and a rightful care for the bodily apparatus. Here is the performance—it is nothing more than a performance, consisting in repeated changing of all the dishes, the removing of every fragment of edibles, and in passing very small separate parcels of food—that it was my lot to endure on an otherwise happy day in a hotel that had little else to distinguish it:

Course 1. Dry bread (no butter)
    Removal
Course 2. Soup (nothing else)
    Removal
Course 3. Fish (very economical), with a potato on the side
    Removal
Course 4. Veal, macaroni
    Removal
Course 5. Spoonful of green beans (nothing else)
    Removal
Course 6. Beef and salad (fragmentary)
    Removal
Course 7. Charlotte russe, bit of cake
    Removal
Course 8. Fruit (slight)
    Removal
Course 9. Morsel of cheese, one cracker
    Removal
Course 10. Coffee
    Relief.

The traveler knows that this species of time-wasting is not unusual; certainly the food is not unusual and does not merit such considerate attention, although it may profit by the magnification. All this contributes nothing to human efficiency—quite the reverse—and certainly nothing to the rightful gusto in the enjoyment of one's subsistence. It is a ceremony. Such laborious uselessness is quite immoral.

I am afraid that our food habits very well represent how far we have moved away from the essentials and how much we have misled ourselves as to the standards of excellence. I looked in a cookbook to learn how to serve potatoes: I found twenty-three recipes, every one of which was apparently designed to disguise the fact that they were potatoes; and yet there is really nothing in a potato to be ashamed of. Of course, this kind of deception is not peculiar to cookery. It is of the same piece as the stamping of the metal building coverings in forms to represent brick and stone, although everybody knows that they are not brick and stone, rather than to make a design that shall express metal and thereby frankly tell the truth; of the same kind also as the casting of cement blocks to represent undressed rock, although every one is aware of the deception, rather than to develop a form that will express cement blocks as brick expresses brick; of the same order as the inflating of good wholesome water by carbonic gas; and all the other deceits in materials on which our common affairs are built. It is, of course, legitimate to present our foods in many forms that we may secure variety even with scant and common materials; but danger may lie in any untruthfulness with which we use the raw materials of life.

So cookery has come to be a process of concealment. Not only does it conceal the materials, but it also conceals the names of them in a ridiculous nomenclature. Apparently, the higher the art of cookery, the greater is the merit of complete concealment. I think that one reason why persons enjoy the simple cooking of farmers and sailors and other elemental folk, is because of its comparative lack of disguise, although they may not be aware of this merit of it. We have so successfully disguised our viands through so many years that it is not "good form" to make inquiries: we may not smell the food, although the odor should be one of the best and most rightful satisfactions, as it is in fruits and flowers. We may smell a parsnip or a potato when it grows in the field, but not when it is cooked.

We add the extrinsic and meaningless odors of spices and flavorings, forgetting that odor no less than music hath occasions; each of the materials has its own odor that the discriminating cook will try to bring out in its best expression. Were we to be deprived of all these exotic seasonings, undoubtedly cookery would be the gainer in the end; nor could we so readily disguise materials that in themselves are not fit to eat. There is a reason why "all foods taste alike," as we often hear it said of the cooking in public places.

Moreover, we want everything that is out of season, necessitating great attention to the arts of preserving and requiring still further fabrication; and by this desire we also lessen the meaning of the seasons when they come in their natural sequence, bringing their treasure of materials that are adapted to the time and to the place. We can understand, then, why it so happens that we neglect the cookery of the common foods, as seeming to be not quite worth the while, and expend ourselves with so much effort on the accessories and the frills. I have been interested to observe some of the instruction in cooking—how it often begins with little desserts, and fudge, and a variety of dib-dabs. This is much like the instruction in manual training that begins with formal and meaningless model work or trivialities and neglects the issues of life. It is much like some of the teaching in agriculture not so many years ago, before we attacked very effectively the serious problems of wheat and alfalfa and forests and markets. Mastery does not lie in these pieces of play work, nor does the best intellectual interest on the part of the student reside in them.

The result is that one finds the greatest difficulty in securing a really good baked potato, a well-cooked steak, or a wholesome dish of applesauce that is not strained and flavored beyond recognition. It is nearly impossible for one to secure an egg fried hard and yet very tender and that has not been "turned" or scorched on the edges—this is quite the test of the skill of the good cook. The notion that a hard-fried egg is dangerously indigestible is probably a fable of poor cookery. One can secure many sophisticated and disguised egg dishes, but I think skill in plainly cooking eggs is almost an unknown art or perhaps a little-practiced art.

Now, it is on these simple and essential things that I would start my instruction in cookery; and this not only for the gain to good eating but also for the advantage of vigor and good morals. I am afraid that our cooking does not set a good example before the young three times every day in the year; and how eager are the young and how amenable to suggestion at these three blessed epochs every day in the year!

Of course, some unsympathetic reader will say that I am drawing a long bow; yet it is only a short way from deception in cookery to the deception in what we call adulteration of food. Undoubtedly, our cookery has prepared the public mind for adulteration. I do not mean to enter the discussion of food adulteration but I will leave with my reader a statement issued by a food chemist but a few years ago, letting him ponder on what had become a staggering infidelity in the use of the good raw materials and hoping that he will try to trace the causes:

Some of the more common forms of food adulterations are as follows:

Hamburg steak prepared at the market is very often found to contain sodium sulphite. Bologna sausage and similar meats sold in this State have, until very recently, usually contained from 1 to 30 percent of added cereal and the water that the cereal would take up.

Prepared flours, like "pancake flour," very often contain little if any buckwheat flour and are made up of the cheapest cereals. Wheat flour is bleached with nitric oxide to make it more pleasing to the eye at the expense of its nutritive value.

The high-priced, fancy French peas are colored green with sulphate of copper.

Bottled ketchup usually contains benzoate of soda as a preservative. This is necessary because the ketchup is so often made from the refuse of the tomato-canning factories and cooking is not sufficient to check the fermentation already started.

Japanese tea is colored with a cyanide of potassium and iron.

Prepared mustard usually contains a large amount of added starch and is colored yellow with tumeric.

69

Coffee, especially ground coffee, has recently been adulterated to a considerable extent with roasted peas.

So-called nonalcoholic bottled beverages often contain alcohol or a habit-forming drug and are usually given an attractive color by adding an aniline dye.

Candy is commonly colored with aniline dyes and often is coated with paraffin to prevent evaporation of moisture. A large amount of the cheaper candies contain substances like glue and soapstone.

The higher-priced molasses usually contain added sulphites.

Flavoring extracts are rarely made from pure products, and most always contain artificial coloring.

Strawberry and raspberry jams and jellies are rarely made from anything but apple jelly with a few berry seeds and coloring matter added. The cheap apple jelly is often imitated by a mixture of glucose, starch, aniline dye, and flavoring.

It is almost impossible to purchase lard that does not contain some added tallow.

The bakeries in the large cities have been the dumping ground for all kinds of decomposed food products, like decayed eggs.

Cheap ice cream of the soda-fountain variety is often made of gelatin, glue, starch.

Cottonseed oil worth twenty cents a quart is commonly sold for olive oil worth one dollar a quart.

Saccharine, one pound of which has the sweetening power of a barrel of sugar, is often used in place of sugar in all forms of prepared sweetened products. Saccharine is a poison and has no food value.

It is our habit to attach all the blame to the adulterators, and it is difficult to excuse them; but we usually find that there are contributory causes and certainly there must be reasons. Has our daily fare been honest?

Not even yet am I done with this plain problem of the daily fare.[8] The very fact that it is daily—thrice daily—and that it enters so much into the thought and effort of every one of us, makes it a subject of the deepest concern from every point of view. The aspect of the case that I am now to reassert is the effect of much of our food preparation in removing us from a knowledge of the good raw materials that come out of the abounding earth.

Let us stop to admire an apple. I see a committee of the old worthies in some fruit show going slowly and discriminatingly among the plates of fruit, discussing the shapes and colors and sizes, catching the fragrances, debating

8. The first sentence under the original subhead (here omitted) "The admiration of good materials," p. 103. The extra return preceding the original subhead is here preserved as section break.

the origins and the histories, and testing them with the utmost precaution and deliberation; and I follow to hear their judgment.

This kind of apple is very perfect in spherical from, deeply cut at the stem, well ridged at the shallow crater, beautifully splashed and streaked with carmine red on a yellowish green undercolor, finely flecked with dots, slightly russet on the shaded side, apparently a good keeper; its texture is fine grained and uniform, flavor mildly subacid, the quality good to very good; if the tree is hardy and productive, this variety is to be recommended to the amateur for further trial! The next sample is somewhat elongated in form, rather below the average in color, the stem very long and well set and indicating a fruit that does not readily drop in windstorm, the texture exceedingly melting but the flavor slightly lacking in character and therefore rendering it of doubtful value for further test. Another sample lacks decidedly in quality, as judged by the specimens on the table, and the exhibitor is respectfully recommended to withdraw it from future exhibitions; another kind has a very pronounced aromatic odor, which will commend it to persons desiring to grow a choice collection of interesting fruits; still another is of good size, very firm and solid, of uniform red color, slightly oblate and therefore lending itself to easy packing, quality fair to good, and if the tree bears such uniform samples as those shown on the table it apparently gives promise of some usefulness as a market sort. My older friends, if they have something of the feeling of the pomologist, can construct the remainder of the picture.

In physical perfectness of form and texture and color, there is nothing in all the world that exceeds a well-grown fruit. Let it lie in the palm of your hand. Close your fingers slowly about it. Feel its firm or soft and mottled surface. Put it against your cheek, and inhale its fragrance. Trace its neutral undercolors, and follow its stripes and mark its dots. If an apple, trace the eye that lies in a molded basin. Note its stem, how it stands firmly in its cavity, and let your imagination run back to the tree from which, when finally mature, it parted freely. This apple is not only the product of your labor, but it holds the essence of the year and it is in itself a thing of exquisite beauty. There is no other rondure and no other fragrance like this.

I am convinced that we need much to cultivate this appreciation of the physical perfectness of the fruits that we grow. We cannot afford to lose this note from our lives, for this may contribute a good part of our satisfaction of being in the world. The discriminating appreciation that one applies to a picture or a piece of sculpture may be equally applied to any fruit that grows on the commonest tree or bush in our field or to any animal that stands on a green pasture. It is no doubt a mark of a well tempered mind that it can understand the significance of the forms in fruits and plants and animals and apply it in the work of the day.

I. WORKMANSHIP

I sometimes think that the rise of the culinary arts is banishing this fine old appreciation of fruits in their natural forms. There are so many ways of canning and preserving and evaporating and extracting the juices, so many disguises and so much fabrication, that the fruit is lost in the process. The tin can and the bottle seem to have put an insuperable barrier between us and nature, and it is difficult for us to get back to a good munch of real apple under a tree or by the fireside. The difficulty is all the greater in our congested city life where orchards and trees are only a vacant memory or stories told to the young, and where the space in the larder is so small that apples must be purchased by the quart. The eating of good apples out of hand seems to be almost a lost art. Only the most indestructible kind, along with leather-skinned oranges and withered bananas, seem to be purchasable in the market. The discriminating apple-eater in the Old World sends to a grower for samples of the kinds that he grows; and after the inquirer has tested them in the family, and discussed them, he orders his winter supply. The American leaves the matter to the cook and she orders plain apples; and she gets them.

I wonder whether in time the perfection of fabrication will not reach such a point that some fruits will be known to the great public only by the picture on the package or on the bottle. Every process that removes us one step farther from the earth is a distinct loss to the people, and yet we are rapidly coming into the habit of taking all things at second hand. My objection to the wine of the grape is not so much a question of abstinence as of the fact that I find no particular satisfaction in the shape and texture of a bottle.

If one has a sensitive appreciation of the beauty in form and color and modeling of the common fruits, he will find his interest gradually extending to other products. Some time ago I visited Hood River Valley in company with a rugged potato grower from the Rocky Mountains. We were amazed at the wonderful scenery, and captivated by the beauty of the fruits. In one orchard the owner showed us with much satisfaction a brace of apples of perfect form and glowing colors. When the grower had properly expounded the marvels of Hood River apples, which he said were the finest in the world, my friend thrust his hand into his pocket and pulled out a potato, and said to the man: "Why is not that just as handsome as a Hood River apple?" And sure enough it was. For twenty-five years this grower had been raising and selecting the old Peachblow potato, until he had a form much more perfect than the old Peachblow ever was, with a uniform delicate pink skin, smooth surface, comely shape, and medium size, and with eyes very small and scarcely sunken; and my Hood River friend admitted that a potato as well as an apple may be handsome and satisfying to the hand and to the eye, and well worth carrying in one's pocket. But this was a high-bred potato, and not one of the common lot.

This episode of the potato allows me another opportunity to enforce my contention that we lose the fruit or the vegetable in the process of cookery. The customary practice of "mashing" potatoes takes all the individuality out of the product, and the result is mostly so much starch. There is an important dietary side to this. Cut a thin slice across a potato and hold it to the light. Note the interior undifferentiated mass, and then the thick band of rind surrounding it. The potato flavor and a large part of the nutriment lie in this exterior. We slice this part away and fry, boil, or otherwise fuss up the remainder. When we mash it, we go still farther and break down the potato texture; and in the modern method we squeeze and strain it till we eliminate every part of the potato, leaving only a pasty mass, which, in my estimation, is not fit to eat. The potato should be cooked with the rind on, if it is a good potato, and if it necessary to remove the outer skin the process should be performed after the cooking. The most toothsome part of the potato is the thick rind and adjacent part, and this I always eat when at home. We have so sophisticated the potato in the modern disguised cookery that we often practically ruin it as an article of food, and we have bred a race of people that sees nothing to admire in a good and well-grown potato tuber.

I now wish to take an excursion from the potato to the pumpkin. In all the range of vegetable products, I doubt whether there is a more perfect example of pleasing form, fine modeling, attractive texture and color, and more bracing odor, than in a well-grown and ripe field pumpkin. Place a pumpkin on your table; run your fingers down its smooth grooves; trace the furrows to the poles; take note of its form; absorb its rich color; get the tang of its fragrance. The roughness and ruggedness of its leaves, the sharp-angled stem strongly set, make a foil that a sculptor cannot improve. Then wonder how this marvelous thing was born out of your garden soil through the medium of one small strand of a succulent stem.

We all recognize the appeal of a bouquet of flowers, but we are unaware that we may have a bouquet of fruits. We have given little attention to arranging them, or any study of the kinds that consort well together, nor have we receptacles in which effectively to display them. Yet, apples and oranges and plums and grapes and nuts, and good melons and cucumbers and peppers and carrots and onions, may be arranged into the most artistic and satisfying combinations.

I would fall short of my obligation if I were to stop with the fruit of the tree and say nothing about the tree or the plant itself. In our haste for lawn trees of new kinds and from the uttermost parts, we forget that a fruit-tree is ornamental and that it provides acceptable shade. A full-grown apple tree or pear tree is one of the most individual and picturesque of trees. The foliage is good, the blossoms as handsome as those of fancy imported things, the fruits always interesting, and the tree is reliable. Nothing is more interesting than an orange tree, in the regions where it grows, with its shining and ever-green leaves and its continuing flowers and fruits. The practice of planting apples and pears and sweet cherries, and other fruit and nut trees, for shade and adornment is much to be commended in certain places.

But the point I wish specially to urge in this connection is the value of many kinds of fruit trees in real landscape work. We think of these trees as single or separate specimens, but they may be used with good result in mass planting, when it is desired to produce a given effect in a large area or in one division of a property. I do not know that any one has worked out full plants for the combining of fruit trees, nuts, and berry-bearing plants into good treatments, but it is much to be desired that this shall be done. Any of you can picture a sweep of countryside planted to these things that would be not only novel and striking, but at the same time conformable to the best traditions of artistic rendering.

I think it should be a fundamental purpose in our educational plans to acquaint the people with the common resources of the region, and particu-larly with those materials on which we subsist. If this is accepted, then we cannot deprive our parks, highways, and school grounds of the trees that bear the staple fruits. It is worthwhile to have an intellectual interest in a fruit tree. I know a fruit grower who secures many prizes for his apples and his pears; when he secures a blue ribbon, he ties it on the tree that bore the fruit.

The admiration of a good domestic animal is much to be desired. It devel-ops a most responsible attitude in the man or the woman. I have observed a peculiar charm in the breeders of these wonderful animals, a certain poise and masterfulness and breadth of sympathy. To admire a good horse and to know just why he admires him is a great resource to any man, as also to feel the responsibility for the care and health of any flock or herd. Fowls, pigs, sheep on their pastures, cows, mules, all perfect of their kind, all sensitive, all of them marvelous in their forms and powers—verily these are good to know.

If the raw materials grow out of the holy earth, then a man should have pride in producing them, and also in handling them. As a man thinketh of his materials, so doth he profit in the use of them. He builds them into him-self. There is a widespread feeling that in some way these materials reflect themselves in a man's bearing. One type of man grows out of the handling of rocks, another out of the handling of fishes, another out of the growing of the products from the good earth. All irreverence in the handling of these materials that come out of the earth's bounty, and all waste and poor workmanship, make for a low spiritual expression.

The farmer specially should be proud of his materials, he is so close to the sources and so hard against the backgrounds. Moreover, he cannot conceal his materials. He cannot lock up his farm or disguise his crops. He lives on his farm, and visibly with his products. The architect does not live in the houses and temples he builds. The engineer does not live on his bridge. The miner does not live in his mine. Even the sailor has his home away from his ship. But the farmer cannot separate himself from his works. Every bushel of buckwheat and every barrel of apples and every bale of cotton bears his name; the beef that he takes to market, the sheep that he herds on his pastures, the horse that he drives—these are his products and they carry his name. He should have the same pride in these—his productions—as another who builds a machine, or another who writes a book about them. The admiration of a field of hay, of a cow producing milk, of a shapely and fragrant head of cabbage, is a great force for good.

It would mean much if we could celebrate the raw materials and the products. Particularly is it good to celebrate the yearly bounty. The Puritans recognized their immediate dependence on the products of the ground, and their celebration was connected with religion. I should be sorry if our celebrations were to be wholly secular.

We have been much given to the display of fabricated materials—of the products of looms, lathes, foundries, and many factories of skill. We also exhibit the agricultural produce, but largely in a crass and rude way to display bulk and to win prizes. We now begin to arrange our exhibitions for color effect, comparison, and educational influence. But we do not justly understand the natural products when we confine them to formal exhibitions. They must be incorporated into many celebrations, expressing therein the earth's bounty and our appreciation of it. The usual and common products, domesticated and wild, should be gathered in these occasions, and not for competition or for prize awards or even for display, but for their intrinsic qualities. An apple day or an apple sabbath would teach the people to express their gratitude for apples. The moral obligation to grow good apples, to handle them honestly, to treat the soil and the trees fairly and reverently, could be developed as a living practical philosophy into the working-days of an apple-growing people. The technical knowledge we now possess requires the moral support of a stimulated public appreciation to make it a thoroughly effective force.

I. WORKMANSHIP

Many of the products and crops lend themselves well to this kind of admiration, and all of them should awaken gratitude and reverence. Sermons and teaching may issue from them. Nor is it necessary that this gratitude be expressed only in collected materials, or that all preaching and all teaching shall be indoors. The best understanding of our relations to the earth will be possible when we learn how to apply our devotions in the open places.

II CONSCIENCE

Now I feel the world's keen sorrow
And the gainless wish to borrow
Some surceasement for the morrow
'Gainst the old pursuing wrong;

But the healing rains are sweeping
And the cleansing ground is sleeping—
So I give me to their keeping
For I know the earth is strong.

—From "Strength," *Wind and Weather* (New York: Scribner, 1916)

The number of essays in this section, six, evinces conscience as an over-riding motif in Bailey's personal and scholarly work. Leading off, "The Separate Soul" functions as both a tribute to the independent-minded John Muirs of the world and an expression of Bailey's hopes and dreams for his retirement from higher education and organizational life. Coming as they do from the chairman of the efficiency-minded Country Life Commission, the sympathies shown here for the unaffiliated man, the independent thinker, may surprise historians who have heretofore represented Bailey as a technocrat. Bailey, in fact, turns many of the cooperative prescriptions of the Country Life Commission on their head here, arguing for the importance of aloneness to the artistic and educative soul. In keeping with the agrarian esprit de corps, "The Separate Soul" questions the recreational inclinations of Thorstein Veblen's so-called leisure class, singling out golf and tennis as emblematic of its idleness and social stratification. In "The Struggle for Existence: War" Bailey develops his critique of militant Social Darwinism. Granted, Bailey writes, war makes heroes of men, but man's final conquest is himself. "The very earth breathes peace," Bailey proclaims, insisting that quiet, peaceable acts form the real bedrock of all that is holy. Quoting Darwin, Bailey posits evolution's ultimate end as successful interdependence rather than violent dominion. In "The Keeping of the Beautiful Earth" Bailey reminds his readers that humanity began in a garden and that beautification becomes a "civic obligation." Anticipating contemporary zoning laws, the author insists no one has the right to spoil a view, erect an unsightly building, or even, by extension, pollute the night sky. Implicit in these idea-kernels is the nascent idea of green architecture and community planning as public expressions of the functionally beautiful. In "The Habit of

Destruction," Bailey lays out the case against rapacious miners and exploiters, challenging them to become environmentally sensitive producers. "All this habit of destructiveness," Bailey writes in a fair summation of *The Holy Earth*, "is uneconomic...unsocial, unmoral." The author asks us to acknowledge our poor stewardship of the earth, our poor "housekeeping," and to admit the need for our "cleaning up"—the metaphor effectively implicating the public in selfish, wanton, childish behavior. The appeal here is primarily to Bailey's female readers, who appeared, Bailey felt, to have a better grasp of reciprocity. As always, the author writes in the vanguard here, as the home economics movement was gathering strength, and along with it, concepts such as "municipal housekeeping," a term espoused by Ellen H. Richards to mobilize women's involvement in uplift and conservation movements outside the home.

The last two readings on conscience appear from Bailey's monograph, *The Country-life Movement in the United States*—largely a book-length summary of the conclusions he reached as chair of the censored Country Life Commission in 1908. "The Country-life Phase of Conservation" argues for the centrality of soil in a popular conservation movement. The soil, Bailey maintains, may be willfully improved or degraded, thus the individual who robs it of its fertility perpetrates a crime against humanity and ought to be held to account. Though the farmer is presented as the best hope for soil stewardship, Bailey also makes it clear that the farmer, too, can be an ugly "monopolist" when his conscience fails him. Finally, in "The Middleman Question," Bailey shows his trust-busting, Progressivist credentials, as, though he characteristically questioned government meddling in rural affairs, he advocates intervention. A "middleman," broadly defined, could and often did include the local shopkeeper as well as the grain elevator operator or railroad; in short, anyone who engaged in opportunistic, obstructionist business practices at the expense of the plowman. Bailey's argument for an antidote—buying locally and directly from the farmer—anticipates contemporary farmer-direct consumer purchases.

The Separate Soul

Many times in this journey have we come against the importance of the individual.[1] We are to develop the man's social feeling at the same time that we allow him to remain separate. We are to accomplish certain social results otherwise than by the process of thronging, which is so much a part of the philosophy of this anxious epoch; and therefore we may pursue the subject still a little further.

Any close and worthwhile contact with the earth tends to make one original or at least detached in one's judgments and independent of group control. In proportion as society becomes organized and involved, do we need the separate spirit and persons who are responsible beings on their own account. The independent judgment should be much furthered by studies in the sciences that are founded on observation of native forms and conditions. And yet the gains of scientific study become so rigidly organized into great enterprises that the individual is likely to be lost in them.

As an example of what I mean, I mention John Muir, who has recently passed away, and who stood for a definite contribution to his generation. He could hardly have made this contribution if he had been attached to any of the great institutions or organizations or to big business. He has left a personal impression and a remarkable literature that has been very little influenced by group psychology. He is the interpreter of mountains, forests, and glaciers.

There is one method of aggregation and social intercourse. There is another method of isolation and separateness. Never in the open country do I see a young man or woman at nightfall going down the highways and the long fields but I think of the character that develops out of the loneliness, in the silence of vast surroundings, projected against the backgrounds, and of the suggestions that must come from these situations as contrasted with

1. From *The Holy Earth* (New York: Scribner, 1915), 130–135; 136–138.

those that arise from the babble of the crowds. There is hardiness in such training; there is independence, the taking of one's own risk and no need of the protection of compensation acts. There is no overimposed director to fall back on. Physical recuperation is in the situation. As against these fields, much of the habitual golf and tennis and other adventitious means of killing time and of making up deficiencies is almost ludicrous.

Many of our reformers fail because they express only a group psychology and do not have a living personal interpretation. Undoubtedly many persons who might have had a message of their own have lost it and have also lost the opportunity to express it by belonging to too many clubs and by too continuous association with so-called kindred spirits, or by taking too much postgraduate study. It is a great temptation to join many clubs, but if one feels any stir of originality in himself, he should be cautious how he joins.

I may also recall the great example of [Louis] Agassiz at Penikese [Island, Massachusetts]. In his last year, broken in health, feeling the message he still had for the people, he opened the school on the little island off the coast of Massachusetts. It was a short school in one summer only, yet it has made an indelible impression on American education. It stimulates one to know that the person who met the incoming students on the wharf was Agassiz himself, not an assistant or an instructor. Out of the great number of applicants, he chose fifty whom he would teach. He wanted to send forth these chosen persons with his message, apostles to carry the methods and the way of approach. (When are we to have the Penikese for the rural backgrounds?)

Sometime there will be many great unattached teachers, who will choose their own pupils because they want them and not merely because the applicants have satisfied certain arbitrary tests. The students may be graduates of colleges or they may be others. They will pursue their work not for credit or for any other reward. We shall yet come back to the masters, and there will be teaching in the marketplaces.

We are now in the epoch of great organization not only in industrial developments but also in educational and social enterprises, in religious work, and in governmental activities. So completely is the organization proceeding in every direction, and so good is it, that one habitually and properly desires to identify oneself with some form of associated work. Almost in spite of oneself, one is caught up into the plan of things, and becomes part of a social, economic, or educational mechanism. No longer do we seek our educational institutions so much for the purpose of attaching ourselves to a master as to pursue a course of study. No more do we sit at the feet of Gamaliel.

In government, the organization has recently taken the form of mechanism for efficiency. We want government and all kinds of organization to be efficient and effective, but administrative efficiency may easily proceed at the expense of personality. Much of our public organization for efficiency is essentially monarchic in its tendency. It is likely to eliminate the most precious resource in human society, which is the freedom of expression of the competent individual. We are piling organization on organization, one supervising and watching and "investigating" the other. The greater the number of the commissions, investigating committees, and the interlocking groups, the more complex does the whole process become and the more difficult is it for the person to find himself. We can never successfully substitute bookkeeping for men and women. We are more in need of personality than of administrative regularity.

This is not a doctrine of laissez-faire or let-alone. The very conditions of modern society demand strong control and regulation and vigorous organization; but the danger is that we apply the controls uniformly and everywhere and eliminate the free action of the individual, as if control were in itself a merit.

In some way we must protect the person from being submerged in the system. We need always to get back of the group to the individual. The person is the reason for the group, although he is responsible to the group.

It is probably a great advantage to our democracy that our educational institutions are so completely organized, for by that means we are able to educate many more persons and to prepare them for the world with a clear and direct purpose in life. But this is not the whole of the public educational process. Some of the most useful persons cannot express themselves in institutions. This is not the fault of the institutions. In the nature of their character, these persons are separate. For the most part, they do not now have adequate means of self-expression or of contributing themselves to the public welfare.

When we shall have completed the present necessity of consolidation, centralization, and organization, society will begin to be conscious of the separate souls, who in the nature of the case must stand by themselves, and it will make use of them for the public good. Society will endow persons, not on a basis of salary, and enable them thereby to teach in their own way and their own time. This will represent one of the highest types of endowment by government and society.

We begin to approach this time by the support, through semipublic agencies, of persons to accomplish certain results or to undertake special pieces of work, particularly of research; but we have not yet attained the higher aim of endowing individuals to express themselves personally. There are liberated personalities, rare and prophetic, who are consumed only in making a living but who should be given unreservedly to the people: the people are much in need.

Never have we needed the separate soul so much as now.

81

II. CONSCIENCE

IF it is so important that we have these separate souls, then must we inquire where they may be found and particularly how we may insure the requisite supply.[2] Isolated separates appear here and there, in all the ranges of human experiences; these cannot be provided or foretold; but we shall need, in days to come, a group or a large class of persons, who in the nature of their occupation, situation, and training are relatively independent and free. We need more than a limited number of strong outstanding figures who rise to personal leadership. We must have a body of unattached laborers and producers who are in sufficient numbers to influence unexpressed public opinion and who will form a natural corrective as against organization men, habitual reformers, and extremists.

It is apparent that such a class must own productive property, be able to secure support by working for themselves, and produce supplies that are indispensable to society. Their individual interests must be greater and more insistent than their associative interests. They should be in direct contact with native resources. This characterization describes the farmer, and no other large or important group.

We have considered, on a former page, that we are not to look for the self-acting individuals among the workingmen as a class. They are rapidly partaking in an opposite development. They are controlled by associative interests. Even under a profit-sharing system they are parts in a close concert.

How to strike the balance between the needful individualism and social crystallization is probably the most difficult question before society. Of the great underlying classes of occupations, farming is the only one that presents the individualistic side very strongly. If individualism is to be preserved anywhere, it must be preserved here. The tendency of our present-day discussion is to organize the farmers as other groups or masses are organized. We are in danger here. Assuredly, the farmer needs better resources in association, but it is a nice question how far we should go and how completely we should try to redirect him. Fortunately, the holding of title to land and the separateness of farm habitations prevent solidification. If, on this individualism and without destroying it, we can develop a co-acting and cooperating activity, we shall undoubtedly be on the line of safety as well as on the line of promise. It would be a pity to organize the farming people merely to secure them their "rights." We ought soon to pass this epoch in civilization. There are no "rights" exclusive to any class. "Rights" are not possessions.

2. The first sentence under the original subhead (here omitted) "The element of separateness in society," p. 136. The extra return preceding the original subhead is here preserved as a section break.

I do not know where the element of separateness in society is to be derived unless it comes out of the earth.

Given sufficient organization to enable the farmer to express himself fully in his occupation and to secure protection, then we may well let the matter rest until his place in society develops by the operation of natural forces. We cannot allow the fundamental supplies from the common earth to be controlled by arbitrary class regulation. It would be a misfortune if the farmer were to isolate himself by making "demands" on society. I hope that the farmer's obligation may be so sensitively developed in him as to produce a better kind of mass cohesion than we have yet known.

The Struggle for Existence: War

We may consider even further, although briefly, the nature of the struggle for existence in its spiritual relation.[3] It would be violence to assume a holy earth and a holy production from the earth, if the contest between the creatures seems to violate all that we know as rightness.

The notion of the contentious and sanguinary struggle for existence finds its most pronounced popular expression in the existence of human war. It is a widespread opinion that war is necessary in the nature of things, and, in fact, it has been not only justified but glorified on this basis. We may here examine this contention briefly, and we may ask whether, in the case of human beings, there are other sufficient means of personal and social development than by mortal combat with one's fellows. We may ask whether the principle of enmity or the principle of fellow feeling is the more important and controlling.

We are not to deny or even to overlook the great results that have come from war. Virile races have forced themselves to the front and have impressed their stamp on society; the peoples have been mixed and also assorted; lethargic folk have been galvanized into activity; iron has been put into men's sinews; heroic deeds have arisen; old combinations and intrigues have been broken up (although new ones take their place). A kind of national purification may result from a great war. The state of human affairs has been brought to its present condition largely as the issue of wars.

On the other hand, we are not to overlook the damaging results, the destruction, the anguish, the check to all productive enterprise, the hatred and revenge, the hypocrisy and deceit, the despicable foreign spy system, the loss of standards, the demoralization, the lessening respect and regard for the rights of the other, the breeding of human parasites that fatten at the fringes of disaster, the levying of tribute, the setting up of unnatural boundaries,

---

3. From *The Holy Earth* (New York: Scribner, 1915), 80–89.

the thwarting of national and racial developments which, so far as we can see, gave every promise of great results. We naturally extol the nations that have survived; we do not know how many superior stocks may have been sacrificed to military conquest, or how many racial possibilities may have been suppressed in their beginnings.

Vast changes in mental attitudes may result from a great war, and the course of civilization may be deflected; and while we adjust ourselves to these changes, no one may say at the time that they are just or even that they are temporarily best. We are never able at the moment to measure the effects of the unholy conquest of peoples who should not have been conquered; these results work themselves out in tribulation and perhaps in loss of effort and of racial standards through many weary centuries. Forces, or even "success," cannot justify theft.

But even assuming the great changes that have arisen from war, this is not a justification of war; it only states a fact, it only provides a measure of the condition of society at any epoch. It is probable that war will still exert a mighty even if a lessening influence; it may still be necessary to resort to arms to win for a people its natural opportunity and to free a race from bondage; and if any people has a right to its own existence, it has an equal right and indeed a duty to defend itself. But this again only indicates the wretched state of development in which we live. Undoubtedly, also, a certain amount of military training is very useful, but there should be other ways, in a democracy, to secure something of this needful training.

The struggle for existence, as expressed in human combat, does not necessarily result in the survival of the most desirable, so far as we are able to define desirability. We are confusing very unlike situations in our easy application of the struggle for existence to war. The struggle is not now between individuals to decide the fitter: it is between vast bodies hurling death by wholesale. We pick the physically fit and send them to the battle line; and these fit are slain. This is not the situation in nature from which we draw our illustrations. Moreover, the final test of fitness in nature is adaptation, not power. Adaptation and adjustment mean peace, not war. Physical force has been immensely magnified in the human sphere; we even speak of the great nations as "powers," a terminology that some day we shall regret. The military method of civilization finds no justification in the biological struggle for existence.

The final conquest of a man is of himself, and he shall then be greater than when he takes a city. The final conquest of a society is of itself, and it shall then be greater than when it conquers its neighboring society.

Man now begins to measure himself against nature also, and he begins to see that herein shall lie his greatest conquests beyond himself; in fact, by this means shall he conquer himself—by great feats of engineering, by completer utilization of the possibilities of the planet, by vast discoveries in the unknown, and by the final enlargement of the soul; and in these fields shall be the heroes. The most virile and upstanding qualities can find expression in the conquest of the earth. In the contest with the planet every man may feel himself grow.

What we have done in times past shows the way by which we have come; it does not provide a program of procedure for days that are coming; or if it does, then we deny the effective evolution of the race. We have passed witchcraft, religious persecution, the inquisition, subjugation of women, the enslavement of our fellows except alone enslavement in war.

Here I come particularly to a consideration of the struggle for existence. Before I enter on this subject, I must pause to say that I would not of myself found an argument either for war or against it on the analogies of the struggle for existence. Man has responsibilities quite apart from the conditions that obtain in the lower creation. Man is a moral agent; animals and plants are not moral agents. But the argument for war is so often founded on this struggle in nature, that the question must be considered.

It has been persistently repeated for years that in nature the weakest perish and that the victory is with the strong, meaning by that the physically powerful. This is a false analogy and a false biology. It leads men far astray. It is the result of a misconception of the teaching of evolution.

Our minds dwell on the capture and the carnage in nature—the hawk swooping on its prey, the cat stealthily watching for the mouse, wolves hunting in packs, ferocious beasts lying in wait, sharks that follow ships, serpents with venomous fangs, the vast range of parasitism; and with the poet we say that nature is "red in tooth and claw." Of course, we are not to deny the struggle of might against might, which is mostly between individuals, and of which we are all aware; but the weak and the fragile and the small are the organisms that have persisted. There are thousands of little and soft things still abundant in the world that have outlived the fearsome ravenous monsters of ages past; there were Goliaths in those days, but the Davids have outlived them, and Gath is not peopled by giants. The big and strong have not triumphed.

The struggle in nature is not a combat, as we commonly understand that word, and it is not warfare. The earth is not strewn with corpses.

I was impressed in reading [Theodore] Roosevelt's *African Game Trails* with the great extent of small and defenseless and fragile animal life that abounds in the midst of the terrible beasts—little, uncourageous things that hide in the crevices, myriads that fly in the air, those that ride on the rhinos, that swim and hide in the pools, and bats that hang in the acacia-trees.

He traveled in the region of the lion, in the region that "holds the mightiest creatures that tread the earth or swim in its rivers; it also holds distant kinsfolk of these same creatures, no bigger than woodchucks, which dwell in crannies of the rocks, and in the tree tops. There are antelope smaller than hares and antelope larger than oxen. There are creatures which are the embodiment of grace; and others whose huge ungainliness is like that of a shape in a nightmare. The plains are alive with droves of strange and beautiful animals whose like is not known elsewhere." The lion is mighty; he is the king of beasts; but he keeps his place and he has no kingdom. He has not mastered the earth. No beast has ever overcome the earth; and the natural world has never been conquered by muscular force.

Nature is not in a state of perpetual enmity, one part with another.

My friend went to a far country. He told me that he was most impressed with the ferocity, chiefly of wild men. It came my time to go to that country. I saw that men had been savage—men are the most ferocious of animals, and the ferocity has never reached its high point of refined fury until today. (Of course, savages fight and slay; this is because they are savages.) But I saw also that these savage men are passing away. I saw animals that had never tasted blood, that had no means of defense against a rapacious captor, and yet they were multiplying. Every stone that I upturned disclosed some tender organism; every bush that I disturbed revealed some timid atom of animal life; every spot where I walked bore some delicate plant, and I recalled the remark of Sir J. William Dawson "that frail and delicate plants may be more ancient than the mountains or plains on which they live"; and if I went on the sea, I saw the medusas as frail as a poet's dream, with the very sunshine streaming through them, yet holding their own in the mighty upheaval of the oceans; and I reflected on the myriads of microscope things that for untold ages had cast the very rock on which much of the ocean rests. The minor things and the weak things are the most numerous, and they have played the greatest part in the polity of nature. So I came away from that far country impressed with the power of the little feeble things. I had a new understanding of the worth of creatures so unobtrusive and so silent that the multitude does not know them.

I saw protective colorings; I saw fleet wings and swift feet; I saw the ability to hide and to conceal; I saw habits of adaptation; I saw marvelous powers of reproduction. You have seen them in every field; you have met them on your casual walks, until you accept them as the natural order of things. And you know that the beasts of prey have not prevailed. The whole contrivance of nature is to protect the weak.

We have wrongly visualized the "struggle." We have given it an intensely human application. We need to go back to Darwin who gave significance to the phrase "struggle for existence." "I use this term," he said, "in a large and metaphorical sense, including dependence of one being on another, and including (which is more important) not only the life of the individual, but success in leaving progeny." The dependence of one being on another, success in leaving progeny—how accurate and how far-seeing was Darwin!

I hope that I speak to naturists and to farmers. They know how diverse are the forms of life; and they know that somehow these forms live together and that only rarely do whole races perish by subjugation. They know that the beasts do not set forth to conquer, but only to gain subsistence and to protect themselves. The beasts and birds do not pursue indiscriminately. A hen hawk does not attack crows or butterflies. Even a vicious bull does not attack fowls or rabbits or sheep. The great issues are the issues of live and let-live. There are whole nations of plants, more unlike than nations of humankind, living together in mutual interdependence. There are nations of quiet and mightless animals that live in the very regions of the mighty and the stout. And we are glad it is so.

Consider the mockery of invoking the struggle for existence as justification for a battle on a June morning, when all nature is vibrant with life and competition is severe, and when, if ever, we are to look for strife. But the very earth breathes peace. The fullness of every field and wood is in complete adjustment. The teeming multitudes of animal and plant have found a way to live together, and we look abroad on a vast harmony, verdurous, prolific, abounding. Into this concord, project your holocaust!

The Keeping of the Beautiful Earth

The proper caretaking of the earth lies not alone in maintaining its fertility or in safeguarding its products.[4] The lines of beauty that appeal to the eye and the charm that satisfies the five senses are in our keeping.

The natural landscape is always interesting and it is satisfying. The physical universe is the source of art. We know no other form and color than that which we see in nature or derive from it. If art is true to its theme, it is one expression of morals. If it is a moral obligation to express the art sense in painting and sculpture and literature and music, so is it an equal obligation to express it in good landscape.

Of the first importance is it that the race keep its artistic backgrounds, and not alone for the few who may travel far and near and who may pause deliberately, but also for those more numerous folk who must remain with the daily toil and catch the far look only as they labor. To put the best expression of any landscape into the consciousness of one's day's work is more to be desired than much riches. When we complete our conquest, there will be no unseemly landscapes.

The abundance of violated landscapes is proof that we have not yet mastered. The farmer does not have full command of his situation until the landscape is a part of his farming. Farms may be units in well-developed and pleasing landscapes beautiful in their combinations with other farms and appropriate to their setting as well as attractive in themselves.

No one has a moral right to contribute unsightly factory premises or a forbidding commercial establishment to any community. The lines of utility and efficiency ought also to be the lines of beauty; and it is due every worker to have a good landscape to look upon, even though its area be very constricted. To produce bushels of wheat and marvels of machinery, to

---

4. From *The Holy Earth* (New York: Scribner, 1915), 115–119.

maintain devastating military establishments, do not comprise the sum of conquest. The backgrounds must be kept.

If moral strength comes from good and sufficient scenery, so does the preservation of it become a social duty. It is much more than a civic obligation. But the resources of the earth must be available to man for his use and this necessarily means a modification of the original scenery. Some pieces and kinds of scenery are above all economic use and should be kept wholly in the natural state. Much of it may yield to modification if he takes good care to preserve its essential features. Unfortunately, the engineer seems not often to be trained in the values of scenery and he is likely to despoil a landscape or at least to leave it raw and unfinished.

On the other hand, there is unfortunately a feeling abroad that any modification of a striking landscape is violation and despoliation; and unwarranted opposition, in some cases amounting almost to prudery, follows any needful work of utilization. Undoubtedly the farmer and builder and promoter have been too unmindful of the effect of their interference on scenery, and particularly in taking little care in the disposition of wastes and in the healing of wounds; but a work either of farming or of construction may add interest and even lines of beauty to a landscape and endow it with the suggestion of human interest. If care were taken in the construction of public and semipublic work to reshape the banks into pleasing lines, to clean up, to care for, to plant, to erect structures of good proportions whether they cost much or little, and to give proper regard to the sensibilities of the communities, most of the present agitation against interference with natural scenery would disappear. One has only to visit the factory districts, the vacation resorts, the tenement areas, the banks of streams and gorges, to look at the faces of cliffs and at many engineering enterprises and at numberless farmyards, to find examples of the disregard of men for the materials that they handle. It is as much our obligation to hold the scenery reverently as to handle the products reverently. Man found the earth looking well. Humanity began in a garden.

The keeping of the good earth depends on preservation rather than on destruction. The office of the farmer and the planter is to produce rather than to destroy; whatever they destroy is to the end that they may produce more abundantly; these persons are therefore natural caretakers. If to this office we add the habit of good housekeeping, we shall have more than one-third of our population at once directly partaking in keeping the earth. It is one of the bitter ironies that farmers should ever have been taken out of their place to wreak vengeance on the earth by means of military devastation. In the past, this ravage has been small in amount because the engines of destruction were weak, but with the perfecting of the modern enginery the havoc is awful and brutal. While we have to our credit the improvement of agriculture and other agencies of conservation, it is yet a fact that man has never been so destructive as now. He is able to turn the skill of his discovery to destructive ends (a subject that we have already approached from another point of view). The keeping of the earth is therefore involved in the organization of society. Military power heads toward destructiveness. Civil power heads toward conservation. The military power may be constructive in times of peace, but its end, if it uses the tools it invents, is devastation and the inflicting of injury. When the civil power is subjugated to the military power, society is headed toward ravage.

To keep and to waste are opposite processes. Not only are we able to despoil the earth by sheer lust of ravage and by blighting the fields with caverns of human slaughter, but we shoot away incredible supplies of copper and petroleum and other unrenewable materials that by every right and equity belong to our successors; and, moreover, we are to make these successors pay for the destruction of their heritage. Day by day we are mortgaging the future, depriving it of supplies that it may need, burdening the shoulders of generations yet unborn.

Merely to make the earth productive and to keep it clean and to bear a reverent regard for its products, is the special prerogative of a good agriculture and a good citizenry founded thereon; this may seem at the moment to be small and ineffective as against mad impersonal and limitless havoc, but it carries the final healing; and while the land worker will bear much of the burden on his back, he will also redeem the earth.

The Habit of Destruction

The first observation that must be apparent to all men is that our dominion has been mostly destructive.[5]

We have been greatly engaged in digging up the stored resources, and in destroying vast products of the earth for some small kernel that we can apply to our necessities or add to our enjoyments. We excavate the best of the coal and cast away the remainder; blast the minerals and metals from underneath the crust, and leave the earth raw and sore; we box the pines for turpentine and abandon the growths of limitless years to fire and devastation; sweep the forests with the besom of destruction; pull the fish from the rivers and ponds without making any adequate provision for renewal; exterminate whole races of animals; choke the streams with refuse and dross; rob the land of its available stores, denuding the surface, exposing great areas to erosion.

Nor do we exercise the care and thrift of good housekeepers. We do not clean up our work or leave the earth in order. The remnants and accumulation of mining camps are left to ruin and decay; the deserted phosphate excavations are ragged, barren, and unfilled; vast areas of forested lands are left in brush and waste, unthoughtful of the future, unmindful of the years that must be consumed to reduce the refuse to mould and to cover the surface respectably, uncharitable to those who must clear away the wastes and put the place in order; and so thoughtless are we with these natural resources that even the establishments that manufacture them—the mills, the factories of many kinds—are likely to be offensive objects in the landscape, unclean, unkempt, displaying the unconcern of the owners to the obligation that the use of the materials imposes and to the sensibilities

5. From *The Holy Earth* (New York: Scribner, 1915), 18–21. This excerpt is drawn from the book's part II, which Bailey titled "Second, The Consequences." "The habit of destruction" begins on page 18 after Bailey's three-paragraph (omitted here) introduction to part II.

of the community for the way in which they handle them. The burden of proof seems always to have been rested on those who partake little in the benefits, although we know that these nonpartakers have been real owners of the resources; and yet so undeveloped has been the public conscience in these matters that the blame—if blame there be—cannot be laid on one group more than on the other. Strange it is, however, that we should not have insisted at least that those who appropriate the accumulations of the earth should complete their work, cleaning up the remainders, leaving the areas wholesome, inoffensive, and safe. How many and many are the years required to grow a forest and to fill the pockets of the rocks, and how satisfying are the landscapes, and yet how desperately soon may men reduce it all to ruin and to emptiness, and how slatternly may then violate the scenery!

All this habit of destructiveness is uneconomic in the best sense, unsocial, unmoral.

Society now begins to demand a constructive process. With care and with regard for other men, we must produce the food and the other supplies in regularity and sufficiency; and we must clean up after our work, that the earth may not be depleted, scarred, or repulsive.

Yet there is even a more defenseless devastation than all this. It is the organized destructiveness of those who would make military domination the major premise in the constitution of society, accompanying desolation with viciousness and violence, ravaging the holy earth, disrespecting the works of the creator, looking toward extirpation, confessing thereby that they do not know how to live in cooperation with their fellows; in such situations, every new implement of destruction adds to the guilt.

In times past we were moved by religious fanaticism, even to the point of waging wars. Today we are moved by impulses of trade, and we find ourselves plunged into a war of commercial frenzy; and as it has behind it vaster resources and more command of natural forces, so is it the most ferocious and wasteful that the race has experienced, exceeding in its havoc the cataclysms of earthquake and volcano. Certainly we have not yet learned how to withstand the prosperity and the privileges that we have gained by the discoveries of science; and certainly the morals of commerce have not given us freedom or mastery. Rivalry that leads to arms is a natural fruit of unrestrained rivalry in trade.

Man has dominion, but he has no commission to devastate: And the Lord God took the man, and put him into the garden of Eden to dress it and to keep it.

Verily, so bountiful hath been the earth and so securely have we drawn from it our substance, that we have taken it all for granted as if it were only a gift, and with little care or conscious thought of the consequences of our use of it.

WE may distinguish three stages in our relation to the planet—the collecting stage, the mining stage, and the producing stage.[6] These overlap and perhaps are nowhere distinct, and yet it serves a purpose to contrast them.

At first man sweeps the earth to see what he may gather—game, wood, fruits, fish, fur, feathers, shells on the shore. A certain social and moral life arises out of this relation, seen well in the woodsmen and the fishers—in whom it best persists to the present day—strong, dogmatic superstitious folk. Then man begins to go beneath the surface to see what he can find—iron and precious stones, the gold of Ophir, coal, and many curious treasures. This develops the exploiting faculties, and leads men into the uttermost parts. In both these stages the elements of waste and disregard have been heavy.

Finally, we begin to enter the productive stage, whereby we secure supplies by controlling the conditions under which they grow, wasting little, harming not. Farming has been very much a mining process, the utilizing of fertility easily at hand and the moving on to lands unspoiled of quick potash and nitrogen. Now it begins to be really productive and constructive, with a range of responsible and permanent morals. We rear the domestic animals with precision. We raise crops, when we will, almost to a nicety. We plant fish in lakes and streams to some extent but chiefly to provide more game rather than more human food, for in this range we are yet mostly in the collecting or hunter stage. If the older stages were strongly expressed in the character of the people, so will this new stage be expressed; and so is it that we are escaping the primitive and should be coming into a new character. We shall find our rootage in the soil.

This new character, this clearer sense of relationship with the earth, should express itself in all the people and not exclusively in farming people and their like. It should be a popular character—or a national character if we would limit the discussion to one people—and not a class character. Now, here lies a difficulty and here is a reason for writing this book: the population of the earth is increasing, the relative population of farmers is decreasing, people are herding in cities, we have a city mind, and relatively fewer people are brought into touch with the earth in any real way. So is it incumbent on us to take special pains—now that we see the new time—that all the people, or as many of them as possible, shall have contact with the earth and that the earth's righteousness shall be abundantly taught.

6. The first sentence under the original subhead (here omitted) "The new hold," p. 22. The extra return preceding the original subhead is here preserved as a section break.

I hasten to say that I am not thinking of any back-to-the-farm movement to bring about the results we seek. Necessarily, the proportion of farmers will decrease. Not so many are needed relatively, for a man's power to produce has been multiplied. Agriculture makes a great contribution to human progress by releasing men for the manufactures and the trades. In proportion as the ratio of farmers decreases is it important that we provide them the best of opportunities and encouragement: they must be better and better men. And if we are to secure our moral connection with the planet to a large extent through them, we can see that they bear a relation to society in general that we have overlooked.

Even the farming itself is changing radically in character. It ceases to be an occupation to gain sustenance and becomes a business. We apply to it the general attitudes of commerce. We must be alert to see that it does not lose its capacity for spiritual contact.

How we may achieve a more widespread contact with the earth on the part of all the people without making them farmers, I shall endeavor to suggest as I proceed; in fact, this is my theme. Dominion means mastery; we may make the surface of the earth much what we will; we can govern the way in which we shall contemplate it. We are probably near something like a stable occupancy. It is not to be expected that there will be vast shifting of cities as the contest for the mastery of the earth proceeds—probably nothing like the loss of Tyre and Carthage, and of the commercial glory of Venice. In fact, we shall have a progressive occupancy. The greater the population, the greater will be the demands on the planet; and, moreover, every new man will make more demands than his father made, for he will want more to satisfy him. We are to take from the earth much more than we have ever taken before, but it will be taken in a new way and with better intentions. It will be seen, therefore, that we are not here dealing narrowly with an occupation but with something very fundamental to our life on the planet.

We are not to look for our permanent civilization to rest on any species of robber-economy. No flurry of coal mining, or gold fever, or rubber collecting in the tropics, or excitement of prospecting for new finds or even locating new lands, no ravishing of the earth or monopolistic control of its bounties, will build a stable society. So is much of our economic and social fabric transitory. It is not by accident that a very distinct form of society is developing in the great farming regions of the Mississippi Valley and in other comparable places; the exploiting and promoting occupancy of those lands is passing and a stable progressive development appears. We have been obsessed of the passion to cover everything at once, to skin the earth, to pass on, even when there was no necessity for so doing. It is a vast pity that this should ever have been the policy of government in giving away great tracts of land by lottery, as if our fingers would burn if we held the lands inviolate until needed by the natural process of settlement. The people should be kept on their lands long enough to learn how to use them. But very well: we have run with the wind, we have staked the land; now we shall be real farmers and real conquerors. Not all lands are equally good for farming, and some lands will never be good for farming; but whether in Iowa, or New England, or old Asia, farming land may develop character in the people.

My reader must not infer that we have arrived at a permanent agriculture, although we begin now to see the importance of a permanent land occupancy. Probably we have not yet evolved a satisfying husbandry that will maintain itself century by century, without loss and without the ransacking of the ends of the earth for fertilizer materials to make good our deficiencies. All the more is it important that the problem be elevated into the realm of statesmanship and of morals. Neither must he infer that the resources of the earth are to be locked up beyond contact and use (for the contact and use will be morally regulated). But no system of brilliant exploitation, and no accidental scratching of the surface of the earth, and no easy appropriation of stored materials can suffice us in the good days to come. City, country, this class and that class, all fall and merge before the common necessity.

It is often said that the farmer is our financial mainstay; so in the good process of time will he be a moral mainstay, for ultimately finance and social morals must coincide.

The gifts are to be used for service and for satisfaction, and not for wealth. Very great wealth introduces too many intermediaries, too great indirectness, too much that is extrinsic, too frequent hindrances and superficialities. It builds a wall about the man, and too often does he receive his impressions of the needs of the world from satellites and sycophants. It is significant that great wealth, if it contributes much to social service, usually accomplishes the result by endowing others to work. The gift of the products of the earth was "for meat": nothing was said about riches.

Yet the very appropriation or use of natural resources may be the means of directing the mind of the people back to the native situations. We have the opportunity to make the forthcoming development of water power, for example, such an agency for wholesome training. Whenever we can appropriate without despoliation or loss, or without a damaging monopoly, we tie the people to the backgrounds.

In the background is the countryman; and how is the countryman to make use of the rain and the abounding soil, and the varied wonder of plant and animal amidst which he lives, that he may arrive at kinship? We are teaching him how to bring some of these things under the dominion of his hands, how to measure and to weigh and to judge. This will give him the essential physical mastery. But beyond this, how shall he take them into himself, how shall he make them to be of his spirit, how shall he complete his dominion? How shall he become the man that his natural position requires of him? This will come slowly, ah, ye!—slowly. The people—the great striving self-absorbed throng of the people—they do not know what we mean when we talk like this, they hear only so many fine words. The naturist knows that the time will come slowly—not yet are we ready for fulfillment; he knows that we cannot regulate the cosmos, or even the natural history of the people, by enactments. Slowly: by removing handicaps here and there; by selection of the folk in a natural process, to eliminate the unresponsive; by teaching, by suggestion; by a public recognition of the problem, even though not one of us sees the end of it.

I hope my reader now sees where I am leading him. He sees that I am not thinking merely of instructing the young in the names and habits of birds and flowers and other pleasant knowledge, although this works strongly toward the desired end; nor of any movement merely to have gardens, or to own farms, although this is desirable provided one is qualified to own a farm; nor of rhapsodies on the beauties of nature. Nor am I thinking of any new plan or any novel kind of institution or any new agency; rather shall we do better to escape some of the excessive institutionalism and organization. We are so accustomed to think in terms of organized politics and education and religion and philanthropies that when we detach ourselves we are said to lack definiteness. It is the personal satisfaction in the earth to which we are born, and the quickened responsibility, the whole relation, broadly developed, of the man and of all men—it is this attitude that we are to discuss.

The years pass and they grow into centuries. We see more clearly. We are to take a new hold.

The Country-life Phase
of Conservation

Neither conservation nor country life is new except in name and as the subject of an organized movement.[7] The end of the original resources has been foreseen from time out of mind, and prophetic books have been written on the subject. The need of a quickened country life has been recognized from the time that cities began to dominate civilization; and the outlook of the high-minded countryman has been depicted from the days of the classical writings until now. On the side of mineral and similar resources, the geologists amongst us have made definite efforts for conservation; and on the side of soil fertility the agricultural chemists and the teachers of agriculture have for a hundred years maintained a perpetual campaign of conservation. So long and persistently have those persons in the agricultural and some other institutions heard these questions emphasized, that the startling assertions of the present day as to the failure of our resources and the coordinate importance of rural affairs with city affairs have not struck me with any force of novelty.

But there comes a time when the warnings begin to collect themselves, and to crystallize about definite points; and my purpose in suggesting this history is to emphasize the importance of the two formative movements now before us by showing that the roots run deep back into human experience. It is no ephemeral or transitory subject that we are now to discuss.

I have said that these are economic and social problems and policies.[8] I wish to enlarge this view. They are concerned with saving, utilizing, and augmenting, and only secondarily with administration. We must first ascertain

---

7. From *The Country-life Movement in the United States* (New York: Macmillan, 1911), 180–200. This excerpt begins with the fourth paragraph of the chapter named above. This sentence is the first under the subheading "These subjects have a history." Except as noted, the extra return preceding the original subheads are deleted throughout.

8. The first sentence under the original subhead (here omitted) "They are not party-politics subjects," p. 182.

the facts as to our resources, and from this groundwork impress the subject on the people. The subject must be approached by scientific methods. The "political" phase, although probably necessary, is only temporary, till we remove impedimenta and clear the way.

It would be unfortunate if such movement became the exclusive program of a political party, for then the question would become partisan and probably be removed from calm or judicial consideration, and the opposition would equally become the program of a party. Every last citizen should be naturally interested in the careful utilization of our native materials and wealth, and it is due him that the details of the question be left open for unbiased discussion rather than to be made the arbitrary program, either one way or another, of a political organization. Conservation is in the end a plain problem involving economic, educational, and social situations, rather than a political issue. The Country Life movement is equally a scientific problem, in the sense that it must be approached in the scientific spirit. It will be inexcusable in this day if we do not go at the subject with only the desire to discover the facts and to arrive at a rational solution, by nonpolitical methods.

The resources that sustain the race are of two kinds, those that lie beyond the power of man to reproduce or increase, and those that may be augmented by propagation and by care.[9] The former are the mines of minerals, metals, and coal, the water, the air, the sunshine; the latter are the living resources, in crop and livestock.

Intermediate between the two classes stands the soil, on which all living resources depend. While the soil is part of the mineral and earthy resources of the planet, it nevertheless can be increased in its producing power. Even after all minerals and metals and coal are depleted, the race may sustain itself in comfort and progress so long as the soil is productive, provided, of course, that water and air and sunshine are still left to us. The greatest of all resources that man can make or mar is the soil. Beyond all the mines of coal and all the precious ores, this is the heritage that must be most carefully saved; and this, in particular, is the country-life phase of the conservation movement.

To my mind, the conservation movement has not sufficiently estimated or emphasized this problem. It has laid stress, I know, on the enormous loss by soil erosion and has said something of inadequate agricultural practice, but the main question is yet practically untouched by the movement, the plain problem of handling the soil by all the millions who, by skill or blundering or theft, produce crops and animals out of the earth. Peoples have

9. The first sentence under the original subhead (here omitted) "The soil is the greatest of all resources," p. 183.

gone down before the lessening fertility of the land, and in all probability other peoples will yet go down. The course of empire has been toward the unplundered lands.

Thinner than a skin of an apple is the covering of the earth that a man tills.[10] The marvelously slight layer that the farmer knows as "the soil" supports all plants and all men, and makes it possible for the globe to sustain a highly developed life. Beyond all calculation and all comprehension are the powers and the mysteries of this soft outer covering of the earth. For all we know, the stupendous mass of materials of which the planet is composed is wholly dead, and only on the surface does any nerve of life quicken it into a living sphere. And yet, from this attenuated layer have come numberless generations of giants of forests and of beasts, perhaps greater in their combined bulk than all the soil from which they have come; and back into this soil they go, until the great life principle catches up their disorganized units and builds them again into beings as complex as themselves.

The general evolution of this soil is toward greater powers; and yet, so nicely balanced are these powers that within his lifetime a man may ruin any part of it that society allows him to hold; and in despair he throws it back to nature to reinvigorate and to heal. We are accustomed to think of the power of man in gaining dominion over the forces of nature, he bends to his use the expansive powers of steam, the energy of the electric current, and he ranges through space in the light that he concentrates in his telescope; but while he is doing all this, he sets at naught the powers in the soil beneath his feet, wastes them, and deprives himself of vast sources of energy. Man will never gain dominion until he learns from nature how to maintain the augmenting powers of the disintegrating crust of the earth.

We can do little to control or modify the atmosphere or the sunlight; but the epidermis of the earth is ours to do with it much as we will. It is the one great earth-resource over which we have dominion. The soil may be made better as well as worse, more as well as less; and to save the producing powers of it is far and away the most important consideration in the conservation of natural resources.

Unfortunately, it is impossible to devise a system of farm accounting that shall accurately represent the loss in producing power of the land (or depreciation in actual capital stock). The rising sentiment on the fertility question is just now reflected in the proposal to ask Congress and the states to make it a misdemeanor for a man to rob his land and to lay out for him a farm scheme. This is a chimerical notion; but the people are bound to express themselves unmistakably in some way on this subject.

10. The first sentence under the original subhead (here omitted) "The soil crust," p. 185.

Even if we should ultimately find that crops do not actually deplete land by the removal of stored plant food in the way in which we have been taught, it is nevertheless true that poor management ruins its productivity; and whatever the phrase we use in our speaking and writing, we shall still need to hold the land usurer to account.

The man who tills and manages the soil owes a real obligation to his fellow men for the use that he makes of his land; and his fellow men owe an equal obligation to him to see that his lot in society is such that he will not be obliged to rob the earth in order to maintain his life.[11] The natural resources of the earth are the heritage and the property of every one and all of us. A man has no moral right to skin the earth, unless he is forced to do it in sheer self-defense and to enable him to live in some epoch of an unequally developed society; and if there are or have been such social epochs, then is society itself directly responsible for the waste of the common heritage. We have given every freeholder the privilege to destroy his farm.

The man who plunders the soil is in very truth a robber, for he takes that which is not his own, and he withholds bread from the mouths of generations yet to be born. No man really owns his acres: society allows him the use of them for his lifetime, but the fee comes back to society in the end. What, then, will society do with those persons who rob society? The pillaging land-worker must be brought to account and be controlled, even as we control other offenders.

I have no socialistic program to propose. The man who is to till the land must be educated: there is more need, on the side of the public welfare, to educate this man than any other man whatsoever. When he knows, and his obligations to society are quickened, he will be ready to become a real conservator; and he will act energetically as soon as the economic pressure for land supplies begins to be acute. When society has done all it can to make every farmer a voluntary conservator of the fatness of the earth, it will probably be obliged to resort to other means to control the wholly incompetent and the recalcitrant; at least, it will compel the soil robber to remove to other occupation, if economic stress does not itself compel it. We shall reach the time when we shall not allow a man to till the earth unless he is able to leave it at least as fertile as he found it.

I do not think that our natural soil resources have yet been greatly or permanently depleted, speaking broadly; and such depletion as has occurred has been the necessary result of the conquest of a continent. But a new situation will confront us, now that we see the end of our raw conquest; and the

11. The first sentence under the original subhead (here omitted) "No man has a right to plunder the soil," p. 188.

old methods cannot hold for the future. The conquest has produced great and strong folk, and we have been conserving men while we have been free with our resources. In the future, we shall produce strong folk by the process of thoroughness and care.

This discussion leads me to make an application to the conservation movement in general.[12] We are so accustomed to think of privileged interests and of corporation control of resources that we are likely to confuse conservation and company ownership. The essence of conservation is to utilize our resources with no waste, and with an honest care for the children of all the generations. But we state the problem to be the reservation of our resources for all the people, and often assume that if all the resources were in private ownership the problem would thereby be solved; but, in fact, the conservation question is one thing and the ownership of property quite another. A corporation may be the best as well as the worst conservator of resources; and likewise, private or individual ownership may be the very worst as well as the best conservator. The individual owner, represented by the "independent farmer" may be the prince of monopolists, even though his operations compass a very small scale. The very fact that he is independent and that he is entrenched behind the most formidable of all barriers, private property rights, insure his monopoly.

In the interest of pure conservation, it is just as necessary to control the single men as the organized men. In the end, conservation must deal with the separate or the individual man; that is, with a person. It matters not whether this person is a part of a trust, or lives alone a hundred miles beyond the frontier, or is the owner of a prosperous farm, if he wastes the heritage of the race, he is an offender.

We are properly devising ways whereby the corporation holds its property or privileges in trust, returning to government (or to society) a fair rental; that is, we are making it responsible to the people. What shall we do with the unattached man, to make him also responsible? Shall we hold the corporate plunderer to strict account, and let the single separate plunderer go scot-free?

The conservation of natural resources, therefore, resolves itself into the philosophy of saving, while at the same time making the most and best progress in our own day.[13] We have not developed much consciousness of saving when we deal with things that come free to our hands, as the sunshine, the

12. The first sentence under the original subhead (here omitted) "Ownership vs. conservation," p. 190.

13. The first sentence under the original subhead (here omitted) "The philosophy of saving," p. 192.

rain, the forests, the mines, the streams, the earth; and the American has found himself so much in the midst of plenty that saving has seemed to him to be parsimony, or at least beneath his attention. As a question of morals, however, conscientious saving represents a very high development. No man has a right to waste, both because the materials in the last analysis are not his own, and because someone else may need what he wastes. A high sense of saving ought to come out of the conservation movement. This will make directly for character efficiency, since it will develop both responsibility and regard for others.

The irrigation and dry-farming developments have a significance far beyond their value in the raising of crops: they are making the people to be conservators of water, and to have a real care for posterity.

Civilization, thus far, is built on the process of waste. Materials are brought from forest, and sea, and mine, certain small parts are used, and the remainder is destroyed; more labor is wasted than is usefully productive; but what is far worse, the substance of the land is taken in unimaginable measure, and dumped wholesale into endless sewer and drainage systems. It would seem as if the human race were bent on finding a process by which it can most quickly ravish the earth and make it incapable of maintaining its teeming millions. We are rapidly threading the country with vast conduits by which the fertility of the land can flow away unhindered into the unreachable reservoirs of the seas.

The fundamental problem for the human race is to feed itself.[14] It has been a relatively easy matter to provide food and clothing thus far, because the earth yet has a small population, and because there have always been new lands to be brought into requisition. We shall eliminate the plagues and the devastations of war, and the population of the earth will tremendously increase in the centuries to come. When the new lands have all been opened to cultivation, and when thousands of millions of human beings occupy the earth, the demand for food will constitute a problem which we scarcely apprehend today. We shall then be obliged to develop self-sustaining methods of maintaining the producing power of land.

We think we have developed intensive and perfected systems of agriculture; but as a matter of fact, and speaking broadly, a permanent organized agriculture is yet unknown. In certain regions, as in Great Britain, the producing power of the land has been increased over a long series of years, but this has been accomplished to a great extent by the transportation of fertilizing materials from the ends of the earth. The fertility of England has

14. The first sentence under the original subhead (here omitted) "The conservation of food," p. 194.

been drawn largely from the prairies and plains of America, from which it has secured its food supplies, from the guano deposits in islands of the seas, from the bones of men in Egypt and the battlefields of Europe.

We begin to understand how it is possible to maintain the producing power of the surface of the earth, and there are certain regions in which our knowledge has been put effectively into operation, but we have developed no conscious plan or system in a large way for securing this result. It is the ultimate problem of the race to devise a permanent system of agriculture. It is the greatest question that can confront mankind; and the question is yet all unsolved.

The best agriculture, considered in reference to the permanency of its results, develops in old regions, where the skinning process has passed, where the hide has been sold, and where people come back to utilize what is left.[15] The skinning process is proceeding at this minute in the bountiful new lands of the United States; and in parts of the older states, and even also in parts of the newer ones, not only the skin but the tallow has been sold.

We are always seeking growing room, and we have found it. But now the Western civilization has met the Eastern, and the world is circumferenced. We shall develop the tropics and push far toward the poles; but we have now fairly discovered the island that we call the earth, and we must begin to make the most of it.

Practically all our agriculture has been developed on a rainfall basis.[16] There is ancient irrigation experience, to be sure, but the great agriculture of the world has been growing away from these regions. Agriculture is still moving on, seeking new regions; and it is rapidly invading regions of small rainfall.

About six-tenths of the land surface of the globe must be farmed, if farmed at all, under some system of water-saving. Of this, about one-tenth is redeemable by irrigation, and the remainder by some system of utilization of deficient rainfall, or by what is inappropriately known as dry-farming. The complementary practices of irrigation and dry-farming will develop a wholly new scheme of agriculture and a new philosophy of country life.

Even in heavy rainfall countries there is often such waste of water from runoff that the lands suffer severely from droughts. No doubt the hilly lands of our best farming regions are greatly reduced in their crop-producing power because people do not prepare against drought as consciously as they

15. The first sentence under the original subhead (here omitted) "The best husbandry is not in the new regions," p. 196.

16. The first sentence under the original subhead (here omitted) "Another philosophy of agriculture," p. 197.

provide against frost. It is often said that we shall water Eastern lands by irrigation, and I think that we shall; but our first obligation is to save the rainfall water by some system of farm management or dry-farming.

Agriculture rests on the saving of water.

THE farmer is rapidly beginning to realize his obligation to society.[17] It is usual to say that the farmer feeds the world, but the larger fact is that he saves the world.

The economic system depends on him. Wall Street watches the crops.

As cities increase proportionately in population, the farmer assumes greater relative importance, and he becomes more and more a marked man.

Careful and scientific husbandry is rising in this new country. We have come to a realization of the fact that our resources are not unlimited. The mining of fertilizing materials for transportation to a few spots on the earth will some day cease. We must make the farming sustain itself, at the same time that it provides the supplies for mankind.

We all recognize the necessity of the other great occupations to a well-developed civilization; but in the nature of the case, the farmer is the final support. On him depends the existence of the race. No method of chemical synthesis can provide us with the materials of food and clothing and shelter, and with all the good luxuries that spring from the bosom of the earth.

I know of no better conservators than our best farmers. They feel their responsibility. Quite the ideal of conservation is illustrated by a farmer of my acquaintance who saves every product of his land and has developed a system of self-enriching livestock husbandry, who has harnessed his small stream to light his premises and do much of his work, who turns his drainage waters into productive uses, and who is now troubled that he cannot make some use of the winds that are going to waste on his farm.

What I have meant to impress is the fact that the farmer is the ultimate conservator of the resources of the earth.[18] He is near the cradle of supplies, near the sources of streams, next the margin of the forests, on the hills and in the valleys and on the plains just where the resources lie. He is in contact with the original and raw materials. Any plan of conservation that overlooks this fact cannot meet the situation. The conservation movement must help the farmer to keep and save the race.

17. The first sentence under the original subhead (here omitted) "The obligation of the farmer," p. 198. The extra return preceding the original subhead is here preserved as a section break.

18. The first sentence under the original subhead (here omitted) "The obligation of the conservation movement," p. 200.

The Middleman Question

I recognize the service of the middleman to society.[19] I know that the distributor and trader are producers of wealth as well as those who raise the raw materials; but this is no justification for abuses. I know that there are hosts of perfectly honest and dependable middlemen. We do not yet know whether the existing system of intermediary distributors and sellers is necessary to future society, but we do not see any other practicable way at present. In special cases, the farmer may reach his own customer; but this condition, as I have suggested, is so small in proportion to the whole number of farmers as not greatly to affect the general situation. We do not yet see any way whereby all farmers can be so organized as to enable them to control all their own marketing. Therefore, we must recognize middleman practice as legitimate.

But even though we yet see no way of general escape from the system, we ought to provide some means of regulating its operation.[20] The present method of placing agricultural produce in the hands of the consumer is for the most part indirect and wasteful. Probably in the majority of cases of dissatisfaction, the person whom we call the middleman does not receive any exorbitant profit, but the cost of the commodities is piled up by a long and circuitous system of intermediate tolls and commissions.

It is commonly advised that farmers "unite" or "organize" to correct middleman and transportation abuses, but these troubles cannot be solved by any combination of farmers because this is not an agricultural question. It is as much a problem for consumers as for producers.[21] It is a part of the

19. This excerpt begins with the fourteenth paragraph, p. 157, of the chapter "The Middleman Question," pp. 149–164. The passage begins with the first sentence under the original subhead (here omitted) "The middleman's part," p. 157 and ends on p. 164.

20. The first sentence under the original subhead (here omitted) "A system of economic waste," p. 158.

21. The first sentence under the original subhead (here omitted) "Cooperation of farmers will not solve it," p. 158.

civilization of our day, completely woven into the fabric of our economic system. The farmer may feel its hardship first because he must bear it, while the consumer, to meet higher prices, demands more pay of his employer or takes another stitch out of somebody else. But it is essentially a problem for all society to solve, not for farmers alone, particularly when it operates on a continental basis. This also indicates the futility of the arbitrary control of prices of the great staples by combinations of farmers.

Of course, temporary or local relief may be secured by organizations of producers here and there, or of consumers here and there (probably consumers can attack the problem more effectively than producers), and by the establishment of public markets; but no organization can permanently handle the question unless the organization is all the people.

The present agitations against middleman practices and stock market gambling ought to compel Congress to pass laws to correct the evils that are correctable by law, and the organizations then should keep such touch on the situation that the laws will be enforced.

It has been suggested that the superabundant middlemen go into farming; but no one can compel them to go to farming, and they might not be successful farmers if they should attack the business, and the farming country might not need them or profit by them, for it is not demonstrated that we need more farmers, although it is apparent that we need better farmers.

It is the business of any government to protect its people.[22] Governments have protected their countries from invasion and war, but the greatest office of government in modern times is to develop its own people and the internal resources of its realm. We are beginning to protect the people from the overlording of railroads, from unfair combinations in trade, and from the tyranny of organized politicians. It is just as much the business of government to protect its people from dishonest and tyrannous middlemen lying beyond the practical reach of individuals. The situation has arisen because of lack of control; there is no conspiracy against the farmer.

It is said that competition will in the end correct the middleman evil, but competition does not correct it; and competition alone, under the present structure of society, will not correct it in most cases because "agreements" between traders restrict or remove competition: the situation does not have within itself the remedies for its own ills.

When we finally eliminate combinations in restraint of trade, the middleman abuses may be in the process of passing out. It is to check dishonesty

22. The first sentence under the original subhead (here omitted) "It is the business of the government," p. 160.

on the one hand and to allow real competition on the other that I am now making suggestions.

I have no suggestion to make as to the nature of the laws themselves.[23] There are many diverse situations to be met; and I intentionally do not make my remarks specific. Of course, any law that really attempts to reach the case must recognize the middleman as exercising a public or semipublic function, and that, as such, he is amenable to control, even beyond the point of mere personal honesty. The licensing of middlemen (a practice that might be carried much further, and which is a first step in reform) recognizes this status; and if it is competent for government to license a middleman, it is also competent for it to exercise some oversight over him. It is not necessary that government declare an agency a monopoly in order to regulate it. Commercial situations that unmistakably involve service to the public are proper for governmental control in greater or lesser degree. The supervision of weights and measures is a good beginning in the regulation of middleman trading. But the enactment of laws, even of good laws, is only another step in the solution. A law does not operate itself, and the common man cannot resort to courts of law to secure justice in such cases as these. There must be a continuing process of government with which to work out the reform and to adjust each case on its merits. Whatever the merits of the laws, their success lies in the continuing application of them to specific cases by persons whose business it is to discern the facts rather than to prove a case.

There are three steps in the control of the middleman: (1) an aroused public conscience on the question; (2) good fundamental laws for interstate phases and similar state laws for local phases; (3) good commissions or other agencies or bodies to which any producer or consumer or middleman may take his case, and which may exercise regulatory functions. The interstate commerce commission has jurisdiction over so much of the problem as relates to the service and rates of common carriers; no doubt, its powers could be extended to other interstate phases. Perhaps departments of agriculture, in states in which public service commissions have not been established, could be given sufficient scope to handle some of the questions.

Of course, some of the middlemen and associated traders will contend that all this interferes with business and with private rights, but no man has a private right to oppress or defraud another or to deprive him of his proper rewards; and we must correct a faulty economic system. There is little danger that the legitimate business of any honest middleman will be interfered with.

23. The first sentence under the original subhead (here omitted) "Must be a continuing process of control," p. 161.

I know that commissions and similar bodies have not always been wholly successful. This is because we have not yet had experience enough, have not consciously trained our people for this kind of work, and have not been able to make watertight laws. Neither do older systems now prove to be adequate. New economic conditions must bring new methods of regulation and control.

I have no desire that society (or government) engage in the middleman business or that it take over private enterprise; but no government can expect to throw back on the producer the responsibility of controlling the middleman. I look for the present agitation to awaken government to the necessity of doing what it is plainly its duty to do. In future, a government that will not protect its people in those cases in which the people, acting to the best of their individual and cooperating capacity, cannot protect themselves, will be known as either a bad government or an undeveloped government.

III EDUCATION

There certainly will come a day
As men become simple and wise
When schools will put their books away
Till they train the hands and the eyes;
Then the school from its heart will say
In love of the winds and the skies:

> I teach
> The earth and the soil
> To them that toil,
> The hill and fen
> To common men
> That live just here.

—From "Country School," *Wind and Weather*
(New York: Scribner, 1916)

The four essays that follow condense Liberty Hyde Bailey's views on natural, scientific, and agricultural education, as they reiterate an essentially agrarian pedagogy favoring experiential learning. The first piece, "The Integument Man," speaks with humor and empathy to all teachers, not just nature-study advocates, emboldening them to risk, to engage, and to teach as much with their heart as with their head—in short, to avoid becoming the titular "Integument Man" prescribing only rote learning. In the second treatise, "The Meaning of the Nature-study Movement" Bailey develops many of the themes of "The Integument Man," offering practical as well as philosophical advice about developmental learning. The pupil, the author insists, has a right to a "poetic interpretation of nature," as their educative world rightly begins in wonder and evolves into science. An agrarian, hands-on education of the open fields and woods is as good for the farmer's son as the urbanite's daughter. It is, Bailey insists, a mass phenomenon capable of transforming education by moving it countryward. In the third essay, "The Fundamental Question in American Country Life," Bailey articulates a key plank in the agrarian platform: that agriculture is not merely a school subject, but a noble civilization that ought to be represented organically, top to bottom, in local schools. This idea, very much lost in the contemporary educative drift toward standardization and testing, argues for greater home-rule. The second half of the essay lays out the author's fears for the then-new agricultural colleges and experiment stations, which he worries will become centralized, overly competitive, and poorly staffed by untrained generalists or obtuse sophisticates without proper regard for an agricultural heritage. In the end, however, the sheer potential of the agricultural revolution that Bailey helped institute is evident in the author's heady statements, especially his claim in "The Fundamental Question in American Country Life" that the American Country Life movement is "probably destined to be the most extensive and important application of the scientific method to social problems that is now anywhere underway." Finally, in "The Outlook to Nature," Bailey points to nature as recreational, educative balm—not a cure for complex, modern lives but a necessary complement. We must, he argues, simplify our lives to find an "inner peace" that transcends material satisfaction. An appreciation of the natural world returns our investment a thousandfold, instructing us in an essential optimism. An educated outlook to nature lends the spirit an exuberant positivism akin to religious faith.

The Integument-Man

I wrote a nature-study leaflet on "How a Squash Plant Gets Out of the Seed." A botanist wrote me that it was a pity to place such an error of statement before the child: it should have read, "How the Squash Plant Gets Out of the Integument."[1]

Of course my friend was correct: the squash plant gets out of an integument. But I was anxious to teach the essence of the squash plant's behavior, not a mere verbal fact—and what child was ever interested in an integument?

It is the old question over again—the question of the point of view and what one is driving at. The method of presentation must first be adapted to the person to be instructed, else the instruction will be of little consequence. A person may be so intent on mere literal accuracy that he overlooks the matters that are really important and even vital.

It is the fear of the Integument-Man that keeps many a good teacher from teaching nature-study. He is afraid that he will make a mistake in statements of fact. Now, the person who is afraid that he will make a mistake is the very person to trust, because he will be careful. Of course he will make mistakes—every one does who really accomplishes anything; but the mistakes will be relatively few: he will at once admit the mistakes and correct them when they are discovered, and the pupils will catch his desire for accuracy and admire the sincerity of his purpose. Pity the man who has never made an error!

The teacher often hesitates to teach nature-study because of the lack of technical knowledge of the subject. This is well; but technical knowledge of the subject does not make a good teacher. Expert specialists are so likely to go into mere details and to pursue particular subjects so far, when teaching beginners, as to miss the leading and emphatic points. They are so cognizant

1. From *The Nature-Study Idea* (New York: Doubleday, 1905), 37–42.

112

of exceptions to every rule that they qualify their statements until the statements have no spirit and no force. There are other ideals than those of mere accuracy. In other words, it is more important that the teacher be a good teacher than a good scientist. One may be so exact that his words mean nothing. But being a good scientist ought not to spoil a good teacher.

The Integument-Man sees the little things. The child sees the big things. Ask a child to describe a house, or to draw one.

The Integument-Man teaches details, and his teaching is "dry." The child wants things in the large; when it gets into the high school or college it may carry analysis and dissection to the limit.

The Integument-Man teaches science, although it is not necessarily the best science. The child wants nature.

The Integument-Man believes that any work, to be of value, must be accurate; and accuracy in nature-study begets accuracy in science, when the pupil takes it up later on. So do I. But the child can be accurate only so far as it can understand and comprehend: it must work in its own sphere; the integuments are not in the child's sphere.

The Integument-Man is fearful of every word that seems to imply motive or direction in plants and the lower animals. "The roots go here and there in search of food" is wrong because roots do not "go." Seeds do not "travel." Plants do not "prepare" for winter. I wonder, then, whether water "runs" or winds "blow." This mere verbal accuracy forgets that the words are only metaphors and parables, their significance determined by custom, and that the essential truth is what we should search for—expressing it, when found, in language that is alive, unmistakable, and conformed to best usage.

The Integument-Man insists on "methods." The other day a young man wanted me to recommend him as a teacher of one of the sciences in a public school. He explained that he had a complete course in this and in that; he could teach the whole subject as laid down in the books; he knew the methods. It was evident that he was well-drilled. He had acquired a fund of well-digested but unrelated facts. These facts were carefully assorted and ticketed, and tucked away in his mental cupboard as embroidered napkins are laid away in a drawer. Poor fellow! Mere details have little educative value. An imperfect method that is adapted to one's use is better than a perfect one that cannot be used. Some school laboratories are so perfect that they discourage the pupil in taking up investigations when thrown on his own resources. Imperfect equipment often encourages ingenuity and originality. A good teacher is better than all the laboratories and apparatus.

I like the man who has had an incomplete course. A partial view, if truthful, is worth more than a complete course, if lifeless. If the man has acquired a power for work, a capability for initiative and investigation, an enthusiasm for the daily life, his incompleteness is his strength. How much there is before him! How eager his eye! How enthusiastic his temper! He is a man with a point of view, not a man with mere facts. This man will see first the large and significant events; he will grasp relationships; he will correlate; later, he will consider the details. He will study the plant before he studies the leaf or germination or the cell. He will discover the bobolink before he looks for its toes. He will care little for mere "methods."

The Integument-Man is afraid that this popular nature-study will undermine and discourage the teaching of science. Needless to say, the fear is absurdly groundless. Science teaching is a part of the very fabric of our civilization. All our goings and our comings are adjusted to it. No sane man wishes to cheapen or discourage the teaching of science. Nature-study is not opposed to it. Nature-study prepares the child to receive the science teaching. Gradually, as the child matures, nature-study may grow into science learning if the child so elects. Science teaching has more to fear from desiccated science teaching than it has from nature-study. Everything that is true and worth the while will endure.

All youths love nature. None of them, primarily, loves science. They are interested in the things they can see. By and by they begin to arrange their knowledge and impressions of these things, and thereby to pursue a science. The idea of the science should come late in the educational development of the youth, for the simple reason that science is only a human way of looking at a subject. There is no natural science, but there has arisen a science of natural things. At first the interest in nature is an affair of the heart, and this attitude should never be stifled, much less eliminated. When the interest passes from the heart to the head, nature-love has given way to science. Fortunately, it can always remain an affair of the heart with a most perfect engraftment of the head, but the teaching of facts alone tends to divorce the two. When we begin the teaching of the youth by the teaching of a science, we are inverting the natural order. A rigidly graded and systematic body of facts kills nature-study; examinations bury it.

Then teach! If you love nature and have living and accurate knowledge of some small part of it, teach! Your reputation is not to be made as a geologist or zoologist or botanist, but as a teacher. When beginning to teach birds, think more of the pupil than of ornithology. The pupil's mind and sympathies are to be expanded: the science of ornithology is not to be extended. Remember that spirit is more important than information. The teacher who thinks first of his subject teaches science; he who thinks first of his pupil teaches nature-study. With your whole heart, teach!

Do not be afraid of the Integument-Man.

The Meaning of the
Nature-study Movement

It is one of the marks of the evolution of the race that we are coming more and more into sympathy with the objects of the external world.[2] These things are a part of our lives. They are central to our thoughts. The happiest life has the greatest number of points of contact with the world, and it has the deepest feeling and sympathy for everything that is. The best thing in life is sentiment; and the best sentiment is that which is born of the most accurate knowledge. I like to make this application of Emerson's injunction to "hitch your wagon to a star"; but it must not be forgotten that one must have the wagon before one has the star. Mere facts are dead, but the meaning of the facts is life. The getting of information is but the beginning of education. "With all thy getting, get understanding."

Of late years there has been a rapidly growing feeling that we must live closer to nature; and we must perforce begin with the child. We attempt to teach this nature-love in the schools, and we call the effort nature-study. It would be better if it were called nature-sympathy.

As yet there are no codified methods of teaching nature-study. The subject is not a formal part of the curriculum; and thereby it is not perfunctory. And herein lies much of its value—in the fact that it cannot be reduced to a system, is not cut and dried, cannot become a part of rigid school methods. Its very essence is spirit. It is as free as its subject matter, as far removed from the museum and the cabinet as the skeleton is from the living animal.

It thus transpires that there is much confusion as to what nature-study is, because of the different attitudes of its various exponents; but these different attitudes are largely the reflections of different personalities and the working out of different methods. There may be twenty best ways of teaching nature-study. It is essentially the expression of one's outlook on the

2. From *The Nature-Study Idea* (New York: Doubleday, 1905), 14–37.

world. We must define nature-study in terms of its purpose, not in terms of its methods. It is not doing this or that. It is putting the child into intimate and essential contact with the things of the external world. Whatever the method, the final result of nature-study teaching is the development of a keen personal interest in every natural object and phenomenon.

There are two or three fundamental misconceptions of what nature-study is or should be; and to these we may now give attention.

Fundamentally, nature-study is seeing what one looks at and drawing proper conclusions from what one sees; and thereby the learner comes into personal relation and sympathy with the object. It is not the teaching of science—not the systematic pursuit of a logical body of principles. Its object is to broaden the child's horizon, not, primarily, to teach him how to widen the boundaries of human knowledge. It is not the teaching of botany or entomology or geology, but of plants, insects, and fields. But many persons who are teaching under the name of nature-study are merely teaching and interpreting elementary science.

Again, nature-study is studying things and the reason of things, not about things. It is not reading from nature books. A child was asked if she had ever seen the Great Dipper. "Oh, yes," she replied, "I saw it in my geography." This is better than not to have seen it at all; but the proper place to have seen it is in the heavens. Nature readers may be of the greatest use if they are made incidental and secondary features of the instruction; but, however good they may be, their influence is pernicious if they are made to be primary agents. The child should first see the thing. It should then reason about the thing. Having a concrete impression, it may then go to the book to widen its knowledge and sympathies. Having seen mimicry in the eggs of the aphis on the willow or apple twig, or in the walking stick, the pupil may then take an excursion with Wallace or Bates to the tropics and there see the striking mimicries of the leaf-like insects. Having seen the wearing away of the boulder or the ledge, he may go to Switzerland with Lubbock and see the mighty erosion of the Alps. Now and then the order may be reversed with profit, but this should be the exception: from the wagon to the star should be the rule.

Yet again, nature-study is not the teaching of facts for the sake of the facts. It is not the giving of information merely—notwithstanding the fact that some nature-study leaflets are information leaflets. We must begin with the fact, to be sure, but the lesson is not the fact but the significance of the fact. It is not necessary that the fact have direct practical application to the daily life, for the object is the effort to train the mind and the sympathies. It is a common notion that when the subject matter is insects, the pupil should be taught the life histories of injurious insects and how to destroy the pests. Now, nature-study may be equally valuable whether the subject is the codlin moth or the ant; but to confine the pupil's attention to insects that are injurious to man is to give him a distorted and untrue view of nature. A bouquet of daisies does not represent a meadow. Children should be interested more in seeing things live than in killing them. Yet I would not emphasize the injunction, "Thou shalt not kill." Nature-study is not recommended for the explicit teaching of morals. I should prefer to have the child become so much interested in living things that it would have no desire to kill them. The gun and slingshot and fishpole will be laid aside because the child does not like them any more. We have been taught that one must make collections if he is to be a naturalist. But collections make museums, not naturalists. The scientist needs these collections; but it does not follow that children always need them. To be taught how to kill is to alienate the pupil's affection and sympathy that it is necessary to kill insects; the farmer had this thought in mind when he said to one of our teachers: "Give us more potato bug and less pussy willow." It is true that we must fight insects, but that is a matter of later practice, not of education. It should be an application of knowledge, not a means of acquiring it. It may be necessary to have war, but we do not teach our children to shoot their playmates.

Nature-study is not merely the adding of one more thing to a curriculum. It is not coordinate with geography or reading or arithmetic. Neither is it a mere accessory, or a sentiment, or an entertainment, or a tickler of the senses. It is not "a study." It is not the addition of more "work." It has to do with the whole point of view of elementary education, and therefore is fundamental. It is the full expression of personality. It is the practical working out of the extension idea that has been so much a part of our time. More than any other recent movement, it will reach the masses and revive them. In time it will transform our ideals and then transform our methods.

Nature-study stands for directness and naturalness. It is astonishing, when one comes to think of it, how indirect and how unrelated to the lives of pupils much of our education has been. Geographies begin with the earth, and finally, perhaps, come down to some concrete and familiar object or scene that the pupil can understand. Arithmetic has to do with brokerage and partnerships and partial payments and other things that mean nothing to the child. Botany has to do with cells and protoplasm and cryptograms. History deals with political affairs, and only rarely comes down to physical facts and to those events that have to do with the real lives of the people; and yet political and social affairs are only the results or expressions of the way in which people live. Readers begin with mere literature or with stories of things that the child will never see or do. Of course these statements are meant to be only general, as illustrating what is even yet a great fault in educational methods. There are many exceptions, and these are becoming commoner. Surely, the best education is that which begins with the materials at hand. A child asks what a stone is before it asks what the earth is.

THERE are two ways of interpreting nature—by way of fact and by way of fancy.[3] To the scientist and to the average man the interpretation by fact is often the only admissible one. He may not be open to argument or conviction that there can be any other truthful way of knowing the external world. Yet the artist and the poet know this world, and they do not know it by mere knowledge or by analysis. It appeals to them in its moods, not in its details. Yet it is as real to them as to the analyst. Too much are we of this generation tied to mere phenomena.

We have the right to a poetic interpretation of nature. The child comes to know nature through its imagination and feeling and sympathy. Note the intent and sympathetic face as the child watches the ant carrying its grains of sand and pictures to itself the home and the bed and the kitchen and the sisters and the school that compromises the little ant's life. What does the flower think? Who are the little people that teeter and swing in the sunbeam? What is the brook saying as it rolls over the pebbles? Why is the wind so sorrowful as it moans on the house corners in the dull November days? There are elves whispering in the trees, and there are chariots of fire rolling on the long low clouds at twilight. Wherever it may look, the young mind is impressed with the mystery of the unknown. The child looks out to Nature with great eyes of wonder.

> Child with the gray-blue eyes
> Gazing so longingly—
> Yonder the great world lies—
> All is unknown to thee!
>
> Child unwedded to care,
> Softly speedeth the hours—
> Thou buildest castles in the air
> And strew'st thy path with flowers.
>
> Build on in thy dreaming,
> Nor thy fancies are vain;
> The best of life's seeming
> Are its castles in Spain!

3. The first sentence under the original subhead (here omitted) "How nature-study may be taught," p. 79. The extra return preceding the original subhead is here preserved as a section break.

The good New England poets, did not they know nature? Have they not left us the very essence and flavor of the fields and the woods and the sky? And yet they were not scientists, not mere collectors of facts. So different are these types of interpretation that we all unconsciously do as I did in my last sentence—we set the poet over against the scientist.

Yet poetry is not mere sentiment. The poet has first known the fact. His poetry is misleading if his observations are wrong. Therefore, as I have said, I should begin my nature-study with facts; for facts are tangible, but sentiments cannot be seen. Whatever else we are, we must have the desire to be definite and accurate. We begin on the earth; later, we may drive our Pegasus to a star.

Do not misunderstand. I would not teach nature-subjects in order that the poetic point of view may be enforced. I plead only that the poetic interpretation is allowable on occasion.

How shall nature-study be taught? By the teacher, not by the book. The teacher will need help. There are books and leaflets that will help him. These publications may be put in the hands of pupils if it is always made plain that the recitation is to be from things which the pupil has seen, not from the book. There can be no textbook of nature-study, for when one studies a book he does not study nature. Nature-study books and leaflets are guides, not texts. The book should be a guide to the animal or plant: the animal or plant should not be a guide to the book.

The teacher will need help both in methods and in facts. The method, however, is not to be a codified series of laws or a hard and fast system; but there should be some underlying pedagogical principle which will run through every item of the work. There will be opportunity for endless variation in the details and in the little applications of the work. The personality of the teacher must always stand out strongly. We need the very best of teachers for nature-study work—those who have the greatest personal enthusiasm, and who are least bound by the traditions of the classroom. The teacher, to be ideal, must have more time, more inspiration, and more knowledge. It is better if the teacher have a large knowledge of science, but nature-study may be taught without great knowledge if one sees accurately and infers correctly from the particular subject in hand.

The teacher should studiously avoid starting with definitions and the setting of patterns. Definitions should be the result or summary of the study, not the beginning of it. Mere patterns should only afford means of comparison, and not be regarded as useful in themselves; and even then they are often misleading. The old idea of the model flower is an unfortunate one, simply because the model flower does not exist in nature. The model flower, the complete leaf, and the like, are inferences; and the pupil should begin with things and not mere ideas. In other words, the ideas should be suggested by the things, and not the things by the ideas. "Here is a drawing of a model flower," the old method says; "go and find the nearest approach to it." "Go and find me a flower," is the true method, "and let us see what it is."

Two factors determine the proper subjects for nature-study. First, the subject must be that in which the teacher is most interested and of which he has the most knowledge; second, the subject must be that which is commonest and which can be most easily seen and appreciated by the pupil, and which is nearest and dearest to his life. The tendency is to go too far afield for the subject matter. We are more likely to know the wonders of China or Brazil than of our own brooks and woods. If the subject matter is of such kind that the children can collect the objects as they come and go from the school, the results will be the better.

With children, begin with naked-eye objects. As the pupil matures and becomes interested, the simple microscope may be introduced now and then. Children of twelve years and more may carry a pocket lens; but the best place to use this lens is in the field. The best nature-study observation is that which is done out-of-doors; but some of it can be made from material brought into the schoolroom.

It is a sound pedagogical principle that the child should not be taught those things that are necessarily foreign to the sphere of its life and experiences. It should not have mere dilutions of science. The young child cannot understand cross-fertilization of flowers, and should not be taught the subject. The subject is beyond the child's realm. When we teach it, we are only translating what grown-up investigators have discovered by means of faithful search. At best, it will only be an exotic thing to the child. Pollen and stamens are not near and dear to the child.

There are three factors in the teaching of nature-study:

1. The fact
2. The reason for the fact
3. The interrogation left in the mind of the pupil.

It is impossible to find a natural history object from which these three factors cannot be drawn, for every object is a fact and every fact has a cause, and children may be interested in both the fact and the cause. It may be better, of course, to choose definite subjects, taking pains, at least at first, to select those having emphatic characters. But even in the dullest days of winter sufficient material may be found to keep the interest aflame. A twig or branch may be at hand. There should be enough specimens to supply each child. Let the teacher ask the pupils what they see. The replies will discover the first factor in the teaching—the fact. However, not every fact is significant to the teacher or to the particular pupils. It remains for the teacher to pick out the fact or answer that is most significant. The teacher should know what is significant and he should keep the point clearly before him. One pupil says that the twig is long; another that it is brown; another that it is crooked; another that it is from an apple tree; another that it has several unlike branchlets or parts. Now, this last reply may appeal to the teacher as a most significant fact. Stop the questioning and open the second epoch in the instruction—the reason why no two parts are alike. As before, from the great number of responses the significant reason may be developed: it is because no two parts have lived under exactly the same conditions. One had more room and more sunlight and it grew larger. The third epoch follows naturally: are there any two objects in nature exactly alike? Let the pupils think about it.

Choose a stone. If similar stones are passed about to the pupils, you ask first for the observation or the fact. One says the stone is long; another, it is light; another, it is heavy; another, that the edges are rounded. This latter fact is very significant. You stop the observation and ask why it is rounded. Someone replies that it is because it is water-worn. Query: Are all stones in brooks rounded? Numberless applications and suggestions can be made from this simple lesson. What becomes of the particles that are worn away? How has soil been formed? How has the surface of the fields been shaped and molded?

It is not necessary that the teacher always know the reason. He can ask the pupils to find out and report next day. It is the strong teacher who can say: "I do not know." If a problem had been sent to Agassiz or Asa Gray and he had not understood it, would he have dissimulated or have evaded in the answer? Would he not have said boldly "I do not know"? Such men delve for knowledge, but for every fact that they discover they turn up a dozen mysteries. Knowledge begins in wonder. The consciousness of ignorance is the first result of wonder, and it leads the pupil on and on: it is the spirit of inquiry.

These illustrations are given merely as examples. They may not be ideal, but they show what can be done with very common material. In fact, the surprise and interest is often all the greater because the objects are so very common and familiar.

To my mind, the best of all subjects for nature-study is a brook. It affords studies of many kinds. It is near and dear to every child. It is an epitome of the nature in which we live. In miniature, it illustrates the forces which have shaped much of the earth's surface. It reflects the sky. It is kissed by the sun. It is rippled by the wind. The minnows play in the pools. The soft weeds grow in the shallows. The grass and the dandelions lie on its sunny banks. The moss and the fern are sheltered in the nooks. It comes from one knows not whence: it flows to one knows not whither. It awakens the desire to explore. It is fraught with mysteries. It typifies the flood of life. It "goes on forever."

In other words, the reason why the brook is such a perfect nature-study subject is the fact that it is the central theme in a scene of life. Living things appeal to children. To relate the nature-study work to living animals and plants is the fundamental idea in [Clifton F.] Hodge's ideal, as expressed, for example, in his book, *Nature Study and Life*. He holds that the appreciation of inanimate things is a later development in the child life than an appreciation of objects that are living. He would, therefore, not begin with weathering of rock and formation of soil, combustion and the like, although he would "not wish to insinuate that the study of living things is all of nature-study." With this I agree for the very young, and I would study a brook or a fence corner or a garden bed or a bird or a plant. However, the teacher and the way of teaching are more important than the subject matter, and there are good nature-study teachers who are better fitted to teach inanimate than animate subjects.

One of the first things that a child should learn when he comes to the study of natural history is the fact that no two objects are alike. This leads to an apprehension of the correlated fact that every animal and plant contends for an opportunity to live, and this is the central fact in the study of living things. The world has a new meaning when this fact is understood. This is the key that unlocks many mysteries, and it is the means of establishing a bond of sympathy between ourselves and the world in which we live.

It is a common mistake to attempt to teach too much at every exercise; and the teacher is also appalled at the amount of information which he must have. Suppose that one teaches two hundred and fifty days in the year. Start out with the determination to drop into the pupils' minds two hundred and fifty suggestions about nature. One suggestion is sufficient for a day. Let them think about it and ponder over it. We stuff our children so full of facts that they cannot digest them. I should prefer ten minutes a day of nature-study to two hours; but I should want it quick and sharp. I should want it designed to develop the observing and reasoning powers of the child and not to give mere information. It should be vivid and spontaneous. Spirit counts for more than knowledge.

Taught in this way, nature-study work is not an additional burden to the teacher, but a relief and a relaxation. It may come at the opening of the school hour, or at the close of a hard period, or at any other time when an opportunity offers. It can often be combined with the regular studies of the school, and in that way it can be introduced in places where it would otherwise meet with objection. For example, the subject matter of the lesson may be used for the exercise in drawing or in geography. Let the child draw the twigs; but always be careful lest the drawing become more important than the twigs.

What may be the result of nature-study? Its legitimate result is education—the developing of mental power, the opening of the eyes and the mind, the civilizing of the individual.[4] As with all education, its central purpose is to make the individual happy; for happiness is nothing more nor less than pleasant and efficient thinking. It is often said that the ignorant man may be as happy as the educated man. Relatively, this is true; absolutely, it is not. A ten-foot well is not so deep as a twenty-foot well; and although the ten-foot well may be full to the brim, it holds only half as much water as the other.

The happiness of the ignorant man is largely the thoughts born of physical pleasures; that of the educated man is the thoughts born of intellectual pleasures. One may find comradeship in a groggery, the other may find it in a dandelion; and inasmuch as there are more dandelions than groggeries (in most communities), the educated man has the greatest chance of happiness.

Some persons object to nature-study because it is not systematic and graded. They think that it leads to disjunctive and discursive work. My first answer is that the discursiveness may be its charm. Thereby comes the contrast with the perfunctory schoolwork; and thereby, also, arises its naturalness. Again, I answer that nature-study exercises are not to be the dominant work in the school. They are, or should be, only incidental. The formal schoolwork will supply the drill in method and system; nature-study will afford relaxation, and it will be valuable because it is short and forceful. But, as a matter of fact, nature-study will nearly always be consecutive in subject matter because the teacher will feel himself most competent in one or two lines and will devote himself chiefly to them; or the consecutiveness may be that of the seasons, following the wildlife of the neighborhood. The gist of it all is that the mere exercises in nature-study are only a means to an end: it is the nature-study spirit, not that exercise nor this, that is to correct and to enliven educational ideals. The given exercise may be secondary to other subjects of the school day, but the point of view—the way of thinking—that it inculcates is fundamental and will pervade the school or the home.

4. The first sentence under the original subhead (here omitted) "What may be the results of nature-study?" p. 29.

My remarks on methods are meant, of course, to apply to children. As the pupil advances, the work will naturally become more systematic, until, in the high school, it may develop into science teaching. Those who complain that nature-study is desultory are really thinking of science, not of nature-study. Although not the teaching of science, as such, nature-study is not unscientific.

Nature-study not only educates, but it educates nature-ward; and nature is ever our companion, whether we will or no. Even though we are determined to shut ourselves in an office, nature sends her messengers. The light, the dark, the moon, the cloud, the rain, the wind, the falling leaf, the fly, the bouquet, the bird, the cockroach—they are all ours.

If one is to be happy, he must be in sympathy with common things. He must live in harmony with his environment. One cannot be happy yonder nor tomorrow: he is happy here and now, or never. Our stock of knowledge of common things should be great. Few of us can travel. We must know the things at home.

Nature love tends toward naturalness, and toward simplicity of living. It tends countryward. One word from the fields is worth two from the city. "God made the country."

I expect, therefore, that much good will come from nature-study. It ought to revolutionize the school life, for it is capable of putting new force and enthusiasm into the school and the child. It is new, and therefore is called a fad. A movement is a fad until it succeeds. We shall learn much, and shall outgrow some of our present notions, but nature-study has come to stay. It is in much the same stage of development that manual training and kindergarten work were twenty-five years ago. We must take care that it does not crystallize into science teaching on the one hand, nor fall into mere sentimentalism on the other.

I would again emphasize the importance of obtaining our fact before we let loose the imagination, for on this point will largely turn the results—the failure or the success of the movement. We must not allow our fancy to run away with us. If we hitch our wagon to a star, we must ride with mind and soul and body all alert. When we ride in such a wagon, we must not forget to put in the tailboard.

Another most important result of the nature-study movement will be its effect, along with manual training and other forces, in gradually overturning present systems of schoolwork. The system of memorizing from books will eventually have to go. The pupil will first be put into sympathetic contact with objects, not put into books. In many ways we are now in a transition period in our school systems. For one thing, we are living in an era of the material equipment of schools—the erecting of magnificent buildings, the gathering of extensive outfits. This is true of colleges and universities as well as of the common schools. When this era is past, we shall have more money to spend for teachers. Teaching will be a profession requiring better training and commanding more pay, and men teachers will come back to it.

In this evolved and emancipated school, the nature-study spirit will prevail, even though the name itself be lost. This spirit stands for naturalness and the natural method, for freedom, spontaneity, individual initiative, because it deals firsthand with actual things. It stands for doing and accomplishing. It is the active and creative method. It is a developing of the powers of the pupil, not hearing him recite. In spirit and method it is opposed to the pouring-in-and-dipping-out process.

My own work in nature-study centers chiefly on its value as a means of improving country living. It may tend distinctly toward the improvement of the farmer, and thereby of farming. Go into a potato-growing community and ask the farmers where the roots of the potato plants are—whether above or below the tubers—and you will puzzle them nearly every time. And yet, a knowledge of the position of the roots is essential to the best potato growing, for upon this position depend in part the principles governing the depth of planting, hilling, and, to some extent, of tilling. At a farmers' meeting in an apple-growing section, I asked how many apple flowers are borne in a cluster. Every man guessed, but no man knew. One man said that the limbs of some of his apple trees had died; he asked me why. I asked him the symptoms: but he did not know as they had any symptoms—they had only died. Had he looked at the limbs? Yes, he had seen them from the barnyard!

Now, I do not care whether nature-study teaches where the potato roots are or not. The point is, that nature-study teaches the importance of actually seeing the thing and then of trying to understand it. The person who actually knows a pussy willow will know how to become acquainted with the potato bug. He will introduce himself.

In recent years there has been great activity in disseminating information amongst the farmers. The results have been gratifying. Not only have farmers learned more, but there has been a general uplift in the tone of many rural communities. But the discouraging fact is that the young people do not often come to the farmers' meetings in any numbers. There will be a constantly recurring crop of ignorance and prejudice. Each crop, to be sure, must be above its predecessor, but yet not living up to the full stature of its opportunities. It is therefore necessary to begin with the new generation—to begin our chimney at the bottom, rather than at the top. People crowd into the cities largely because of the intellectual entertainment that they find there. If their own intellectual horizon is enlarged, they may find entertainment in the country.

The teacher, the clergyman, the progressive merchant or farmer here and there, are the persons that are willing to help along the work of uplifting the rural communities. Education is the only salvation for the farmer—not the development of facts, merely, but the development of power through the enlargement of capability. The results will come slowly. We must not be impatient. There are centuries of inertia to be overcome. The best and most permanent things are of slow growth.

Nature-study teaching may seem to be an indirect way of reaching the farmer; but it is not. It is direct because it strikes at the very root of the difficulty. One of the pleasantest comments which we have had on our nature-study work came from a country teacher who said that because she had used it her pupils were no longer ashamed of being farmers' children. If only that much can be accomplished for each country child, the result will be enough for one generation. What can be done for the country child can be done, in a different sphere, for the city child. Fifty years hence the harvest will be seen.

The nature-study effort sets our thinking in the direction of our daily doing. It relates the schoolroom to the life that the child is to lead. It makes the common and familiar affairs seem to be worth the while. Essentially, it is not an ideal of the school any more than it is for the home; but so completely do we delegate all work of teaching and instructing to the school, that nature-study effort comes to be, in practice, a schoolroom subject. I wish that every parent, as well as every professional teacher, could see the importance of first instructing the child in the very things that it is doing and the very objects that it is seeing. The ideal of the parent or the teacher should be to bring the child into sympathetic relations with its world; but whatever may be in the mind and hope of the teacher, so far as the child is concerned the nature sympathy must come as a natural effect of actual observation of definite objects and phenomena.

If, in conclusion, I were asked for a condensed statement of the nature-study idea, I should choose the following definition of it by Professor Thomas H. Macbride, of the University of Iowa:

> I should say that by nature-study a good teacher means such study of the natural world as leads to sympathy with it. The keynote, in my opinion, for all nature-study is sympathy. Such study in the schools is not botany; it is not zoology; although, of course, not contravening either. But by nature-study we mean such a presentation, to young people, of the outside world that our children learn to love all nature's forms and cease to abuse them. The study of natural science leads, to be sure, to these results, but its methods are long and have a different primary object.

The Fundamental Question
in American Country Life

How to make country life what it is capable of becoming is the question before us; and while we know that the means is not single or simple, we ought to be able to pick out the first and most fundamental thing that needs now to be done.[5]

It is perfectly apparent that the fundamental need is to place effectively educated men and women into the open country. All else depends on this. No formal means can be of any permanent avail until men and women of vision and with trained minds are at hand to work out the plans in an orderly way.

And yet it is frequently said that the first necessity is to provide more income for the farmer; but this is the result of a process, not the beginning of it. And again it is said that organization is the first necessity, even to make it possible to use the education. If organization is necessary to make the best use of education, then it assumes education as its basis. Educated men will make organization possible and effective, but economic organization will not insure education except remotely, as it becomes a means of consolidating an unorganic society.

But there is no longer any need to emphasize the value of education. It would now be difficult to find an American farmer who requires convincing on this point. Yet I have desired to say that there is no other agency, using education in its broad sense, that can by any possibility be placed ahead of it.

Agriculture is now a school subject.[6] It is recognized to be such by state syllabi, in the minds of the people, and in the minds of most school men. It is finding its way into high schools and other schools here and there.

---

5. From *The Country-life Movement in the United States* (New York: Macmillan, 1911), 61–68, 79–84.
6. The first sentence under the original subhead (here omitted) "Agriculture in the public schools," p. 62.

III. EDUCATION

There is no longer much need to propagate the idea that agriculture is a school subject. It is now our part to define the subject, organize it, and actually to place it in the schools.

We must understand that the introduction of agriculture into the schools is not a concession to farming or to farmers. It is a school subject by right.

It is the obligation of a school to do more than merely to train the minds of its students. The school cannot escape its social responsibilities; it carries these obligations from the very fact that it is a school supported by public money.

The schools, if they are to be really effective, must represent the civilization of their time and place. This does not mean that every school is to introduce all the subjects that engage men's attention, or that are capable of being put into educational form; it means that it must express the main activities, progress, and outlook of its people. Agriculture is not a technical profession or merely an industry, but a civilization. It is concerned not only with the production of materials, but with the distribution and selling of them, and with the making of homes directly on the land that produces the material. There cannot be effective homes without the development of a social structure.

Agriculture therefore becomes naturally a part of a public school system when the system meets its obligation. It is introduced into the schools for the good of the schools themselves. It needs no apology and no justification; but it may need explanation in order that the people may understand the situation.

If agriculture represents a civilization, then the homemaking phase of country life is as important as the field farming phase. As is the home, so is the farm; and as is the farm, so is the home. Some of the subjects that are usually included under the current name of home economics, therefore, are by right as much a part of schoolwork as any other subjects; they will be a part of city schools as much as of country schools if the city schools meet their obligations. They are not to be introduced merely as concessions to women or only as a means of satisfying popular demand; they are not to be tolerated: they are essential to a public school program.

The American college of agriculture phase of education is now well established.[7] It is the most highly developed agricultural education in the world. It is founded on the democratic principle that the man who actually tills the soil must be reached, an idea that may not obtain in other countries.

---

7. The first sentence under the original subhead (here omitted) "The American contribution," p. 65.

128

We are now attempting to extend this democratic education by means of agriculture to all ages of our people, and there is promise that we shall go farther in this process than any people has yet gone; and this fact, together with the absence of a peasantry, with the right of personal landholding, and with a voice in the affairs of government, should give to the people of the United States the best country life that has yet been produced.

America's contribution to the country-life situation is a new purpose and method in education, which is larger and freer than anything that has yet been developed elsewhere, and which it is difficult for the Old World fully to comprehend.

The founding of the great line of public-maintained colleges and experiment stations means the application of science to the reconstruction of a society; and it is probably destined to be the most extensive and important application of the scientific method to social problems that is now anywhere underway.

It is not to extol our education experiment that I am making this discussion, but to measure the situation; and I think that there are perils ahead of us, which we should now recognize.[8]

There are two grave dangers in the organization of the present situation: (1) the danger that we shall not develop a harmonious plan, and thereby shall introduce competition rather than cooperation between agencies; (2) the danger that the newer agencies will not profit fully by our long experience in agriculture teaching.

An internal danger is the giving of instruction in colleges of agriculture that is not founded on good preparation of the student or is not organized on a sound educational basis. Winter course and special students may be admitted, and extension work must be done; but the first responsibility of a college of agriculture is to give a good educational course: it deals with education rather than with agriculture, and its success in the end will depend on the reputation it makes with school men.

There is also danger that new institutions will begin their extension work in advance of their academic educational work; whereas, extension and propaganda can really succeed only when there is a good background of real accomplishment at home.

There is necessity that we now reorganize much of our peripatetic teaching. It is no longer sufficient to call persons together and exhort them and talk to them. We have come about to the end of agricultural propaganda. All field and itinerant effort should have a follow-up system with the purpose

8. The first sentence under the original subhead (here omitted) "The dangers of the situation," p. 66.

to set every man to work on his own place with problems that will test him. We have been testing soils and crops and fertilizers and livestock and machines: it is now time to test the man.

There is also danger that we consolidate too many rural schools in towns. If it is true that the best country life is developed when persons live actually on their farms, then we should be cautious of all movements that tend to centralize their interests too far from home, and particularly to centralize them in a town or in a village. The good things should come to the farm rather than that the farm should be obliged to go to the good things.[9]

THE demand for agriculture-education is now widespread; the subject is becoming "popular."[10] All kinds of plans are being tried or discussed.

Persons do not seem to realize that we have had about one hundred years of experience in the United States in agriculture education, and that this experience ought to point the way to success, or at least to the avoiding of serious errors. The agricultural colleges have come up through a long and difficult route, and their present success is not accidental, nor is it easy to duplicate or imitate. First and last, about every conceivable plan has been tried by them, or by others in their time or preceding them; and this experience ought to be utilized by the other institutions that are now being projected in all parts of the country.

Plans that certainly cannot succeed are now being projected. The projectors seem to proceed on the idea that it requires no background of experience to enable an institution to teach agriculture, whereas agriculture education is the most difficult and also the most expensive of all education yet undertaken.

To teach agriculture merely by giving a new direction or vocabulary to botany, chemistry, geology, physics, and the like is not to teach agriculture at all, although it may greatly improve these subjects themselves. To put a school of agriculture in the hands of some good science teacher in a general college faculty with the idea that he can cover the agricultural work and at the same time keep up his own department, is wholly ineffective (except temporarily) and out of character with the demands of the twentieth century (but in high schools a good science teacher may handle the work, or an agriculture teacher may carry the science). To suppose that "agriculture" is one

9. The pages that originally followed this sentence, inclusive of the subheadings "The present educational institutions," "The need of plans to coordinate this educational work," "Outline of a state plan," and "A state extension program," pp. 71–79, are here leapfrogged for the sake of concision.

10. The first sentence under the original subhead (here omitted) "The lessons of experience," p. 79. The extra return is here preserved as a section break.

subject for a college course, to be sufficiently represented by a "chair," is to miss the point of modern progress. To give only laboratory and recitation courses may be better than nothing, but land teaching, either as a part of the institution or on adjacent farms, must be incorporated with the customary schoolwork if the best results are to be secured. To make a school farm pay for itself and for the school is impossible unless the school is a very poor or exceedingly small one; and yet this old fallacy is alive at the present day. To have a distant farm to visit and look at, in order to "apply" the "teachings" of chemistry, botany, and the like, falls far short of real agriculture instruction. To develop a "model farm" that shall be a pattern to the multitude in exact farming is an exploded notion: there are many farmers' farms that are better adapted to such purpose (the demonstration farm is the modern adaptation of the idea, and it is educationally sound).

To teach agriculture of college grade requires not only persons who know the subject, but an organization well-informed on the educational administration that is required. There must be a body of experience in this line of work behind any teaching on a college plane that shall be really useful; when this body of experience does not exist, the work must necessarily grow slowly and be under the most expert direction. The presumption is still against successful agriculture work in the literary and liberal arts institutions, because such teaching demands a point of view on education that the men in these institutions are likely not to possess. Agriculture cannot be introduced in the same way that a department or chair of history or mathematics can be organized; it requires a different outlook on educational procedure, a different order of equipment and of activities, and its own type of administration.

I am much afraid that some of the newer unattached institutions, in their eagerness to make departures and to be self-sufficient, will not profit by our long development, and that the secondary schools and others may make many of the mistakes that the regular colleges of agriculture long ago have made. The presumption is against any school that expects to develop merely a local enterprise, without reference to other schools or to experience.

I am sure we all want to encourage the introduction of agriculture into all educational institutions, but we should not be misled merely by the word "agriculture"; and in the interest of good work we should be careful not to encourage any enterprise of this kind until convinced that it has been well-studied and that it will be administered in the interest of rural progress.

The Outlook to Nature

So great has been the extension of knowledge, and so many the physical appliances that multiply our capabilities, that we are verily burdened with riches.[11] We are so eager to enter all the strange and ambitious avenues that open before us that we overlook that soil at our feet. We live in an age of superlatives, I had almost said of super-superlatives, so much so that even the superlatives now begin to pall. The reach for something new has become so much a part of our lives that we cease to recognize the fact and accept novelty as a matter of course. If we shall fail to satisfy ourselves with the new, the strange, and the eccentric, perhaps we shall be able to extract new delights from them because in their turn the commonplaces will again be the superlatives, and we shall be content with the things that come naturally and in due order. Certain it is that every sensitive soul feels this longing for something simple and elemental in the midst of the voluminous and intricate, something free and natural that shall lie close to the heart and really satisfy our best desires.

It is not likely that we shall greatly simplify our outward physical and business affairs. Probably it is not desirable that we should do so, for we must maintain our executive efficiency. We have seen a marvelous development of affairs, expressed in the renovation of a hundred old occupations and the creation of a thousand new ones. Most of these occupations and businesses are clear gain to the world, and we may expect them to endure. This rise of affairs has emphasized the contrasts of business and of home. Machinery and complexity belong to affairs; but a simpler and directer mental attitude should belong to our personal and private hours. Perhaps

11. The excerpt begins with the fourth paragraph of the chapter "The Commonplace," p. 4. The title of the volume from which this passage is drawn, *Outlook to Nature* (New York: Macmillan, 1905), is here used in place of the less descriptive original chapter title, "The Commonplace." The passage includes pp. 4–12.

our greatest specific need is a wholesome return to nature in our moments of leisure—all the more important now that the moments of leisure are so few. This return to nature is by no means a cure-all for the ills of civilization, but it is one of the means of restoring the proper balance and proportion of our lives. It stands for the antithesis of acting and imitation, for a certain pause and repose, for a kind of spiritual temper, for the development of the inner life as contrasted with the externals.

The outlook to nature is, of course, the outlook to optimism, for nature is our governing condition and is beyond the power of man to modify or correct. We look upward and outward to nature. Some persons have supposed, however, that the "contentment" preached by the nature-lover implies unvexed indifference to the human affairs of the time, and that therefore it makes for a kind of serene and weak utopianism; but, to my mind, the outlook to nature makes for just the reverse of all this. If nature is the norm, then the necessity for correcting and amending the abuses that accompany civilization becomes baldly apparent by very contrast. The repose of the nature-lover and the assiduous exertion of the man of affairs are complementary, not antithetical, states of mind. The return to nature affords the very means of acquiring the incentive and energy for ambitious and constructive work of a high order; it enforces the great truth that, in the affairs of men, continued progress is conditioned upon a generous discontent and diligent unrest.

By nature, I mean the natural out-of-doors—the snow and the rain, the sky, the plants, the animals, the running brooks, and every landscape that is easy of access and undefiled. Every person desires these things in greater or lesser degree: this is indicated by the rapidly spreading suburban movement, by the vacationing in the country, and by the astonishing multiplication of books about nature. Yet there are comparatively very few who have any intimate contact with nature, or any concrete enjoyment from it, because they lack information that enables them to understand the objects and the phenomena.

The currents of civilization tend always to take us out of our environment rather than fit us into it. We must recast our habits of thought so as to set our faces nature-ward. This is far more important than any effort at mere simplicity or toward lopping off the redundancies: it is fundamental direction and point of view.

The outlook to nature is the outlook to what is real, and hearty, and spontaneous. Our eager civilization prematurely makes us mentally old. It may be true that the span of one's life is increasing, but at twenty we have the knowledge and the perplexities that our grandfathers had only at forty. Our children may now be older when they are graduated from school, but the high school course of today is more complex than was the college course of fifty years ago. All this has a tendency to lessen the years of free and joyous youth. You have only to see the faces of boys and girls on your city streets to discover how old the young have grown to be. In home and school our methods have been largely those of repression: this is why the natural buoyant outburst that I saw on the city thoroughfare challenged such instant attention and surprise. We need to emphasize the youthful life.

Therefore, I preach the things that we ourselves did not make; for we are all idolaters—the things of our hands we worship. I preach the near-at-hand, however plain and ordinary—the sky in rain and sun; the bird on its nest and the nest on its bough; the rough bark of the trees; the frost on bare thin twigs; the mouse skittering to its burrow; the insect seeking its crevice; the smell of the ground; the sweet wind; the leaf that clings to its twig or that falls when its work is done. Wisdom flows from these as it can never flow from libraries and laboratories. "There be four things," say the Proverbs, "which are little upon the earth, by they are exceeding wise:

> The ants are a people not strong, yet they prepare their meat in the summer;
> The conies are but a feeble folk, yet they make their houses in the rocks;
> The locusts have no king, yet go they forth all of them by bands;
> The spider taketh hold with her hands, and is in the kings' palaces.

IV COMMUNITY

In stranger lands beyond the sea
With a speech I could not know
Some kindred soul has walked with me
Where the tireless pathways go;
High on tops of the rounding downs
And shores of the singing bays
Far in streets of the talking towns
We have walked our speechless ways.

And these are the ceaseless kindred souls
That I meet on life's highway—
We meet and touch and they reach their goals
And I bid them all Good-Day.

—From "The Great High-Roads," *Wind and Weather*
(New York: Scribner, 1916)

In the following five essays, Liberty Hyde Bailey approaches an agrarian's sense of community from very different angles, though in each case he intimates the time-honored questions: *Who are we?* and *Who are we fighting for?* In "The Brotherhood Relation" and "The Neighbor's Access to the Earth," the author uses the then-novel term "biocentric" to suggest a revolutionary philosophy by which humans are equal to nature and by which the environmental steward becomes an integral agent of greater civic good. In this biocentric paradigm, the farmer is at once independent and beholden, as he is the "bottom" or foundational man. "The Neighbor's Access to the Earth" completes the syllogism—if the farmer's work is divine and his place in society protected, and if the society he toils for is truly egalitarian, then the urbanite and the suburbanite should likewise have access to the balm of the agrarian lifestyle. "The naturist," Bailey insists, "is not selfish." In advancing the cause of social justice, Bailey advocates a move away from large homes and estates and toward a more equitable division of community resources. The back-to-the-land movement, Bailey cautions, needn't exclusively mean back-to-the-farm, as the urbanite could recreate, vacation, or simply live outside the cities and derive pseudo-agricultural satisfactions. As Bailey famously writes in *The Holy Earth,* "If it were possible for every person to own a tree and to care for it, the good results would be beyond estimation." In the third essay, "Country and City," Bailey conjures Thoreau's notion of the "poetical farmer" and further contemplates the poetic sense of the plowman's lifestyle. The author exhorts his readers to experience the outdoors, to become native to a place, and to get their shoes muddy.

In the last two essays of this section, violent competition is represented as a threat to a peaceable agrarian republic. In "The Principle of Enmity," from Bailey's wartime book *Universal Service: The Hope of Humanity*, he honors the essential sacrifice of the serviceperson. At the same time, he fingers urban industrialism, rife with greed and commercialism, as the cause of needless destruction. In "Democracy, What It Is," from *What Is Democracy?*, Bailey puts a finer point on the distinction between *democracy*—the will of the people—and *despotism*. The essay concludes with a remarkably current litany of antithetical terms, defining democracy, poignantly, by what it is not.

The Brotherhood Relation

A constructive and careful handling of the resources of the earth is impossible except on a basis of large cooperation and of association for mutual welfare.[1] The great inventions and discoveries of recent time have extensive social significance.

Yet we have other relations than with the physical and static materials. We are parts in a living sensitive creation. The theme of evolution has overturned our attitude toward this creation. The living creation is not exclusively man-centered: it is biocentric. We perceive the essential continuity in nature, arising from within rather than from without, the forms of life proceeding upwardly and onwardly in something very like a mighty plan of sequence, man being one part in the process. We have genetic relation with all living things, and our aristocracy is the aristocracy of nature. We can claim no gross superiority and no isolated self-importance. The creation, and not man, is the norm. Even now do we begin to guide our practices and our speech by our studies of what we still call the lower creation. We gain a good perspective on ourselves.

If we are parts in the evolution, and if the universe, or even the earth, is not made merely as a footstool, or as a theater for man, so do we lose our cosmic selfishness and we find our place in the plan of things. We are emancipated from ignorance and superstition and small philosophies. The present widespread growth of the feeling of brotherhood would have been impossible in a self-centered creation: the way has been prepared by the discussion of evolution, which is the major biological contribution to human welfare and progress. This is the philosophy of the oneness in nature and the unity in living things.

1. From *The Holy Earth* (New York: Scribner, 1915), 30–41.

IV. COMMUNITY

THE surface of the earth is particularly within the care of the farmer.[2] He keeps it for his own sustenance and gain, but his gain is also the gain of all the rest of us. At the best, he accumulates little to himself. The successful farmer is the one who produces more than he needs for his support; and the overplus he does not keep; and, moreover, his own needs are easily satisfied. It is of the utmost consequence that the man next the earth shall lead a fair and simple life; for in riotous living he might halt many good supplies that now go to his fellows.

It is a public duty so to train the farmer that he shall appreciate his guardianship. He is engaged in a quasi-public business. He really does not even own his land. He does not take his land with him, but only the personal development that he gains from it. He cannot annihilate his land, as another might destroy all his belongings. He is the agent or the representative of society to guard and to subdue the surface of the earth; and he is the agent of the divinity that made it. He must exercise his dominion with due regard to all these obligations. He is a trustee. The productiveness of the earth must increase from generation to generation: this also is his obligation. He must handle all his materials, remembering man and remembering God. A man cannot be a good farmer unless he is a religious man.

If the farmer is engaged in a quasi-public business, shall we undertake to regulate him? This relationship carries a vast significance to the social order, and it must color our attitude toward the man on the land. We are now in that epoch of social development when we desire to regulate by law everything that is regulatable and the other things besides. It is recently proposed that the Congress shall pass a law regulating the cropping scheme of the farmer for the protection of soil fertility. This follows the precedent of the regulation, by enactment, of trusts and public utilities. It is fortunate that such a law cannot be passed, and could not be enforced if it were passed; but this and related proposals are crude expressions of the growing feeling that the farmer owes an obligation to society, and that this obligation must be enforced and the tiller of the soil be held to account.

We shall produce a much better and safer man when we make him self-controlling by developing his sense of responsibility than when we regulate him by exterior enactments.

In the realm of control of the farming occupation we shall invoke other than legal means, and perhaps these means will be suggestive for other situations. These means may be somewhat indefinite in the lawbook sense, but they may attain to a better human result. We shall reach the question by

2. The first sentence under the original subhead (here omitted) "The farmer's relation," p. 32. The extra return preceding the original subhead is here preserved as a section break.

surer ways than the crudities of legislation. We shall reach the man, in this field, rather than his business. We have begun it by accepting it as one part of our duty to the race to provide liberally at public expense for the special education of the man on the land. This is the reason, even if we have not formulated it to ourselves, why society is willing to go farther in the education of the farming people than in the popular education of other ranges of the people. This, of course, is the fundamental way; and if there are any governments that attempt to safeguard this range directly by laws rather than by education, then they have not arrived at a long view of the situation.

We invoke regulatory law for the control of the corporate activities; but we must not forget the other kinds of activities contributing to the making of society, nor attempt to apply to them the same methods of correction.

Into this secular and more or less technical education we are now to introduce the element of moral obligation, that the man may understand his peculiar contribution and responsibility to society; but this result cannot be attained until the farmer and every one of us recognize the holiness of the earth.

The farmer and every one of us—every citizen—should be put right toward the planet, should be quicked to his relationship to his natural background. The whole body of public sentiment should be sympathetic with the man who works and administers the land for us; and this requires understanding. We have heard much about the "marginal man," but the first concern of society should be for the bottom man.

If this philosophy should really be translated into action, the farmer would nowhere be a peasant, forming merely a caste, and that a low one, among his fellows. He would be an independent cooperating citizen partaking fully of the fruits of his labor, enjoying the social rewards of his essential position, being sustained and protected by a body of responsive public opinion. The farmer cannot keep the earth for us without an enlightened and very active support from every other person, and without adequate safeguards from exploitation and from unessential commercial pressure.

This social support requires a ready response on the part of the farmer; and he must also be developed into his position by a kind of training that will make him quickly and naturally responsive to it. The social fascination of the town will always be greater than that of the open country. The movements are more rapid, more picturesque, have more color and more vivacity. It is not to be expected that we can overcome this fascination and safeguard the country boy and girl merely by introducing more showy or active enterprises into the open country. We must develop a new background for the country youth, establish new standards, and arouse a new point of view. The farmer will not need all the things that the city man thinks the farmer needs. We must stimulate his moral response, his appreciation of the worthiness of the things in which he lives, and increase his knowledge of all the objects and affairs amongst which he moves. The backbone of the rural question is at the bottom a moral problem.

We do not yet know whether the race can permanently endure urban life, or whether it must be constantly renewed from the vitalities in the rear. We know that the farms and the back spaces have been the mother of the race. We know that the exigencies and frugalities of life in these backgrounds beget men and women to be serious and steady and to know the value of every hour and of every coin that they earn; and whenever they are properly trained, these folk recognize the holiness of the earth.

For some years I have had the satisfaction to speak to rural folk in many places on the holy earth and to make some of the necessary applications.

Everywhere I have met the heartiest assent from these people. Specially do they respond to the suggestion that if the earth is hallowed, so are the native products of the earth hallowed; and they like to have the mystery—which is the essential sentiment—of these things brought home to them with frequency. I will here let my reader have a letter that one of these persons wrote me, and I print it without change. On inquiry, the writer of it told me that he is a farmer, has never followed any other occupation, was brought up "in the woods," and has had practically no education. I did not ask him, but I judge from the narrative style that he has been a reader or a hearer of the Old Testament; and here is the letter:

As you say, too many people confound farming, with that sordid, selfish, money-getting game, called "business," whereas, the farmer's position is administrative, being in a way a dispenser of the "Mysteries of God," for they are mysteries. Every apple is a mystery, and every potato is a mystery, and every ear of corn is a mystery, and every pound of butter is a mystery, and when a "farmer" is not able to understand these things he is out of place.

The farmer uses the soil and the rains and the snows and the frosts and the winds and the sun; these are also the implements of the Almighty, the only tools He uses, and while you were talking that day, it brought to mind the recollection of an account I once read of an occurrence which took place in the vicinity of Carlsruhe, in Germany, about thirty years ago, and I want to tell you about it. An old man and his two sons, who were laborers on a large farm there, went out one morning to mow peas, with scythes, as was the method in use at that time, and soon after they began work, they noticed a large active man coming along a pathway which bordered the field on one side, and when he came to where they were, he spoke to them, very pleasantly, and asked them some questions about their work and taking the scythe from the hands of the older man he mowed some with it and finally returned it and went his way.

After a time when the owner of the farm came out to oversee the work they told him of the occurrence, and asked him if he could tell who the stranger might be, and he told them that he was Prince Bismarck, the Chancellor of the empire, who was staying at his country home at Carlsruhe, and was out for his morning walk, and they were astonished, and the old man was filled with a great pride, and he felt himself elevated above all his fellows, and he wouldn't have sold his scythe for half the money in Germany, and his descendants to this day boast of the fact that their father and Bismarck mowed with the same scythe. Now if it was sufficient to stimulate the pride of this old laborer, if it was sufficient to create for him a private aristocracy, if it was sufficient to convert that old rusty scythe into a priceless heirloom to be treasured up and transmitted from father to son, if it was sufficient for all these things that he had once held a momentarily unimportant association with the man of "blood and iron," how much more inconceivably and immeasurably high and exalted is the station of the farmer who is, in a measure, a fellow craftsman of the God of Nature, of the great First Cause of all things, and people don't know it. No wonder the boys leave the farm!

THIS, then, is the landsman's obligation, and his joyful privilege.[3] But it must not be supposed that he alone bears the responsibility to maintain the holiness of the divine earth. It is the obligation also of all of us, since every one is born to the earth and lives upon it, and since every one must react to it to the extent of his place and capabilities. This being so, then it is a primary need that we shall place at the use of the people a kind of education that shall quicken those attachments.

Certainly all means of education are useful, and every means should be developed to its best; and it is not to be expected that all the people shall pursue a single means: but to the nation and to the race a fundamental training must be provided.

We are now in the time of developing a technical education in agriculture, to the end that we may produce our land supplies. Already this education is assuming broad aspects, and we begin to see that it has very important bearing on public policies. It is a new form of exercise in natural science—the old education in this great realm having become so specialized and departmentalized as to lose much of its value as a means of popular training.

It is a happy augury that in North America so many public men and administrators have taken the large view of education by means of agriculture, desiring, while training farmers of those who would be farmers, to make it a means of bringing the understanding of the people back to the land.

---

3. The first sentence under the original subhead (here omitted) "The underlying training of the people," p. 39. The extra return preceding the original subhead is here preserved.

The Americans are making a very remarkable contribution here, in a spirit of real statesmanship. In the long run, this procedure will produce a spirit in the people that will have far-reaching importance in the development of national character, and in a relation to the backgrounds of which very few of us yet have vision.

It will be fortunate if we can escape the formalizing and professionalizing of this education, that has cast such a blight on most of the older means of training the young, and if we can keep it democratic and free in spirit.

We shall need to do the same in all the subjects that lie at the foundations— in all the other crafts; all these crafts are of the earth. They support the physical man and the social fabric, and make the conditions out of which all the highest achievements may come.

Every person in a democracy has a right to be educated by these means; and a people living in a democracy must of necessity understand the significance of such education. This education should result or function politically. It is not sufficient to train technically in the trades and crafts and arts to the end of securing greater economic efficiency—this may be accomplished in a despotism and result in no self-action on the part of the people. Every democracy must reach far beyond what is commonly known as economic efficiency, and do everything it can to enable those in the backgrounds to maintain their standing and their pride and to partake in the making of political affairs.

The Neighbor's Access
to the Earth

When one really feels the response to the native earth, one feels also the obligation and the impulse to share it with the neighbor.[4] The earth is not selfish. It is open and free to all. It invites everywhere. The naturist is not selfish—he shares all his joys and discoveries, even to the extent of publishing them. The farmer is not selfish with his occupation—he freely aids every one or any to engage in his occupation, even if that one becomes his competitor. But occupations that are some degrees removed from the earth may display selfishness; trade and, to a large extent, manufacture are selfish, and they lock themselves in. Even the exploiting of the resources of the earth may be selfish, in the taking of the timber and the coal, the waterpowers and the minerals, for all this is likely to develop to a species of plunder. The naturist desires to protect the plants and the animals and the situations for those less fortunate and for those who come after. There are lumbermen and miners with the finest sense of obligation. There are other men who would take the last nugget and destroy the last bole.

We are to recognize the essential integrity of the farming occupation, when developed constructively, as contrasted with the vast system of improbity and dishonor that arises from depredation and from the taking of booty.

The best kind of community interest attaches to the proper use and partitioning of the earth, a communism that is dissociated from propaganda and programs. The freedom of the earth is not the freedom of license: there is always the thought of the others that are dependent on it. It is the freedom of utilization for needs and natural desires, without regard to one's place among one's fellows, or even to one's condition of degradation or state of sinfulness. All men are the same when they come back to the meadows,

4. From *The Holy Earth* (New York: Scribner, 1915), 42–65.

143

to the hills, and to the deep woods: He maketh his sun to rise on the evil and the good, and sendeth rain on the just and the unjust.

The lesson of the growing, abounding earth is of liberality for all, and never exploitation or very exclusive opportunities for the few. Even if the weaker anywhere perish in the contest for food, they are nevertheless given the opportunity to contest on terms equal to their abilities; and at all events, we come, in the human sphere, to the domination of sweet reason rather than to competition in sheer force. When, by means of reasonable education, this simple relation is understood by mankind and begins to express itself spontaneously, we shall find our voluminous complex of laws to regulate selfishness gradually disappearing and passing into the limbo.

It is now easy to understand the sinfulness of vast private estates that shut up expanses of the surface of the earth from the reach and enjoyment of others that are born similarly to the privileges of the planet. There is no warrant in nature for guarantee deeds to such estates. It is true, of course, that land estates should not be equal, for capacities for use are not equal, and abilities and deserts are not equal. It is legitimate to reward those who otherwise render great service, and this reward may lie in unusual privileges. The present emoluments in the way of incomes bear little relation to service or even to merit.

We have not yet escaped the idea that vested rights—and particularly personal realty—are inviolable. Certainly these rights must be protected by law, otherwise there can be no stability and regularity in affairs; but there is no inalienable right in the ownership of the surface of the earth. Readjustments must come, and even now they are coming slowly, and here and there in the interest of the neighbor; and in the end there will be no private monopoly of public or natural resources.

The cure for these ills does not lie, however, in the ownership of all the land by "the government," at least not in our time and perhaps never. It is well for a person to have his own plot for his lifetime, with the right to use it as he will so long as he does not offend, or does not despoil it for those who follow: it steadies him, and it identifies him with a definite program in life.

We usually speak as if all good results in the distribution of the natural bounty will ensue if "the government" or "the state" owns the resources; but government ownership of resources and direction of industries may not mean freedom or escape for the people. It depends entirely on the kind of government—not on its name or description, but on the extent to which the people have been trained to partake on their own initiative. The government may be an autocracy or only another form of monopoly.

The aristocracy of land has much to its credit. Great gains in human accomplishment have come out of it; but this does not justify it for the future.

The aristocracy of land is a very dangerous power in human affairs. It is all the more dangerous when associated with aristocracy of birth and of factitious social position, which usually accompany it. A people may be ever so free in its advantages and in its theoretical political organization, and yet suffer overwhelming bondage if its land is tied up in an aristocratic system, and particularly if that system is connected into a social aristocracy. And whenever rigid aristocracy in land connects itself with the close control of politics, the subjection becomes final and complete.

What lies within a nation or a people may lie in enlarged form between the nations or the peoples. Neighborliness is international. Contest for land and sea is at the basis of wars. Recognizing the right of any people to its own life, we must equally recognize its right to a sufficient part of the surface of the earth. We must learn how to subdivide it on the basis of neighborliness, friendship, and conference; if we cannot learn this, then we cannot be neighbors but only enemies. The proposal now before Congress to cede to Canada the Alaskan Panhandle, or a part of it, is an evidence of this growth of international morals, extended to the very basis on which nations have been the least ready to cooperate.

If we may fraternalize territory, so shall we fraternalize commerce. No people may rightly be denied the privilege to trade with all other peoples. All kinds of useful interchange are civilizers and peacemakers; and if we carry ourselves to others when we carry our produce and our wares, so do any of us need that others shall bring their produce and their wares to us. It would be a sorry people that purchased no supplies from without. Every people, small or large, has right of access to the sea, for the sea belongs to mankind. It follows that no people has a right to deprive any other people of the shore, if that people desires the contact.

We now begin to understand the awful sin of partitioning the earth by force.

THE question then arises whether lands and other natural resources shall now be divided and redistributed in order that the share-and-share of the earth's patrimony shall be morally just.[5] Undoubtedly the logic of the situation makes for many personal points of very close contact with the mother earth, and contact is usually most definite and best when it results from what we understand as ownership. This, in practice, suggests many small parcels of land—for those who would have their contact by means of land, which is the directest means—under personal fee. But due provision must

5. The first sentence following the original subhead (here omitted) "The subdividing of the land," p. 48. The extra return preceding the original subhead is here preserved as a break.

always be made, as I have already indicated, for the man who makes unusual contribution to the welfare of his fellows, that he may be allowed to extend his service and attain his own full development; and moreover, an established order may be not be overturned suddenly and completely without much damage, not only to personal interests but to society. Every person should have the right and the privilege to a personal use of some part of the earth; and naturally the extent of his privilege must be determined by his use of it.

It is urged that lands can be most economically administered in very large units and under corporate management; but the economic results are not the most important results to be secured, although at present they are the most stressed. The ultimate good in the use of land is the development of the people; it may be better that more persons have contact with it than that it shall be executively more effectively administered. The morals of land management are more important than the economics of land management; and of course my reader is aware that by morals I mean the results that arise from a right use of the earth rather than the formal attitudes toward standardized or conventional codes of conduct.

If the moral and the economic ends can be secured simultaneously, as eventually they will be secured, the perfect results will come to pass; but any line of development founded on accountant economics alone will fail.

Here I must pause for an explanation in self-defense, for my reader may think I advise the "little farm well tilled" that has so much captured the public mind. So far from giving such advice, I am not thinking exclusively of farming when I speak of the partitioning of the land. One may have land merely to live on. Another may have a wood to wander in. One may have a spot on which to make a garden. Another may have a shore, and another a retreat in the mountains or in some far space. Much of the earth can never be farmed or mined or used for timber, and yet these supposed waste places may be very real assets to the race: we shall learn this in time. I am glad to see these outlying places set aside as public reserves; and yet we must not so organize and tie up the far spaces as to prevent persons of little means from securing small parcels. These persons should have land that they can handle and manipulate, in which they may dig, on which they may plant trees and build cabins, and which they may feel is theirs to keep and to master, and which they are not obliged to "improve." In the parks and reserves the land may be available only to look at, or as a retreat in which one may secure permission to camp. The regulations are necessary for these places, but these places are not sufficient.

If it were possible for every person to own a tree and to care for it, the good results would be beyond estimation.

Now, farming is a means of support; and in this case, the economic possibilities of a particular piece of land are of primary consequence. Of course, the most complete permanent contact with the earth is by means of farming, when one makes a living from the land; this should produce better results than hunting or sport; but one must learn how to make this connection. It is possible to hoe potatoes and to hear the birds sing at the same time, although our teaching has not much developed this completeness in the minds of the people.

I hope, therefore, that the farmer's piece of land will be economically good (that it may make him a living and produce a surplus for some of the rest of us), and that the farmer may be responsive to his situation. The size of the farm that is to support a family, and the kinds of crops that shall be grown and even the yields that shall be secured to the acre, are technical problems of agriculture. In this New World, with expensive labor and still with cheap land, we cannot yet afford to produce the high yields of some of the Old World places—it may be better to till more land with less yield to the acre. But all this is aside from my present purpose; and this purpose is to suggest the very real importance of making it possible for an increasing proportion of the people to have close touch with the earth in their own rights and in their own names.

We recognize different grades or kinds of land occupancy, some of it being proprietorship and some of it tenancy and some of it mere shareholding. Thus far have we spoken of the partitioning of the land mostly in its large social and political relations; but to society also belongs the fertility of the land, and all efforts to conserve this fertility are public questions in the best sense. In America we think of tenant occupancy of land as dangerous because it does not safeguard fertility; in fact, it may waste fertility. This is because the practice in tenancy does not recognize the public interest in fertility, and the contract or agreement is made merely between the landowner and the tenant, and is largely an arrangement for skinning the land. It is only when the land itself is a party in the contract (when posterity is considered) that tenancy is safe. Then the tenant is obliged to fertilize the land, to practice certain rotations, and otherwise to conserve fertility, returning to the land the manurial value of products that are sold. When such contracts are made and enforced, tenancy farming does not deplete the land more than other farming, as the experience in some countries demonstrates. It is hardly to be expected, however, that tenant occupancy will give the man as close moral contact with the earth and its materials as will ownership; yet a well-developed tenancy is better than absentee farming by persons who live in town and run the farm by temporary hired help. The tenancy in the United States is partly a preliminary stage to ownership: if we can fulfill the moral obligation to society in the conserving of fertility and other natural resources, tenancy may be considered as a means to an end. Persons who work the land should have the privilege of owning it.

It may be urged by those who contend that land should be held by society, that this regulation of tenancy provides a means of administering all farm lands by government in the interest of maintenance of fertility. Leaving aside the primary desirability, as I see it, of reserving individual initiative, it is to be said that this kind of regulation of the tenant is possible only with a livestock husbandry; nor do we yet have sufficient knowledge to enable us to project a legal system for all kinds of agriculture; or again is it applicable to widely differing conditions and regions. A keener sense of responsibility will enable owner and tenant to work out better methods in all cases, but it is now impossible to incorporate complete control methods into successful legislative regulations. The increasing competition will make it ever more difficult for the careless man to make a good living by farming, and he will be driven from the business; or if he is not driven out, society will take away his privilege.

Yet we are not to think of society as founded wholly on small separate tracts, or "family farms," occupied by persons who live merely in contentment; this would mean that all landsmen would be essentially laborers. We need to hold on the land many persons who possess large powers of organization, who are managers, who can handle affairs in a bold way; it would be fatal to the best social and spiritual results if such persons could find no adequate opportunities on the land and were forced into other occupations. Undoubtedly we shall find ourselves with very unlike land units, encouraged and determined by the differing conditions and opportunities in different regions; and thereby shall we also avoid the great danger of making our fundamental occupation to produce a uniform and narrow class spirit.

We need the great example of persons who live separately on their lands, who desire to abide, who are serious in the business, and who have sufficient proprietary rights to enable them to handle the natural resources responsibly. There is a type of well-intentioned writers that would have the farmers live in centers in order that they may have what are called "social" advantages, betaking themselves every morning to the fields when the dew is on the grass and the birds sing, hastening back every evening (probably when the clock points to five) to engage in the delightful delirium of card parties and moving picture shows (of course gathering the golden harvest in the meantime). Other writers are to have the farms so small that the residences will be as close as on a village street, and a trolley car will run through, and I suppose the band will play!

IF, then, we are to give the people access to the holy earth, it means not only a new assent on the part of society but a new way of partitioning the surface.[6] This is true whether we consider the subject wholly from the viewpoint of making natural resources utilizable or from the added desire to let the people out to those resources.

The organization of any affair or enterprise determines to a great extent the character of the result; and the organization rests directly on the subdivision into parts. The dividing of a business into separate responsibilities of different departments and sub-departments makes for easy access and for what we now know as efficiency; the dividing of a nation into states or provinces and counties and many lesser units makes political life possible; the setting off a man's farm into fields, with lanes and roads connecting, makes a working enterprise. The more accurately these subdivisions follow natural and living necessities, the greater will be the values and the satisfactions that result from the undertaking.

Here is the open country, behind the great cities and the highly specialized industries. There are hills in it, great and small. There are forests here, none there; sands that nobody wants; fertile lands that everybody wants; shores inviting trade; mineral wealth; healing waters; power in streams; fish in ponds and lakes; building stone; swamps abounding in life; wild corners that stimulate desire; sceneries that take the soul into the far places. These are the fundamental reserves and the backgrounds. The first responsibility of any society is to protect them, husband them, bring them into use, and at the same time to teach the people what they mean.

To bring them from rapacious citizens who have small social conscience, it is necessary to have good access. It is necessary to have roads. These roads should be laid where the resources exist, direct, purposeful. In a flat and uniform country, road systems may well be rectangular, following section lines and intermediate lines; but the rectangularity is not the essential merit—it is only a serviceable way of subdividing the resources. To find one's direction, north or south, is convenient, but it may clearly be subordinated to the utilization and protection of the supplies. The section line division may accomplish this or it may not, and it is likely to place roads in wrong locations and to render the country monotonous and uninteresting.

But in the broken country, in the country of tumbled hills and crooked falling streams, of slopes that would better be left in the wild, and of lands that are good and fruitful for the plow, the roads may go the easy grades;

---

6. The first sentence following the original subhead (here omitted) entitled "A new map," p. 55. The extra return preceding the original subhead is here preserved as section break.

but they ought also to go in such a plan as to open up the country to the best development, to divide its resources in the surest way for the greatest number of persons, and to reduce profitless human toil to the minimum—and this is just what they may not do. They may go up over bare and barren hills merely to pass a few homesteads where no homesteads ought to be, roads that are always expensive and never good, that accomplish practically nothing for society. They leave good little valleys at one side, or enter them over almost impossible slopes. There are resources of physical wealth and of wonderful scenery that they do not touch, that would be of much value if they were accessible. The farming country is often not divided in such a way as to render it either most readily accessible or to make it the most useful as an asset for the people.

To connect villages and cities by stone roads is good. But what are we to do with all the back country, to make it contribute its needful part to feed the people in the days that are to come, and to open it to the persons who ought to go? We cannot accomplish this to the greatest purpose by the present road systems, even if the roads themselves are all made good.

When the traveler goes to a strange country, he is interested in the public buildings, the cities, and some of the visible externals; but if he wants to understand the country, he must have a detailed map of its roads. The automobile maps are of no value for this purpose, for they show how one may pass over the country, not how the country is developed. As the last nerve fiber and the last capillary are essential to the end of the finger and to the entire body, so the ultimate roads are essential to the myriad farms and to the national life. It is difficult in any country to get these maps, accurately and in detail; but they are the essential guidebooks.

We undertake great conquests of engineering, over mountains and across rivers and through the morasses; but at the last we shall call on the engineer for the greatest conquest of all—how to divide the surface of the earth so that it shall yield us its best and mean to us the most, on the easiest grades, in the most practicable way, that we may utilize every piece of land to fullest advantage.

This means a new division and perhaps a redistribution of lands in such a way that the farmer will have this due proportion of hill and of valley, rather than that one shall have all valley and another all hardscrabble on the hill or all waste land in some remote place. It means that there will be on each holding the proper relation of tilled land and pasture land and forest land, and that the outlets for the farmer and his products will be the readiest and the simplest that it is possible to make. It means that some roads will be abandoned entirely, as not worth the cost, and society will make a way for farmers living on impossible farms to move to other lands; and that there will be no "backroads," for they will be the marks of an undeveloped society. It means that we shall cease the pretense to bring all lands into farming, whether they are useful for farming or not; and that in the back country beyond the last farms there shall be trails that lead far away.

In the farm region itself, much of the old division will pass away, being uneconomical and nonsocial. The abandonment of farms is in some cases a beginning of the process, but it is blind and undirected. Our educational effort is at present directed toward making the farmer prosperous on his existing farm, rather than to help him to secure a farm of proper resources and with proper access. As time goes on, we must reassemble many of the land divisions, if each man is to have adequate opportunity to make the most effective application of his knowledge, the best use of himself, and the greatest possible contribution to society. It would be well if some of the farms could be dispossessed of their owners, so that areas might be recombined on a better basis.

This is no utopian or socialistic scheme, nor does it imply a forcible interference with vested rights. It is a plain statement of the necessities of the situation. Of course it cannot come about quickly or as a result of direct legislation; but there are various movements that may start it—it is, in fact, already started. All the burning rural problems relate themselves in the end to the division of the land. In America, we do not suffer from the holding of the land in a few families or in an aristocratic class; that great danger we have escaped, but we have not yet learned how to give the land meaning to the greatest number of people. This is a question for the best political program, for we look for the day when statesmanship shall be expressed in the details of common politics.

We now hear much about the good roads question, as if it were a problem only of highway construction: it is really a question of a new map.

It would be a great gain if many persons could look forward to the ownership of a bit of the earth, to share in the partition, to partake in the brotherhood.[7] Some day we shall make it easy rather than difficult for this to be brought about.

Society, in its collective interest, also has necessities in the land. There is necessity of land to be owned by cities and other assemblages for water reservoirs, and all the rights thereto; for school grounds, playgrounds, reformatory institutions, hospitals, drill grounds, sewage disposal areas, irrigation developments, drainage reclamations; for the public control of

---

7. The first sentence after the original subhead (here omitted) entitled "The public program," p. 61. The extra return before the original subhead is here preserved as a break.

banks and borders of streams and ponds, for the shores of all vast bodies of water, for pleasure parks, recreation, breathing spaces in the great congestions, highways and other lines of communication; for the sites of public buildings, colleges and experiment stations, bird and beast refuges, fish and game reservations, cemeteries. There are also the rights of many semipublic agencies that need land—of churches, of fraternal organizations, of incorporated seminaries and schools, of waterpower and oil and coal developments, of manufacturing establishments, of extensive quarries, and of commercial enterprises of very many kinds. There is also the obligation of the general government that it shall have reserves against future needs, and that it shall protect the latent resources from exploitation and from waste. Great areas must be reserved for forests, as well as for other crops, and, in the nature of the case, these forest spaces in the future must be mostly in public ownership.

Great remainders should be held by the people to be sold in small parcels to those who desire to get out to the backgrounds but who do not want to be farmers, where they may spend a vacation or renew themselves in the soil or under the trees, or by the green pastures or along the everlasting streams. It is a false assumption which supposes that if land cannot be turned into products of sale it is therefore valueless. The present active back-to-the-land movement has meaning to us here. It expresses the yearning of the people for contact with the earth and for escape from complexity and unessentials. As there is no regular way for attaining these satisfactions, it has largely taken the form of farming, which occupation has also been reestablished in popular estimation in the same epoch. It should not be primarily a back-to-the-farm movement, however, and it is not to be derided. We are to recognize its meaning and to find some way of enabling more of the people to stand on the ground.

Aside from all this, land is needed for human habitation, where persons may have space and may have the privilege of gathering about them the goods that add value to life. Much land will be needed in future for this habitation, not only because there will be more people, but also because every person will be given an outlet. We know it is not right that any family should be doomed to the occupancy of a very few dreary rooms and deathly closets in the depths of great cities, seeing that all children are born to the natural sky and to the wind and to the earth. We do not yet see the way to allow them to have what is naturally theirs, but we shall learn how. In that day we shall take down the wonderful towers and cliffs in the cities, in which people work and live, shelf on shelf, but in which they have no home. The great city expansion in the end will be horizontal rather than perpendicular. We shall have many knots, clustered about factories and other enterprises, and we shall learn how to distribute the satisfactions in life rather than merely to assemble them. Before this time comes, we shall have passed the present insistence on so-called commercial efficiency, as if it were the sole measure of a civilization, and higher ends shall come to have control. All this will rest largely on the dividing of the land.

It is the common assumption that the solution of these problems lies in facilities of transportation, and, to an extent, this is true; but this assumption usually rests on the other assumption, that the method of the present city vortex is the method of all time, with its violent rush into the vortex and out of it, consuming vastly of time and energy, preventing home leisure and destroying locality feeling, herding the people like cattle. The question of transportation is indeed a major problem, but it must be met in part by a different philosophy of human effort, settling the people in many small or moderate assemblages rather than in a few mighty congestions. It will be better to move the materials than to move the people.

The great cities will grow larger; that is, they will cover more land. The smaller cities, the villages, the country towns will take on greatly increased importance. We shall learn how to secure the best satisfactions when we live in villages as well as when we live in cities. We begin to plan our cities and to a small extent our villages. We now begin to plan the layout of the farms, that they may accomplish the best results. But the cities and the towns depend on the country that lies beyond; and the country beyond depends on the city and the town. The problem is broadly one problem: the problem of so dividing and subdividing the surface of the earth that there shall be the least conflict between all these interests, that public reservations shall not be placed where it is better to have farms, that farming developments may not interfere with public utilities, that institutions may be so placed and with such area as to develop their highest usefulness, that the people desiring outlet and contact with the earth in their own right may be accorded that essential privilege. We have not yet begun to approach the subject in a fundamental way, and yet it is the primary problem of the occupancy of the planet.

To the growing movement for city planning should be added an equal movement for country planning; and these should not proceed separately, but both together. No other public program is now more needed.

Country and City

I am always interested in Thoreau's "poetical farmer," not because I recommend his kind of farming, but because of his philosophical point of view:[8]

> [George] Minott is perhaps the most poetical farmer, the one who most realizes to me the poetry of the farmer's life, that I know. He does nothing with haste and drudgery, but everything as if he loved it. He makes the most of his labor, and takes infinite satisfaction in every part of it. He is not looking forward to the sale of his crops, but he is paid by the constant satisfaction which his labor yields to him. He has not too much land to trouble him, too much work to do, no hired man nor boy, but simply to amuse himself and live. He cares not so much to raise a large crop as to do his work well. He knows every pin and nail in his barn. If any part of it is to be floored, he lets no hired man rob him of that amusement, but he goes slowly to the woods, and at his leisure selects a pitch pine tree, cuts it, and hauls it or gets it hauled to the mill, and so he knows the history of his barn floor. Farming is an amusement which has lasted him longer than gunning or fishing. He is never in a hurry to get his garden planted, and yet it is always planted soon enough, and none in the town is kept so beautifully clean. He always prophesies a failure of his crops, and yet is satisfied with what he gets. His barn floor is fastened down with oak pins, and he prefers them to iron spikes, which he says will rust and give way. He handles and amuses himself with every ear of his corn crop as much as a child with its playthings, so his small crop goes a great way. He might well cry if it were carried to market. The seed of weeds is no longer in his soil. He loves to walk in a swamp in windy weather, and hear the wind groan through the pines. He indulges in no luxury of food, or dress, or furniture, yet he is not penurious, but merely simple. If his sister dies before him, he may have to go to the almshouse in his old age, yet he is not poor, for he does not want riches.

---

8. This excerpt begins on page 131 of the lengthy chapter titled "Country and City" from *Outlook to Nature* (New York: Macmillan, 1905). This passage runs through the conclusion of the original "Country and City" chapter on page 142.

Therefore I preach the open country, because it is natural and without affectation. There is very much in the city that we need, but this is so well accepted that there is no occasion to emphasize it: we need to emphasize the things that are free and that are remote from contention and noise.[9] I preach the plain and frugal living of the plain people. Yesterday the bill of fare that was put before me at the hotel contained, by actual count, the names of 567 articles. To judge by the names, most of them were inedible. Ten articles are sufficient, and twenty are luxury. I preach the steadiness of country life, its freedom from speculativeness and from great temptation to evildoing. We need the example of all simple and direct lives, even if we lose some of the "polished" manners. We need the freshness and the spontaneity, and the power to rely on oneself. The day of homespun is past, and the day of the machine has come: danger is that the machine and the formal affairs shall come between us and the essentials. We are too likely to work by proxy and through servants.

With the increasing complexities of civilization, it may be impossible to simplify the machinery of our political life; yet we all have the desire to do so, and we feel that the more direct the institutions the more efficient and enduring they are. The native institutions have largely determined the methods and points of view in great geographical regions; the New England town meeting, with its ideal democracy; the southern courthouse, with its social stratification; the central west schoolhouse, repeating the democracy of New England but with freer individualism; the arid west ditch meeting, repeating again the democracy, but made strenuous by the urgency of a single vital problem. It is doubtful whether a nation of cities could be a democracy.

I think that we need the example and influence of men who do not live on salary. I have said that one reason why boys leave the farm is because in other occupations they are offered wages or salaries, and the risk of livelihood is thereby reduced; but the very lessening of this risk sacrifices much of a man's self-reliance—it loses him his independence, not only in directly securing the means of support, but, what is more serious, in his attitude toward society. Salary practice is a concomitant of organization, and it goes with social stratification. The man who receives salary exclusively depends on someone else, and his opinions are controlled, or at least modified, thereby. Often to a very large extent he loses his autonomy. There is a general feeling among salaried men that they must engage in other business in unsalaried hours, not always so much, I think, because they desire to add to

---

9. The first sentence following the original subhead (here omitted) entitled "We Need The Country," pp. 134.

their income, as to satisfy the longing for some greater measure of independence. The farmer is about the only man left who lives directly on his own efforts, without the aid of salary, speculation, or nonintrinsic profits that accrue from trade. There is a tendency to organize agriculture, and thereby to develop salaries in it; this tendency is no doubt to be commended, yet I look with some apprehension to the effect that it may have on independent effort and opinion.

We need the native love of home. The city or town young man is too often a man of the streets or of the clubs, and he does not marry early. The farm boy does not fear to take the responsibility of a family, and he does not wait till his income is large and his best energies and ideals are dissipated.

We need the healthfulness and the buoyancy of the country and the open air. It is often said that, as a matter of fact, the city man is physically more perfect than the countryman. This may be true; but it is because the city man takes better care of himself and of his surroundings, not because the city itself is more healthful than the country. The open country should be the ideal place for the making and preserving of physical robustness. Recent statistics in England and Wales show that the comparative mortality figures are lowest for clergymen and farmers, being closely followed by teacher and agricultural laborers, and then, at some distance, by carpenters, lawyers, shopkeepers, and others. Certainly all our people need the open air and the out-of-doors. This is probably truer for Americans than for others. A matron of a large boarding school for girls told me recently that many of the pupils come to her so thinly clad that she is obliged to keep her houses too warm for health in order to make the girls comfortable. This school is an expensive one and the girls come from well-to-do families; it is not a question of expense: the matron said that by many mothers it is not considered "good form" for girls to dress warm. The girls are clad in gauzy shivery stuff, and they therefore become hothouse subjects, withdrawing from the cold and discomforted by every change of temperature.

We magnify the comfort of living indoors. We have made the inside of the house so attractive and suggestive of ease that the temptation is to go outside as little as possible, as if the out-of-doors is to be avoided. The abundance of books may keep us indoors. We have so many books even about the out-of-doors that we do not need to go outdoors to learn about it. Americans are fond of saying that the Europeans are far behind us in developing the physical comforts of the home. I also am proud of this; but I sometimes wonder whether this is not due in part to our dread of the out-of-doors, and whether this very physical perfection of the house may not still further emphasize the breach that has grown up between ourselves and nature. Most of the interest in nature is more or less sentimental and theoretical and long-range, and ceases when we are in danger of getting our shoes muddy. There is, to be sure, a tendency in American house-building toward an outdoor feeling, but this usually does not extend beyond the veranda, which is really built for protection. We have not yet proceeded so far as the usable garden room—in this respect the Europeans lead us. The sedentary indoor life has its sure effects, and we try to correct these effects by means of drugs; and the American is known by his nostrums.

We must constantly return to the native and the indigenous in order to correct our civilization and to direct it. We are in danger of overrefining: we need to go to the primitive for strength and renewal. A new and strong kind of nativeness is no doubt developing in the cities; but we also need the kind of nativeness and essentialness that develops in the country. I am always conscious that there is no soil in the city, but only dirt: the ground must be covered until it is blotted out. When we get away from the soil we begin to get away from simplicity and directness. We all perceive a growing tendency countryward, coming in response to a universal soul hunger that the strenuous and complex life does not fully satisfy. Sooner or later, most men come to feel as did the city schoolboy who declared that some day he would live in the real country and would build his house out-of-doors.

The Principle of Enmity

This day are millions of men ready to give their lives. This day will thousands be sacrificed. These are stupendous facts.[10]

The pity of it is that they are sacrificed for the ancient Principle of Enmity or Antagonism. On no other principle or theory could they be sacrificed. They throw away their bodies—bodies that have been nurtured in pain and in hope, that have grown and matured through long watchful years—that a form of governmental organization may be maintained, a cult of racial selfishness, a range of commercial unmorality, a kind of enterprise that is not sound else it could not lead to human slaughter.

And yet there is something inspiring in this readiness with which human beings give themselves over to annihilations in support of what they conceive to be an unalterable principle. They fling themselves into the welter even with eagerness. One wonders what vast plans might be accomplished if even one-tenth of this energy were placed in cooperative effort for public good, rather than for the public destruction.

It is apparent that here we have the operation of two forces—the Principle of Enmity on the one hand, and the Will to Serve on the other. It is plain, also, that these forces are essentially opposite and antagonistic. Which of them is to obtain the mastery? It is our part to disentangle them and to aid the forward one to grow.

It is in a day of vast organization for self-interest that this willing sacrifice is made, in a day when hard money-getting for personal use is pursued under the name of business, in a day when the ends of the planet are ransacked for private gain, when the earth is laid bare, when the weak are crowded to the wall, when legitimized competition is warfare.

---

10. From *Universal Service: The Hope of Humanity* (New York: Sturgis & Walton, 1918), 3–16.

The justification of a political or regulatory movement lies strongly as to whether it will "help business." To be guided by the public press, one would think that the justification of all public action lies in what is called "prosperity." To this fetish the politician appeals. The number of persons "in business" is indeed great, and the welfare of the population is greatly dependent on it; yet it is not a safe assumption that these particular interests have the walk-away or that their welfare should be the controlling consideration in society. The commercial movement may be the stimulation of a people, but the eventual balance sheet of mankind will not be made in case. Democracy cannot be expressed in terms of trade.

Business has no divine right, any more than has rulership. All self-assumed "rights" in the governance and control of the people must go to the discard.

The business world is at constant conflict, with the conflict of insatiable self-welfare. The price-cutting, the rebating, the freeze-out, the grab, the cornering of produce and commodities, the theft under forms of law, the law-making in the interest of the special advantage, the ruin of the competitor, the avarice of wealth, the desire to live beyond one's deserts, the professions that prey on their fellows, the deals in restraint of fair opportunity and combinations in obstruction of trade, the complacent gift of some of the gain to the public in forms of holy charity—all this is of the same breed that leads to war; and today we wage war to maintain a traditional governmental system and to protect ourselves in a dominion of trade. Peace does not lie in the present organization of society. The moralities of industrialism do not yet allow for it.

Religious animosities that lead to war are mostly over-past. The seven seas are discovered. The contest for dominion over new regions has been largely left for many years to the field of diplomacy. We are now in the Age of Riches.

The nations are not at peace with each other even when there is no open armed conflict. The military establishments attest this fact. Hard commercial rivalry attests it, with the preferential tariffs and reprisals, and some of the quarantine on products. The play of diplomacy is apparently in part a play for advantage. The "understandings" and secret strategies, the alliances, on the pernicious theory of "balance of power," are on their face the evidences of enmity.

We speak as if anything short of armed conflict is peace. This language really confuses the whole subject and obscures the causes. Armed outbursts are the occasional eruptions of a laval internal state: this state may exist even if no explosions take place, and so long as it exists there is no peace. To stop war or to avoid war is not to have peace.

IV. COMMUNITY

In commercial business is the reign of power, of power as much sought and as much prized as sovereigns seek the power of armies: it is power that the race has coveted and then worshipped, the ability to overwhelm, to submerge, to put out of the running, and if it is successful, it is accorded to be righteous. Men do not hesitate to take advantage of war itself to exercise the power to accumulate gain, speculating on misfortune. In its worst development it is expressed in the blood money wrung by the invading victor at arms, on the principle that if you are strong enough to knock a man down you are entitled to steal his watch.

And yet, in the midst of this vast self-seeking, organized into worldwide systems, millions are giving away their lives. The gift and the enmity seem to be complementary qualities. These lives, however, belong to all of us. Is society to receive an adequate return for them?

THE enmity that we indulge in war is only an enlargement of that which we indulge in much of our commerce and trade; one form of warfare leads to another, and war breeds war; and as there are rules of the game to gloss the brutalities of the one, so there are courtesies and certain formalities to give character to the other. In the one case we speak of The Enemy; in the other we speak of The Competitor. These antagonisms as against one another are probably founded largely in our antagonisms to the earth, represented in our destruction of it by every means within our power and by every device that our cunning can invent. There is no end to which the race would not go in its devastation of the earth if more gold and goods were forthcoming, regardless of those yet to come in the countless generations.

These conflicts are in the traditions of the race, in the family feuds, the tribal animosities, group pugilisms, the clans, the racial antipathies, the national overprides.

Indeed, nationalism itself is freely expressed in trade movements. The "spheres of influence," the commercial treaties, loans, suzerainty over smaller peoples, interference in the policy of other nations, the concessions to nationals, the snuffing out of weak governments, are largely or even mostly the result of trade influence, giving preference or advantage to one people or one group as against another. National expansion is primarily economic; and the "open-door" policy is difficult to secure and to maintain.

National isolations are still evident, in spite of all the good efforts in the interest of common understanding. If these increasing efforts are to meet with the best rewards, any practice or system of political or commercial espionage must be roundly challenged. We recognize the spread of worldwide friendships that result from the buying and selling of products and commodities, and we look for the time when these interchanges will really bring the peoples together; very important is it, therefore, that the background situations of trade should tend more and more in the direction of cooperation.

The giving and requiring of passports, in its rigid application, is another strange survival in the twentieth century. Credentials for ambassadors, delegates, and others are of course necessary; but when shall we cease to require consent for persons to pass the ports of another country?

The present tendency of governments to engage directly in business, rather than regulation and in enforcement of law, shows clearly the drift of the time, whereby commercial issues assume the right of way. Even the new educational movement, in the form of "home project work," stressed the organization of the enterprise on methods of business rather than on the study of nature. The necessity to maintain oneself in the midst of the increasing complexities and the desire to appropriate the things which science and invention have accumulated, impel both young and old and drive us into vast materialism.

It is to be understood that I make no proposals looking toward the weakening of trade. I have no new or sudden program, but I hope for a gradual shift in the point of view. It is not to be expected that competition can be eliminated in human affairs, but certainly we may hope that cooperation will become the major principle. I expect this cooperation to arise out of the present competitive system; we see unmistakable signs of such movements even in business itself.

Self-preservation is indeed a precious principle and it is established in the nature of things; but we mislead ourselves when we apply this biological phrase to the fierce competitions of business—these competitions are not self-preservation in the natural history sense. Similarly the principle of struggle for existence has been misapplied to the contests of ambition; we have even tried to dignify war by the use of this catchword, forgetting that there is no war in nature. Much of our action is excused on the misnaming of the so-called natural laws.

Democracy, What It Is

Now, therefore, may we see more clearly, the scaffolding having been removed. We behold a structure much simpler, and therefore much more beautiful, than we had conceived.[11]

Democracy is a state of society. It is such a constitution of the social order as allows each member to develop his personality to the full and at the same time to participate in public affairs on his own motion. The demos is self-controlling.

So, likewise, is peace a state of society. Certainly it is not an agreement not to fight, not even a successful conciliation, not a treaty or an understanding. A treaty of peace is only a pledge of the contending parties that under certain conditions they will behave themselves. Peace inheres in the nature of the social organization. It is not eternal, nor extraneous, nor a symptom. It is one of the fruitions of democracy, and evidence that people have arrived at enduring values and have learned self-control.

Democratic society expresses itself in many ways: in government and other national action, in religion, in an educational intention, in some particular social order.

Democracy is primarily a sentiment—a sentiment of personality. It is the expression of the feeling that every person, whatever his birth or occupation, shall develop the ability and have the opportunity to take part. Its motive is individualism on the one hand and voluntary public service on the other—the welfare and development of the individual and of all individuals.

The wealth of a democracy lies in its people, not in its government or its goods. The product of democracy is self-acting men and women. The well-being and progress of society require that every citizen, of whatever age,

11. From *What Is Democracy?* (Ithaca, NY: Comstock Publishing, 1918), 35–43. The word *democracy*, implicit in the original chapter title, has been added to the essay title here for clarity.

may have the opportunity to discover himself or herself and to make use of himself largely in his own way. Any theory of the state as the end of society or as the motive of government leads away from democracy as darkness leads away from light. It may be said that the State can bequeath privileges to its people and can develop the highest forms of prosperity; very good, yet its very perfection is its condemnation, its strength is its weakness, and it will explode of its own pressure. The citizen must be able to think of himself in other terms than in terms of the state. The state is not the end of society any more than the church is the end of religion.

A democratic society can exist only on the basis of active and enthusiastic public service. Essentially this service is voluntary, yet it may be required of those who do not volunteer. This service is far broader and deeper than military service alone.

The service of democracy is not the blind allegiance to an autocrat, whether that autocrat is a state, a party, or a king. Otherwise it is only subjugation.

Democracy rests on living conditions and on civic opportunities. It is rooted in the daily life, in what a person is able to acquire in goods, in his intellectual progress, in what he is competent and at liberty to think, in his freedom of movement, in his spiritual aspiration, in his expression of himself. The person is to be placed in the most advantageous environment.

If the person is to be placed in the most advantageous conditions and environment, so will he desire a similar privilege for his neighbor and voluntarily assume the responsibility of which I speak. The yielding of advantage to another, the giving up of granted "rights" that another may have a larger life, are in the very essence of the democratic state.

As the man and the woman and child are part of the social order, so must the social order be cohesive; otherwise it is anarchy. Democracy is highly organic; but its organization is for the good of all, not for the propagation of a party or the maintenance of a dominating family, or for power or supremacy or dynasty, or for any other conquest than the conquest of the soul. Overhead dominion not delegated by the people is obviated or eliminated. Its laws will be powerful and effective because they rest in the will of the people. It is the special privilege of the democrat to uphold the constituted government. Democracy, as represented in republican forms, is not a pile of pebbles or a bundle of sticks. Its parts are grown coherently together. It can operate as a unit. The War will show that it is capable of rapid, definite, and effective action.

So the organization of democracy is for public weal and benefit, never for dominion, never for aggrandizement, never for one part of the demos and not for the whole. Government is not an aim in itself.

Government organs may become bureaus, bureaucratic rather than democratic, jealous of their rights and power, immured in their privileges as if they created them, unpossessed of the will to yield. It is this readiness to yield to outside council, rather than to pressure, that marks government in a democracy; yet government is likely to place greater value on mere regularity and invariableness, which it calls by the sacred word "consistency," than on flexibility to meet clear public needs and to hold the interest of the plain man.

Democracy, as distinguished from government, is an end or aim. It is a mission. It is not a byproduct of industrialism; it is not an accident or an incident; it is not an adjustment of business; it is not an arrangement between organized interests. A country is democratic only when its people think in terms of democracy. Public sentiment is the most powerful force in democracy.

Responsibility, not freedom, is the key word in democracy—responsibility for one's self, for the good of the neighbor, for the welfare of the demos. Until every citizen feels this responsibility as an inescapable personal obligation, there is not complete democracy.

Cooperation, not competition, is the password. It is the natural result of the responsibility each citizen assumes. Verily, the basis of democracy is service.

The organization of war is not democratic: quite the contrary. If militarism is to be the method of civilization, then democracy is plainly unattainable. Yet vast democratic gains may come out of war. Americans are entitled to hope for at least two great gains for themselves in the present War [World War I], aside from helping to make the world safe for democracy: the setting of personal standards for soldiers, who constitute millions of energized young citizens; the raising of the moral tone of society by means of many kinds of big-hearted cooperation. All these gains are conditioned on the real idealism in which we went to war.

The only freedom is organized freedom that kindly involves the whole people. Personal freedom, involving not service, means civic and social disunion, every man looking for advantage or acting for himself. When selfish persons come together, they organize their selfishness and pass laws to protect it.

Citizenship is a reality. It has value. It is not alone a protection to an individual. He assumes obligations. He is called on when need be, to protect the society that has protected him; and he is under obligation at all times to cooperate in it. If one's country is right, it never means so much to the citizen as in time of war.

So, therefore, are we to distinguish democracy from politics; for politics, as men have come to know it, is a game played for advantage. Not until present forms of party lines have subsided or disappeared in the nations of the world will the best democracy appear and persist.

In time of war, party governments are abrogated, or should be so, indicating that political partisanship is inadequate to the handling of great fundamental problems.

The fundamental concept in a democracy is that government and the other forms of public action are expressions that inhere in the people themselves. Then, therefore, the free education of all the people into large views of life is essential if the people are to be responsive and competent. The intention of this education is personal and social, not to safeguard and support a superimposed state.

It may help us to concrete the subject if we set over against democracy some of the things and ideas that we consider to be its opposites or at least of antagonistic genera. These antonyms and antitheses are a precious lot, and they smell with age. Here are some of them: medievalism, autocracy, absolutism, tyranny, despotism, dictatorship, domination and rule, dominion, supremacy, sovereignty, aggression and conquest, colonization for profit, militarism, caesarism, imperialism, royal favor, overlordship, divine right, hereditary privilege, nabobery, pan-nationalism, exploitation, aristocracy, oligarchy, bureaucracy, officialism, toryism, dynasticism, paternalism, balance of power, intrigue, arbitrary powers of all kinds and classes, covered diplomacy, international burglary, plutocracy, patronage, subjugation, conspiracy and espionage, slavery and peonage and serfdom, peasanthood, vassalage—how the ages of struggle for breath roll before us!—piracy, bondage and mastery, monopoly, reactionism, jingoism, bossism, standpatism, organizationism, fanaticism, fatalism, dogmatism, intolerance, superstition, infallibility, group control, materialism, nihilism, anarchy, selfishness, ignorance. There are those who think that democracy is not inevitable: perhaps not, yet one cannot contemplate this list of monsters with which the world has grappled without the feeling that there is a perfecting principle in humanity which holds its course across the centuries.

The words for democracy are fewer than those for its opposite, and yet democracy makes progress and eventually will overthrow them all.

In a democracy, the people is the state. The character and the quality of the people determine the nature of the state.

I find the root of democracy in spiritual religion rather than in political freedom or organized industrial efficiency. Democracy is a spiritual power or product in a people. It is invisible. Spiritual forces are stronger than guns.

It expresses itself in humbleness of spirit. When any people assumes an attitude of superiority, we know thereby that it is not a democracy: Pride goeth before destruction, and a haughty spirit before a fall.[12]

---

12. The last paragraph of the chapter has been omitted for concision.

V NATURE

But nature knew
Of all that grew
No thing is in vain:
The restless tease
Of busy bees
Had rendered gain.

As you and me,
So flower and bee
Hath life to give;
Nor pride nor pelf
Each of itself
Hath right to live.

—From "Utility," *Wind and Weather*
(New York: Scribner, 1916)

T he four essays following roundly consider the succor of nature. While
much of Bailey's writing might be included under the umbrella "nature," these pieces explicitly address how man may be instructed and in-
spired by the natural world. In "Ways to Approach Nature," Bailey recalls
the importance of one unplowed pasture from his youth, an "Elysian field"
for the mysteries and miracles it contained. In conjuring his home ground,
Bailey makes the case for natural history and for nativeness in making a
place's deep acquaintance. Here the classic agrarian virtues of humility,
early rising, and reverential regard are exemplified, especially in the recollection of Bailey's trip to California's Mt. Shasta. In the second selection,
"The Forest," Bailey explores the "background spaces" crucial to our national psyche. Echoing Thoreau's essay "Walking" as well as the visionary
historiographies of Frederick Jackson Turner, the author argues that "men
go off in vague heresies" when they lose contact with the ancient, vegetative
primeval. He stands for listening to nature's "little voices"; we ought to be
glad, Lib Bailey writes, for the underdeveloped country remaining, which
gives birth to our better natures. In the third excerpt, "The Spiritual Contact
with Nature," the author's agrarianism surfaces in his aversion to the largely
urban "make-believe" worlds frugality and simplicity combat. Importantly,
Bailey uses "The Spiritual Contact with Nature" to question the wisdom
of the biblical "eye for an eye, tooth for a tooth" edict. The naturist, he

maintains, transcends such crudities while cultivating "the tenderest regard for every living thing." Rather than subscribe, whole hog, to the doctrine of the "survival of the fittest," Bailey suggests human beings ought to strive for a higher regard for life. Life should be a process of adaptation and accommodation rather than a "contest in ambition." Finally, in "The Holy Earth, the Statement" Bailey sets forth an eco-theological manifesto, a new kind of scripture, describing humankind's essential relationship to the earth. The earth, he argues, is not evil or treacherous, but essentially good. Humanity is a part of nature, therefore humanity is also good, but no more and no less than the plants and animals. Though humanity itself is not inherently sinful, Bailey concludes, its actions toward the planet may be evil if not conducted in the proper spirit or with the proper regard. The earth, because it is holy and larger than any single person, trumps personal salvation. Greed, getting, and other forms of crass commercial morality should be avoided at all costs as vestiges of our baser instincts.

The Ways to Approach Nature

When a youth, I was told that it was impossible for me to study geology to any purpose, because there were no outcroppings of rocks in my region.[1] So I grew up in ignorance of the fact that every little part of the earth's surface has a history, that there are reasons for sandbanks and for bogs as well as for stratified rocks. This is but another illustration of the old book slavery, whereby we are confined to certain formal problems, whether or not these problems have any relation to our conditions.

The landscape is composed chiefly of three elements—the surface of the earth, the sky, the vegetation. I well remember what a great surprise it was to learn that the sculpting of the fields can be understood, and that the reasons for every bank and knoll and mud hole can be worked out. There was a field back of the barn that contained hundreds of narrow knolls, averaging three to four feet high. At one side of every knoll was a narrow deep pocket that until midsummer was filled with water. The field was so rough that it could not be plowed, and so it was continuously used as a pasture. It was an Elysian field for a boy. Every pool was a world of life, with strange creatures and mysterious depths, and every knoll was a point of vantage. Near one edge of the field ran a rivulet, and beyond the rivulet were great woods. What was beyond the woods, I could only surmise. I recall how year by year I wondered at this field, until it became a sort of perpetual and unexplainable mystery, and somehow it came to be woven as a natural part of the fabric of my life. To this day I try once each year to visit this dear old field, even though it is long since leveled. All the sweep

1. The above excerpt picks up with the second full sentence of the first paragraph, p. 50. The umbrella title for this excerpt is drawn from the subheading by the same name on page 37 in Part I, "The Commonplace," from *Outlook to Nature* (New York: Macmillan, 1905). The passage includes pp. 50–61.

of my childhood comes back to me unbidden. The field is still a pasture, but generations of cows have passed on since then. Yet, as much as this field meant to me, I do not remember to have had any distant feeling that there was any cause for the pools and the knolls. My father cut the field from the forest, yet I do not remember that I ever asked him why this field was so; and I never heard any persons express any curiosity about it. We all seemed to have accepted it, just as we accept the air. As I think of it now, this field must have been the path of a tornado that turned over the trees; and long before the settlers came, the prostrate trunks had decayed and a second forest has grown. Would that I could have known that simple explanation! One sentence would have given me the clue. How the mystery of the ancient forest would have conjured a new world of marvel and discovery!

When I had written this sketch of my pasture field, I called in a little school girl and read it to her. I wanted to hear her estimate of it—for children are the best critics and also honest ones.

"That's a nice story," she said, "but I don't want to study such things in school."

"And why not?" I asked.

"Because they are hard and dry," she said.

Poor child! She was thinking of her books!

I would preach the sky. When in the open country we are impressed most with the sense of room and with the sky. City persons have no sky, but only fragments of a leaky roof; for the city is one structure and needs only a roof to make it a single building. They have no free horizon line, no including circle laid on the earth, no welkin. There are no clouds—only an indefined something that portends rain or hides the sun. One must have free vision if he is to know the sky. He must see the clouds sweep across the firmament, changing and dissolving as they go. He must look deep into the zenith, beyond the highest cirrus. We have almost lost the habit of looking up:

> Look unto the heavens, and see;
> And behold the skies, which are higher than thou.

Or, if we note the sky, it is chiefly a midday or sunset recognition. Our literature is rich in sunsets, but poorer in sunrises. Civilization has led us away from the morning, and at the same time it has led us away from youthfulness. We have telescoped the day far into the night, and morning is becoming obsolete. We are owls. I know that this cannot be helped; but it can be mentioned. I have asked person after person whether he ever saw the sun

169

rise. The large number have said no; and most of those who had seen the sun rise had seen it against their will and remembered it with a sense of weariness. Here, again, our farm boy has the advantage; he leads something like a natural life. I doubt whether a man can be a poet if he has not known the sunrise.

The sky is the one part of the environment that is beyond our reach. We cannot change it; we cannot spoil it; we cannot paint signs on it. The sky is forever new and young; the seasons come out of it; the winds blow out of it; the weather is born from it:

> Hast though entered the treasuries of the snow,
> Or hast thou seen the treasuries of the hail?

I preach the mountains, and everything that is taller than a man. Yet it is to be feared that many persons see too many mountains and too many great landscapes, and that the "seeing" of nature becomes a business as redundant and wearisome as other affairs. One who lives on the mountains does not know how high they are. Let us have one inspiration that lifts us clear of ourselves: this is better than to see so many mountains that we remember only their names. The best objects that you can see are those in your own realm; but your own realm becomes larger and means more for the sight of something beyond.

It is worthwhile to cherish the few objects and the phenomena that have impressed us greatly, and it is well to recount them often, until they become part of our being. One such phenomenon is idealized in my own memory. It was the sight of sunrise on Mt. Shasta, seen from the southeastern side from a point that was wholly untouched by travelers. From this point only the main dome of the mountain is seen. I had left the Southern Pacific train at Upton's and had ridden on a flatcar over a lumber railroad some eighteen miles to the southeast. From this destination, I drove far into the great forest, over the volcano dust that floated through the woods like smoke as it was stirred up by our horses and wagon wheels. I was a guest for the night in one of those luxurious lodges which true nature lovers, wishing wholly to escape the affairs of the cities, build in remote and inaccessible places. The lodge stood on a low promontory, around three sides of which a deep swift mountain stream rain in wild tumult. Giant shafts of trees, such shafts as one sees only in the stupendous forests of the far West, shot straight into the sky from the very cornices of the house. It is always a marvel to the easterner how shafts of such extraordinary height could have been nourished by the very thin and narrow crowns that they bear. One always wonders, also, at the great distance the sap water must carry its freight of mineral from root to leaf and its heavier freight from leaf to root.

We were up before dawn. We made a pot of coffee, and the horses were ready—fine mounts, accustomed to woods trails and hard slopes. It was hardly light enough to enable us to pick our way. We were two pigmies, so titanic was the forest. The trails led us up and up, under pitchy boughs becoming fragrant, over needle-strewn floors still heavy with darkness, disclosing glimpses now and then of gray light showing eastward between the boles. Suddenly the forest stopped, and we found ourselves on the crest of a great ridge: and sheer before us stood the great cone of Shasta, cold and gray and silent, floating on a sea of darkness from which even the highest tree crowns did not emerge. Scarcely had we spoken in the course of our ascent, and now words would be sacrilege. Almost automatically we dismounted, letting the rains fall over the horses' necks, and removed our hats. The horses stood, and dropped their heads. Uncovered, we sat ourselves on the dry leaves and waited. It was the morning of creation. Out of the pure stuff of nebulae the cone had just been shaped and flung adrift until a world should be created on which it might rest. The gray light grew into white. Wrinkles and features grew into the mountain. Gradually a ruddy light appeared in the east. Then a flash of red shot out of the horizon, stuck on a point of the summit, and caught from crag to crag and snow to snow until the great mass was streaked and splashed with fire. Slowly the darkness settled away from its base; a tree emerged; a bird chirped; and the morning was new!

Now a great netherworld began to rise up out of chaos. Far hills rose first through rolling billows of mist. Then came wide forests of conifer. As the panorama rose, the mountain changed from red to gold. The stars had faded out and left the great mass to itself on the bosom of the rising world— the mountain fully created now and established. Spriggy bushes and little leaves—little green-brown leaves and tender tufts of herbs—trembled out of the woods. The illimitable circle of the world stretched away and away, its edges still hung in the stuff from which it had just been fashioned. Then the forest awoke with calls of birds and the penetrating light, and the creation was complete![2]

---

2. The final, summary paragraph on pp. 61–62, beginning, "I have now reviewed some of the characteristics of the sympathetic attitude toward nature..." has been omitted from this passage as a redundancy.

The Forest

"This is the forest primeval." These are the significant words of the poet in *Evangeline*.[3] Perhaps more than any single utterance they have set the American youth against the background of the forest.

The backgrounds are important. The life of every one of us is relative. We miss our destiny when we miss or forget our backgrounds. We lose ourselves. Men go off in vague heresies when they forget the conditions against which they live. Judgments become too refined and men tend to become merely disputatious and subtle.

The backgrounds are the great unoccupied spaces. They are the large environments in which we live but which we do not make. The backgrounds are the sky with its limitless reaches; the silences of the sea; the tundra in pallid arctic nights; the deserts with their prismatic colors; the shores that gird the planet; the vast mountains that are beyond reach; the winds, which are the universal voice in nature; the sacredness of the night; the elemental simplicity of the open fields; and the solitude of the forest. These are the facts and situations that stand at our backs, to which we adjust our civilization, and by which we measure ourselves.

The great conquest of mankind is the conquest of his natural conditions. We admire the man who overcomes: the sailor or navigator in hostile and unknown seas; the engineer who projects himself hard against the obstacles; the miner and the explorer; the builder; the farmer who ameliorates the earth to man's use.

But even though we conquer or modify the physical conditions against which we are set, nevertheless the backgrounds will remain. I hope that

---

3. A portion of the original title as it appeared in *The Holy Earth* is here excised. The original subheading title read "The background spaces: The forest," pp. 150–155. This passage also includes the subheading "The background spaces—the open fields," pp. 164–166, where noted.

we may always say "The forest primeval." I hope that some reaches of the sea may never be sailed, that some swamps may never be drained, that some mountain peaks may never be scaled, that some forests may never be harvested. I hope that some knowledge may never be revealed.

Look at your map of the globe. Note how few are the areas of great congestion of population and of much human activity as compared with the vast and apparently empty spaces. How small are the spots that represent the cities and what a little part of the earth are the political divisions that are most in the minds of men! We are likely to think that all these outlying and thinly peopled places are the wastes. I suspect that they contribute more to the race than we think. I am glad that there are still some places of mystery, some reaches of hope, some things far beyond us, some spaces to conjure up dreams. I am glad that the earth is not all Iowa or Belgium or the Channel Islands. I am glad that some of it is the hard hills of New England, some the heathered heights of Scotland, some the cold distances of Quebec, some of it the islands far off in little-traversed seas, and some of it also the unexplored domains that lie within eyesight of our own homes. It is well to know that these spaces exist, that there are places of escape. They add much to the ambition of the race; they make for strength, for courage, and for renewal.

In the cities I am always interested in the variety of the contents of the store windows. Variously fabricated and disguised, these materials come from the ends of the earth. They come from the shores of the seas, from the mines, from the land, from the forests, from the arctic, and from the tropic. They are from the backgrounds. The cities are great, but how much greater are the forests and the sea!

No people should be forbidden the influence of the forest. No child should grow up without a knowledge of the forest; and I mean a real forest and not a grove or village trees or a park. There are no forests in cities, however many trees there may be. As a city is much more than a collection of houses, so is a forest much more than a collection of trees. The forest has its own round of life, its characteristic attributes, its climate, and its inhabitants. When you enter a real forest you enter the solitudes, you are in the unexpressed distances. You walk on the mold of years and perhaps of ages. There is no other wind like the wind of the forest; there is no odor like the odor of the forest; there is no solitude more complete; there is no song of a brook like the song of a forest brook; there is no call of a bird like that of a forest bird; there are no mysteries so deep and which seem yet to be within one's realization.

While a forest is more than trees, yet the trees are the essential part of the forest; and no one ever really knows or understands a forest until he first understands a tree. There is no thing in nature finer and stronger than the bark of a tree; it is a thing in place, adapted to its ends, perfect in its conformation, beautiful in its color and its form and the sweep of its contour; and every bark is peculiar to its species. I think that one never really likes a tree until he is impelled to embrace it with his arms and to run his fingers through the grooves of its bark.

Man listens in the forest. He pauses in the forest. He finds himself. He loses himself in the town and even perhaps in the university. He may lose himself in business and in great affairs; but in the forest he is one with a tree, he stands by himself and yet has consolation, and he comes back to his own place in the scheme of things. We have almost forgotten to listen; so great and ceaseless is the racket that the little voices pass over our ears and we hear them not. I have asked person after person if he knew the song of the chipping sparrow, and most of them are unaware that it has any song. We do not hear it in the blare of the city street, in railway travel, or when we are in a thunderous crowd. We hear it in the still places and when our ears are ready to catch the smaller sounds. There is no music like the music of the forest, and the better part of it is faint and far away or high in the tops of trees.

The forest may be an asylum. "The groves were God's first temples." We need all our altars and more, but we need also the sanctuary of the forest. It is a poor people that has no forests. I prize the farms because they have forests. It is a poor political philosophy that has no forests. It is a poor nation that has no forests and no workers in wood.

In many places there are the forests. I think that we do not get the most out of them. Certainly they have two uses: one for the products, and one for the human relief and the inspiration. I should like to see a movement looking toward the better utilization of the forests humanly, as we use school buildings and church buildings and public halls. I wish that we might take our friends to the forests as we also take them to see the works of the masters. For this purpose, we should not go in large companies. We need sympathetic guidance. Parties of two and four may go separately to the forests to walk and to sit and to be silent. I would not forget the forest in the night, in the silence and the simplicity of the darkness. Strangely few are the people who know a real forest at dark. Few are those who know the forest when the rain is falling or when the snow covers the earth. Yet the forest is as real in all these moments as when the sun is at full and the weather is fair.

I wish that we might know the forest intimately and sensitively as a part of our background. I think it would do much to keep us close to the verities and the essentials.

174

HERE not long ago was the forest primeval.[4] Here the trees sprouted, and grew their centuries, and returned to the earth. Here the midsummer brook ran all day long from the faraway places. Here the night winds slept. Here havened the beasts and fowls when storms pursued them. Here the leaves fell in the glory of the autumn, here other leaves burst forth in the miracle of spring, and here the pewee called in the summer. Here the Indian tracked his game.

It was not so very long ago. That old man's father remembers it. Then it was a new and holy land, seemingly fresh from the hand of the creator. The old man speaks of it as of a golden time, now far away hallowed; he speaks of it with an attitude of reverence. "Ah yes," my father told me; and calmly with bared head he relates it, every incident so sacred that not one hairbreadth must he deviate. The church and the master's school and the forests—these three are strong in his memory.

Yet these are not all. He remembers the homes cut in the dim wall of the forest. He recalls the farms full of stumps and heaps of logs and the ox teams on them, for these were in his boyhood. The ox team was a natural part of the slow moving conquest in those rugged days. Roads betook themselves into the forest, like great serpents devouring as they went. And one day, behold! the forest was gone. Farm joined farm, the village grew, the old folk fell away, new people came whose names had to be asked.

And I thought me why these fields are not as hallowed as were the old forests. Here are the same knolls and hills. In this turf there may be still the fibers of ancient trees. Here are the paths of the midsummer brooks, but vocal now only in the freshets. Here are the winds. The autumn goes and the spring comes. The pewee calls in the groves. The farmer and not the Indian tracks the plow.

Here I look down on a little city. There is a great school in it. There are spires piercing the trees. In the distance are mills, and I see the smoke of good accomplishment roll out over the hillside. It is a self-centered city, full of pride. Every milepost praises it. Toward it all the roads lead. It tells itself to all the surrounding country. And yet I cannot but feel that these quiet fields and others like them have made this city; but I am glad that the fields are not proud.

One day a boy and one day a girl will go down from these fields, and out into the thoroughways of life. They will go far, but these hills they will still call home.

4. The first sentence following the original subhead (here omitted) entitled "The background spaces: The open fields," p. 164. It is clear from their shared subheading, "The background spaces...," that this piece and the previous, "The Forest," ought to be considered as a whole, hence they are run-in here.

V. NATURE

From these uplands the waters flow down into the streams that move the mills and that float the ships. Loads of timber still go hence for the construction down below. Here go building stones and sand and gravel—gravel from the glaciers. Here goes the hay for ten thousand horses. Here go the wheat, and here the apples, and the animals. Here are the votes that hold the people steady.

Somewhere there is the background. Here is the background. Here things move slowly. Trees grow slowly. The streams change little from year to year, and yet they shape the surface of the earth in this hill country. In yonder fencerow the catbird has built since I was a boy, and yet I have wandered far and I have seen great changes in yonder city. The well sweep has gone but the well is still there: the wells are gone from the city. The cows have changed in color, but still they are cows and yield their milk in season. The fields do not perish, but time eats away the city. I think all these things must be good and very good or they could not have persisted in all this change.

In the beginning! Yes, I know, it was holy then. The forces of eons shaped it: still was it holy. The forest came: still holy. Then came the open fields.

The Spiritual Contact
with Nature

A useful contact with the earth places man not as superior to nature but as a superior intelligence working in nature as conscious and therefore as a responsible part in a plan of evolution, which is a continuing creation. It distinguishes the elemental virtues as against the acquired, factitious, and pampered virtues.[5] These strong and simple traits may be brought out easily and naturally if we incorporated into our schemes of education the solid experiences of tramping, camping, scouting, farming, handcraft, and other activities that are not mere refinements of subjective processes.

Lack of training in the realities drives us to find satisfaction in all sorts of make-believes and in play-lives. The "movies" and many other developments of our time make an appeal wholly beyond their merits, and they challenge the methods and intentions of education.

There are fundamental satisfactions than "thrills." There is more heart ease in frugality than in surfeit. There is no real relish except when the appetite is keen. We are now provided with all sorts of things that nobody ever should want.

The good spiritual reaction to nature is not a form of dogmatism or impressionism. It results normally from objective experience, when the person is ready for it and has good digestion. It should be the natural emotion of the man who knows his objects and does not merely dream about them. There is no hallucination in it. The remedy for some of the erratic "futurism" and for forms of illusion is to put the man hard against the facts: he might be set to studying bugs or soils or placed between the handles of a plow until such time as objects begin to take their natural shape and meaning in his mind.

It is not within my purview here to consider the abstract righteous relation of man to the creation, nor to examine the major emotions that result

5. From *The Holy Earth* (New York: Scribner, 1915), 75–79.

from a contemplation of nature. It is only a very few of the simpler and more practical considerations that I may suggest.

The training in solid experience naturally emphasizes the righteousness of plain and simple eating and drinking, and of frugality and control in pleasures. Many of the adventitious pleasures are in the highest degree pernicious and are indications of weakness.

Considering the almost universal opinion that nature exhibits the merciless and relentless struggle of an eye for an eye and a tooth for a tooth, it is significant that one of the most productive ways of training a youth in sensitiveness and in regard for other creatures is by means of the nature contact. Even if the person is taught that the strong and ferocious survive and conquer, he nevertheless soon comes to have the tenderest regard for every living thing if he has the naturist in him. He discards the idea that we lose virility when we cease to kill, and relegates the notion to the limbo of deceits. This only means that unconsciously he has experienced the truth in nature, and in practice has discarded the erroneous philosophy contained in books even though he may still give these philosophies his mental assent.

It is exactly among the naturists that the old instinct to kill begins to lose its force and that an instinct of helpfulness and real brotherhood soon takes its place. From another source, the instinct to kill dies out among the moralists and other people. And yet it is passing strange how this old survival—or is it a reversion?—holds its place amongst us, even in the higher levels. The punishment of a life for a life is itself a survival. Entertainment even yet plays upon this old memory of killing, as in books of adventure, in fiction, in games of children, and worst of all on the stage where this strange anachronism, even in plays that are not historic, is still portrayed in pernicious features and in a way that would rouse any community and violate law if it were enacted in real life.

It is difficult to explain these survivals when we pretend to be so much shocked by the struggle for existence. We must accept the struggle, but we ought to try to understand it. The actual suffering among the creatures as the result of this struggle is probably small, and the bloody and ferocious contest that we like to picture to ourselves is relatively insignificant. There is a righteous element in the struggle; or, more truthfully, the struggle itself is right. Every living and sentient thing persists by its merit and by its right. It persists within its sphere, and usually not in the sphere of some other creature. The weeding-out process is probably related in some way with adaptability, but only remotely with physical strength. It is a process of applying the test. The test is applied continuously, and not in some violent upheaval.

If one looks for a moral significance in the struggle for existence, one finds it in the fact that it is a process of adjustment rather than a contest in ambition.

The elimination of the unessentials and of the survivals of a lower order of creation that have no proper place in human society, is the daily necessity of the race. The human struggle should not be on the plane of the struggle in the lower creation, by the simple fact that the human plane is unlike; and those who contend that we should draw our methods of contest from wild nature would therefore put us back on the plane of the creatures we are supposed to have passed. If there is one struggle of the creeping things, if there is one struggle of the fish of the sea and another of the beasts of the field, and still another of the fowls of the air, then surely there must be still another for those who have dominion.

The Holy Earth, the Statement

So bountiful hath been the earth and so securely have we drawn from it our substance, that we have taken it all for granted as if it were only a gift, and with little care or conscious thought of the consequences of our use of it; nor have we very much considered the essential relation that we bear to it as living parts in the vast creation.[6]

It is good to think of ourselves—of this teeming, tense, and aspiring human race—as a helpful and contributing part in the plan of a cosmos, and as participators in some far-reaching destiny. The idea of responsibility is much asserted of late, but we relate it mostly to the attitude of persons in the realm of conventional conduct, which we have come to regard as very exclusively the realm of morals; and we have established certain formalities that satisfy the conscience. But there is some deeper relation than all this, which we must recognize and the consequences of which we must practice. There is a directer and more personal obligation than that which expends itself in loyalty to the manifold organizations and social requirements of the present day. There is a more fundamental cooperation in the scheme of things than that which deals with the proprieties or which centers about the selfishness too often expressed in the salvation of one's soul.

We can be only onlookers on that part of the cosmos that we call the far heavens, but it is possible to cooperate in the processes on the surface of the sphere. This cooperation may be conscious and definite, and also useful to the earth; that is, it may be real. What means this contact with our natural situation, this relationship to the earth to which we are born, and what signify this new exploration and conquest of the planet and these accumulating prophecies of science? Does the mothership of the earth have any real meaning to us?

6. This sentence marks the beginning of Part I of *The Holy Earth* (New York: Scribner, 1915) which is listed in the original table of contents as "First, the Statement." "The Holy Earth" has been added to the chapter title here to resupply the context made explicit in the original. This passage includes material under four separate subheadings, inclusive of pp. 1–16.

All this does not imply a relation only with material and physical things, nor any effort to substitute a nature religion. Our relation with the planet must be raised into the realm of spirit; we cannot be fully useful otherwise. We must find a way to maintain the emotions in the abounding commercial civilization. There are two kinds of materials—those of the native earth and the idols of one's hands. The latter are much in evidence in modern life, with the conquests of engineering, mechanics, architecture, and all the rest. We visualize them everywhere, and particularly in the great centers of population. The tendency is to be removed farther and farther from the everlasting backgrounds. Our religion in detached.

We come out of the earth and we have a right to the use of the materials; and there is no danger of crass materialism if we recognize the original materials as divine and if we understand our proper relation to the creation, for then will gross selfishness in the use of them be removed. This will necessarily mean a better conception of property and of one's obligation in the use of it. We shall conceive of the earth, which is the common habitation, as inviolable. One does not act rightly toward one's fellows if one does not know how to act rightly toward the earth.

Nor does this close regard for the mother earth imply any loss of mysticism or of exaltation: quite the contrary. Science but increases the mystery of the unknown and enlarges the boundaries of the spiritual vision. To feel that one is a useful and cooperating part in nature is to give one kinship, and to open the mind to the great resources and the high enthusiasms. Here arise the fundamental common relations. Here arise also the great emotions and conceptions of sublimity and grandeur, of majesty and awe, the uplift of vast desires—when one contemplates the earth and the universe and desires to take them into the soul and to express oneself in their terms; and here also the responsible practices of life take root.

So much are we now involved in problems of human groups, so persistent are the portrayals of our social afflictions, and so well do we magnify our woes by insisting on them, so much in sheer weariness do we provide antidotes to soothe our feelings and to cause us to forget by means of many empty diversions, that we may neglect to express ourselves in simple free personal joy and to separate the obligation of the individual from the irresponsibilities of the mass.

It suits my purpose to quote the first sentence in the Hebrew scripture: In the beginning God created the heaven and the earth.[7]

7. The first sentence following the original subhead (here omitted) "In the beginning," p. 5. The extra return preceding the original subhead is here preserved as a section break.

V. NATURE

This is a statement of tremendous reach, introducing the cosmos; for it sets forth in the fewest words the elemental fact that the formation of the created earth lies above and before man, and that therefore it is not man's but God's. Man finds himself upon it, with many other creatures, all parts in some system which, since it is beyond man and superior to him, is divine.

Yet the planet was not at once complete when life had appeared upon it. The whirling earth goes through many vicissitudes; the conditions on its fruitful surface are ever changing; and the forms of life must meet the new conditions: so does the creation continue, and every day sees the genesis in process. All life contends, sometimes ferociously but more often bloodlessly and benignly, and the contention results in momentary equilibrium, one set of contestants balancing another; but every change in the outward conditions destroys the equation and a new status results. Of all the disturbing living factors, man is the greatest. He sets mighty changes going, destroying forests, upturning the sleeping prairies, flooding the deserts, deflecting the courses of the rivers, building great cities. He operates consciously and increasingly with plan aforethought; and therefore he carries heavy responsibility.

This responsibility is recognized in the Hebrew scripture, from which I have quoted; and I quote it again because I know of no other scripture that states it so well. Man is given the image of the creator, even when formed from the dust of the earth, so complete is his power and so real his dominion: And God blessed them: and God said unto them, Be fruitful, and multiply, and replenish the earth, and subdue it: and have dominion over the fish of the sea, and over the fowl of the air, and over every living thing that moveth upon the earth.

One cannot receive all these privileges without bearing the obligation to react and to partake, to keep, to cherish, and to cooperate. We have assumed that there is no obligation to an inanimate thing, as we consider the earth to be: but man should respect the conditions in which he is placed; the earth yields the living creature; man is a living creature; science constantly narrows the gulf between the animate and the inanimate, between the organized and the inorganized; evolution derives the creatures from the earth; the creation is one creation. I must accept all or reject all.

IT is good to live.[8] We talk of death and of lifelessness, but we know only of life. Even our prophecies of death are prophecies of more life. We know no better world: whatever else there may be is of things hoped for, not of

---

8. The first sentence following the original subhead (here omitted) "The earth is good," p. 7. The extra return preceding the original subhead is here preserved as a section break.

things seen. The objects are here, not hidden nor far to seek: And God saw everything that he had made, and, behold, it was very good.

These good things are the present things and the living things. The account is silent on the things that were not created, the chaos, the darkness, the abyss. Plato, in the *Republic,* reasoned that the works of the creator must be good because the creator is good. This goodness is in the essence of things; and we sadly need to make it a part in our philosophy of life. The earth is the scene of our life, and probably the very source of it. The heaven, so far as human beings know, is the source only of death; in fact, we have peopled it with the dead. We have built our philosophy on the dead.

We seem to have overlooked the goodness of the earth in the establishing of our affairs, and even in our philosophies. It is reserved as a theme for preachers and for poets. And yet, the goodness of the planet is the basic fact in our existence.

I am not speaking of good in an abstract way, in the sense in which some of us suppose the creator to have expressed himself as pleased or satisfied with his work. The earth is good in itself, and its products are good in themselves. The earth sustains all things. It satisfies. It matters not whether this satisfaction is the result of adaptation in the process of evolution; the fact remains that the creation is good.

To the common man the earth propounds no system of philosophy or of theology. The man makes his own personal contact, deals with the facts as they are or as he conceives them to be, and is not swept into any system. He has no right to assume a bad or evil earth, although it is difficult to cast off the hindrance of centuries of teaching. When he is properly educated he will get a new resource from his relationships.

It may be difficult to demonstrate this goodness. In the nature of things we must assume it, although we know that we could not subsist on a sphere of the opposite qualities. The important consideration is that we appreciate it, and this not in any sentimental and impersonal way. To every bird the air is good; and a man knows it is good if he is worth being a man. To every fish the water is good. To every beast its food is good, and its time of sleep is good. The creatures experience that life is good. Every man in his heart knows that there is goodness and wholeness in the rain, in the wind, the soil, the sea, the glory of sunrise, in the trees, and in the sustenance that we derive from the planet. When we grasp the significance of this situation, we shall forever supplant the religion of fear with a religion of consent.

We are so accustomed to these essentials—to the rain, the wind, the soil, the sea, the sunrise, the trees, the sustenance—that we may not include them in the categories of the good things, and we endeavor to satisfy ourselves with many small and trivial and exotic gratifications; and when these

183

gratifications fail or pall, we find ourselves helpless and resourceless. The joy of sound sleep, the relish of a sufficient meal of plain and wholesome food, the desire to do a good day's work and the recompense when at night we are tired from the doing of it, the exhilaration of fresh air, the exercise of the natural powers, the mastery of a situation or a problem—these and many others like them are fundamental satisfactions, beyond all pampering and all toys, and they are of the essence of goodness. I think we should teach all children how good are the common necessities and how very good are then things that are made in the beginning.

WE hear much about man being at the mercy of nature, and the literalist will contend that there can be no holy relation under such conditions.[9] But so is man at the mercy of God.

It is blasphemous practice that speaks of the hostility of the earth, as if the earth were full of menaces and cataclysm. The old fear of nature, that peopled the earth and sky with imps and demons, and that gave a future state to Satan, yet possesses the minds of men, only that we may have ceased to personify and to demonize our fears, although we still persistently contrast what we call the evil and the good. Still do we attempt to propitiate and appease the adversaries. Still do we carry the ban of the early philosophy that assumed materials and "the flesh" to be evil, and that found a way of escape only in renunciation and asceticism.

Nature cannot be antagonistic to man, seeing that man is a product of nature. We should find vast joy in the fellowship, something like the joy of Pan. We should feel the relief when we no longer apologize for the creator because of the things that are made.

It is true that there are devastations of flood and fire and frost, scourge of disease, and appalling convulsions of earthquake and eruption. But man prospers; and we know that the catastrophes are greatly fewer than the accepted bounties. We have no choice but to abide. No growth comes from hostility. It would undoubtedly be a poor human race if all the pathway had been plain and easy.

The contest with nature is wholesome, particularly when pursued in sympathy and for mastery. It is worthy a being created in God's image. The earth is perhaps a stern earth, but it is a kindly earth.

Most of our difficulty with the earth lies in the effort to do what perhaps ought not to be done. Not even all the land is fit to be farmed. A good part of agriculture is to learn how to adapt one's work to nature, to fit the crop

9. The first sentence following the original subhead (here omitted) "It is kindly," p. 10. The extra return preceding the original subhead is here preserved as a section break.

scheme to the climate and to the soil and the facilities. To live in right relation with his natural conditions is one of the first lessons that a wise farmer or any other wise man learns. We are at pains to stress the importance of conduct; very well: conduct toward the earth is an essential part of it.

Nor need we be afraid of any fact that makes one fact more or less in the sum of contacts between the earth and the earth-born children. All "higher criticism" adds to the faith rather than subtracts from it, and strengthens the bond between. The earth and its products are very real.

Our outlook has been drawn very largely from the abstract. Not being yet prepared to understand the condition of nature, man considered the earth to be inhospitable, and he looked to the supernatural for relief; and relief was heaven. Our pictures of heaven are of the opposites of daily experience—of release, or peace, of joy uninterrupted. The hunting grounds are happy and the satisfaction has no end. The habit of thought has been set by this conception, and it colors our dealings with the human questions and to much extent it controls our practice.

But we begin to understand that the best dealing with problems on earth is to found it on the facts of earth. This is the contribution of natural science, however abstract, to human welfare. Heaven is to be a real consequence of life on earth; and we do not lessen the hope of heaven by increasing our affection for the earth, but rather do we strengthen it. Men now forget the old images of heaven, that they are mere sojourners and wanderers lingering for deliverance, pilgrims in a strange land. Waiting for this rescue, with posture and formula and phrase, we have overlooked the essential goodness and quickness of the earth and the immanence of God.

This feeling that we are pilgrims in a vale of tears has been enhanced by the widespread belief in the sudden ending of the world, by collision or some other impending disaster, and in the common apprehension of doom; and lately by speculations as to the aridation and death of the planet, to which all of us have given more or less credence. But most of these notions are now considered to be fantastic, and we are increasingly confident that the earth is not growing old in human sense, that its atmosphere and its water are held by the attraction of its mass, and that the sphere is at all events so permanent as to make little difference in our philosophy and no difference in our good behavior.

I am again impressed with the first record in *Genesis* in which some mighty prophet-poet began his account with the creation of the physical universe.

So do we forget the old-time importance given to mere personal salvation, which was permission to live in heaven, and we think more of our present situation, which is the situation of obligation and of service; and he who loses his life shall save it.

We begin to foresee the vast religion of a better social order.

V. NATURE

VERILY, then, the earth is divine, because man did not make it.[10] We are here, part in the creation. We cannot escape. We are under obligation to take part and to do our best, living with each other and with all the creatures. We may not know the full plan, but that does not alter the relation. When once we set ourselves to the pleasure of our dominion, reverently and hopefully, and assume all its responsibilities, we shall have a new hold on life.

We shall put our dominion into the realm of morals. It is now in the realm of trade. This will be very personal morals, but is will also be national and racial morals. More iniquity follows the improper and greedy division of the resources and privileges of the earth than any other form of sinfulness.

If God created the earth, so is the earth hallowed; and if it is hallowed, so must we deal with it devotedly and with care that we do not despoil it, and mindful of our relations to all beings that live on it. We are to consider it religiously: Put off thy shoes from off thy feet, for the place whereon thou standest is holy ground.

The sacredness to us of the earth is intrinsic and inherent. It lies in our necessary relationship and in the duty imposed upon us to have dominion, and to exercise ourselves even against our own interest. We may not waste that which is not ours. To live in sincere relations with the company of created things and with conscious regard for the support of all men now and yet to come, must be of the essence of righteousness.

This is a larger and more original relation than the modern attitude of appreciation and admiration of nature. In the days of the patriarchs and prophets, nature and man shared in the condemnation and likewise in the redemption. The ground was cursed for Adam's sin. Paul wrote that the whole creation groaneth and travaileth in pain, and that it waiteth for the revealing. Isaiah proclaimed the redemption of the wilderness and the solitary place with the redemption of man, when they shall rejoice and blossom as the rose, and when the glowing sand shall become a pool and the thirsty ground springs of water.

The usual objects have their moral significance. An oak tree is to us a moral object because it lives its life regularly and fulfils its destiny. In the wind and in the stars, in forest and by the shore, there is spiritual refreshment: And the spirit of God moved upon the face of the waters.

I do not mean all this, for our modern world, in any vague or abstract way. If the earth is holy, then the things that grow out of the earth are also holy. They do not belong to man to do with them as he will. Dominion does not carry personal ownership. There are many generations of folk yet

---

10. The first sentence following the original subhead (here omitted) "The Earth is holy," p. 14. The extra return preceding the original subhead is here preserved as a section break.

to come after us who will have equal right with us to the products of the globe. It would seem that a divine obligation rests on every soul. Are we to make righteous use of the vast accumulation of knowledge of the planet? If so, we must have a new formulation. The partition of the earth among the millions who live on it is necessarily a question of morals; and a society that is founded on an unmoral partition and use cannot itself be righteous and whole.

VI FARM

The blood of old plowmen runs hard in my arm
Of axemen and yeomen and battlemen all
Who fought and who flinched not by marish or wall
Who met the bold day and chased ev'ry alarm;
My fatherkind sleep, but I hear the old call
And fight the hot battle by forge and by farm—
For these are my lands
And these are my hands
And I am bone of the folk that resistlessly stands.

—From "Farmer's Challenge," *Wind and Weather*
  (New York: Scribner, 1916)

The four essays that follow digest Liberty Hyde Bailey's views on agriculture and country folk. In the first, "The Democratic Basis in Agriculture," Bailey explores through an agrarian lens the twin "evils" of monopoly and bureaucracy. In this remarkable essay, published not long after the passage of the Smith-Lever Act of 1914, which further insinuated the long arm of government into farmers' fields, Bailey fears the legislative "monster" he helped make. He cautions against overcentralization, hyperprescription, and bureaucracy, in particular. "The best project anywhere," he writes, "is a good man or woman working in a program, but unhampered." There is a strong sense of foreboding—unusual for Bailey—in the dangers of institutionalized agriculture, making this a compelling piece for critics of land-grant agricultural education. In the second essay, "The National Movement," the author worries that the goodness of the Country Life movement will be "overexploited" for its literary and pop cultural cachet; he agonizes over its potential co-option by "demagogues" and "fakirs." In the last half of the essay, the author gets to the crux of the matter; namely, that "the fundamental weakness in our civilization is the fact that the city and the country represent antagonistic forces." The country, Bailey argues, echoing Emerson, is essentially exploited by the city for its commodities; the city acts as parasite. The analogy here is appropriately biological, as later rural observers would apply a similarly physiological metaphor to describe the rural "brain drain." City men should think twice, though, about changing the status quo by themselves going into farming, as few are equipped, Bailey cautions, to do the work of the experienced land-man. Instead, he suggests

188

an apprenticeship on a working farm or movement to rural "villages" or small towns where agrarian urbanites could engage in commerce supportive of the agriculturalist. Echoing today's cynicism about suburban life, Bailey makes a clear distinction between the suburban gardener and the large-scale producer. In the third essay, "Women's Contribution to the Country-life Movement," Bailey shows why the ameliorative efforts of the Country Life Commission were cheered by women especially. Though Bailey's characterization of the farm wife may seem anachronistic, closer examination of his endorsement of women's educational, intellectual, and recreational opportunities shows why Bailey was considered a meddling urban radical by some stuck-in-the-mud farmers who feared gender equity. The last selection, "One Hundred and Twenty-nine Farmers," follows logically from "Women's Contribution," as it quotes actual letters from farm men and women across the country. Though mixed in its genre—part literary essay and part sociological survey—Bailey's penchant for straight-from-the-horse's-mouth reportage shines through. As so many of the Country Life Commission questionnaires have been lost or destroyed, these earnest responses constitute an invaluable historical record of farming in the early twentieth century and the myriad satisfactions of downhome agrarianism, then as now.

The Democratic Basis
in Agriculture

For years without number—for years that run into the centuries when men have slaughtered each other on many fields, thinking that they were on the fields of honor, when many awful despotisms have ground men into the dust, the despotisms thinking themselves divine—for all these years there have been men on the land wishing to see the light, trying to make mankind hear, hoping but never realizing.[1] They have been the pawns on the great battlefields, men taken out of the peasantries to be hurled against other men they did not know and for no rewards except further enslavement. They may even have been developed to a high degree of manual or technical skill that they might the better support governments to make conquests. They have been on the bottom, upholding the whole superstructure and pressed into the earth by the weight of it. When the final history is written, the lot of the man on the land will be the saddest chapter.

But in the nineteenth century, the man at the bottom began really to be recognized politically. This recognition is of two kinds—the use that a government can make in its own interest of a highly efficient husbandry, and the desire to give the husbandman full opportunity and full justice. I hope that in these times the latter motive always prevails. It is the only course of safety.

Great public service institutions have now been founded in the rural movement. The United States Department of Agriculture has grown to be one of the notable government establishments of the world, extending itself to a multitude of interests and operating with remarkable effectiveness. The chain of colleges of agriculture and experiment stations, generously cooperative between nation and state, is unlike any other development anywhere, meaning more, I think, for the future welfare and peace of the people than

---

1. From *The Holy Earth* (New York: Scribner, 1915), 139–149. For concision, the excerpt begins with the second sentence of the third paragraph of the subhead "The democratic basis in agriculture," p. 140.

any one of us yet foresees. There is the finest fraternalism, and yet without clannishness, between these great agencies, setting a good example in public service. And to these agencies we are to add the state departments of agriculture, the work of private endowments although yet in its infancy, the growing and very desirable contact with the rural field of many institutions of learning. All these agencies comprise a distinctly modern phase of public activity.

A new agency has been created in the agricultural extension act which was signed by President Wilson on the 8th of May in 1914. The farmer is to find help at his own door. A new instrumentality in the world has now received the sanction of a whole people and we are just beginning to organize it. The organization must be extensive, and it ought also to be liberal. No such national plan on such a scale has ever been attempted; and it almost staggers one when one even partly comprehends the tremendous consequences that in all likelihood will come of it. The significance of it is not yet grasped by the great body of the people.

Now, the problem is to relate all this public work to the development of a democracy. I am not thinking so much of the development of a form of government as of a real democratic expression on the part of the people. Agriculture is our basic industry. As we organize its affairs, so to a great degree shall we secure the results in society in general. It is very important in our great experiment in democracy that we do not lose sight of the first principle in democracy, which is to let the control of policies and affairs rest directly back on the people.

We have developed the institutions on public funds to train the farmer and to give him voice. These institutions are of vast importance in the founding of a people. The folk are to be developed in themselves rather than by class legislation, or by favor of government, or by any attitude of benevolence from without.

Whether there is any danger in the organization of our new nationalized extension work, and the other public rural agencies, I suppose not one of us knows. But for myself, I have apprehension of the tendency to make some of the agricultural work into "projects" at Washington and elsewhere. If we are not careful, we shall not only too much centralize the work, but we shall tie it up in perplexing red tape, official obstacles, and bookkeeping. The merit of the projects themselves and the intentions of the officers concerned in them are not involved in what I say; I speak only of the tendency of all government to formality and to crystallization, to machine work and to armchair regulations; and even at the risk of a somewhat lower so-called "efficiency," I should prefer for such work as investigating and teaching in agriculture, a dispersion of the initiative and responsibility, letting the coordination and standardizing arise very much from conference and very little from arbitrary regulation.

The best project anywhere is a good man or woman working in a program, but unhampered.

If it is important that the administration of agricultural work be not overmuch centralized at Washington, it is equally true that it should not be too much centralized in the states. I hear that persons who object strongly to federal concentration may nevertheless decline to give the countries and the communities in their own states the benefit of any useful starting power and autonomy. In fact, I am inclined to think that here at present lies one of our greatest dangers.

A strong centralization within the state may be the most hurtful kind of concentration, for it may more vitally affect the people at home. Here the question, remember, is not the most efficient formal administration, but the best results for the people. The farm bureau work, for example, can never produce the background results of which it is capable if it is a strongly entrenched movement pushed out from one center, as from the college of agriculture or other institution. The college may be the guiding force, but it should not remove responsibility from the people of the localities, or offer them a kind of cooperation that is only the privilege of partaking in the college enterprises. I fear that some of our so-called cooperation in public work of many kinds is little more than to allow the cooperator to approve what the official administration has done.

In the course of our experience in democracy, we have developed many checks against too great centralization. I hope that we may develop the checks effectively in this new welfare work in agriculture, a desire that I am aware is also strong with many of those who are concerned in the planning of it.

Some enterprises may be much centralized, whether in a democracy or elsewhere; an example, is the postal service: this is on the business side of government. Some enterprises should be decentralized; an example is a good part of the agricultural service: this is on the educational side of government. It is the tendency to reduce all public work to uniformity; yet there is no virtue in uniformity. Its only value is as a means of an end.

Thus far, the rural movement has been wholesomely democratic. It has been my privilege for one-third of a century to have known rather closely many of the men and women who have been instrumental in bringing the rural problem to its present stage of advancement. They have been public-minded, able, far-seeing men and women, and they have rendered an unmeasurable service. The rural movement has been brought to its present state without any demand for special privilege, without bolstering by factitious legislation, and to a remarkable degree without self-seeking. It is based on a real regard for the welfare of all the people, rather than for rural people exclusively.

Thrice or more in this book I have spoken as if not convinced that the present insistence on "efficiency" in government is altogether sound. That is exactly the impression I desire to convey. As the term is now commonly applied, it is not a measure of good government.

Certain phrases and certain sets of ideas gain dominance at certain times. Just now the idea of administrative efficiency is uppermost. It seems necessarily to be the controlling factor in the progress of any business or any people. Certainly, a people should be efficient; but an efficient government may not mean an efficient people—it may mean quite otherwise or even the reverse. The primary purpose of government in these days, and particularly in this country, is to educate and to develop all the people and to lead them to express themselves freely and to the full, and to partake politically. And this is what governments may not do, and this is where they may fail even when their efficiency in administration is exact. A monarchic form may be executively more efficient than a democratic form; a despotic form may be more efficient than either. The justification of a democratic form of government lies in the fact that it is a means of education.

The final test of government is not executive efficiency. Every movement, every circumstance that takes starting power and incentive away from the people, even though it makes for exacter administration, is to be challenged. It is specially to be deplored if this loss of starting power affects the persons who deal firsthand with the surface of the planet and with the products that come directly out of it.

There is a broad political significance to all this. Sooner or later the people rebel against entrenched or bureaucratic groups. Many of you know how they resist even strongly centralized departments of public instruction, and how the effectiveness of such departments may be jeopardized and much lessened by the very perfectness of their organization; and if they were to engage in a custom of extraneous forms of newsgiving in the public press, the resentment would be the greater. In our rural work we are in danger of developing a piece of machinery founded on our fundamental industry; and if this ever comes about, we shall find the people organizing to resist it.

The reader will understand that in this discussion I assume the agricultural work to be systematically organized, both in nation and state; this is essential to good effort and to the accomplishing of results: but we must take care that the formal organization does not get in the way of the good workers, hindering and repressing them and wasting their time.

We want governments to be economical and efficient with funds and in the control of affairs; this also is assumed: but we must not overlook the larger issues. In all this new rural effort, we should maintain the spirit of teamwork and of coaction, and not make the mistake of depending too much on the routine of centralized control.

In this country we are much criticized for the cost of government and for the supposed control of affairs by monopoly. The cost is undoubtedly too great, but it is the price we pay for the satisfaction of using democratic forms. As to the other disability, let us consider that society lies between two dangers—the danger of monopoly and the danger of bureaucracy. On the one side is the control of the necessities of life by commercial organization. On the other side is the control of the necessities of life, and even of life itself, by entrenched groups that ostensibly represent the people and which it may be impossible to dislodge. Here are the Scylla and the Charybdis between which human society must pick its devious way.

Both are evil. Of the two, monopoly may be the lesser: it may be more easily brought under control; it tends to be more progressive; it extends less far; it may be the less hateful. They are only two expressions of one thing, one possibly worse than the other. Probably there are peoples who pride themselves on more or less complete escape from monopoly who are nevertheless suffering from the most deadening bureaucracy.

Agriculture is in the foundation of the political, economic, and social structure. If we cannot develop starting power in the background people we cannot maintain it elsewhere. The greatness of all this rural work is to lie in the results and not in the methods that absorb so much of our energy. If agriculture cannot be democratic, then there is no democracy.

The National Movement

The present revival of rural interest is immediately an effort to improve farming; but at bottom it is a desire to stimulate new activity in a more or less stationary phase of civilization.[2] We may overexploit the movement, but it is sound at the center. For the next twenty-five years we may expect it to have great influence on the course of events, for it will require this length of time to balance up society. Politicians will use it as a means of riding into power. Demagogues and fakirs will take advantage of it for personal gain. Tradesmen will make much of it. Writers are even now beginning to sensationalize it.

But there will also arise countrymen with statesmanship in them; if not so, then we cannot make the progress that we need. The movement will have its significant political aspect, and we may look for governors of states and perhaps more than one President of the United States to come out of it. In the end, the farmer controls the politics because he makes the crops on which the wealth of the country depends. There is probably a greater proportion of taxpayers among voting farmers than among city people.

Considered in total results, educational and political as well as social and economic, the country-life movement in North America is probably farther advanced than in any other part of the world. It may not have such striking manifestations in some special lines, and our people may not need so much as other peoples that these particular lines be first or most strongly attacked. The movement really has been underway for many years, but it has only recently found separate expression. Most of the progress has been fundamental, and will not need to be done over again. The movement is well afoot among the country people themselves, and they are doing some of the

2. From *The Country-Life Movement in the United States* (New York: Macmillan, 1911), 4–7; 16–30.

clearest thinking on the situation. Many of our own people do not know how far we have already come.

Such undercurrent movements are usually associated with transition epochs.[3] In parts of the Old World the nexus in the social structure has been the landlord, and the change in land tenure systems has made a social reorganization necessary. There is no political land tenure problem in the United States, and therefore there is no need, on that score, of the cooperation of small owners or would-be owners to form a new social crystallization. But there is a land problem with us, nevertheless, and this is at the bottom of our present movement: it is the immanent problem of remaining more or less stationary on our present lands, rather than moving on to untouched lands, when the ready-to-use fertility is reduced. We have had a new-land society, with all the marks of expansion and shift. We are now coming to a new era; but, unlike new eras in some other countries, it is not complicated by hereditary social stratification. Our real agricultural development will now begin.

In the discussion of these rural interests, old foundations and old ideas in all probability will be torn up. We shall probably discard many of the notions that now are new and that promise well. We may face trying situations, but something better will come out of it. It is now a time to be conservative and careful, and to let the movement mature.[4]

CIVILIZATION oscillates between two poles.[5] At the one extreme is the so-called laboring class, and at the other are the syndicated and corporate and monopolized interests. Both these elements or phases tend to go to extremes. Many efforts are being made to weld them into some sort of share-earning or commonness of interest, but without very great results. Between these two poles is the great agricultural class, which is the natural balance force or the middle wheel of society. These people are steady, conservative, abiding by the law, and are to a greater extent than we recognize, a controlling element in our social structure.

The man on the farm has the opportunity to found a dynasty. City properties may come and go, rented houses may be removed, stocks and bonds

3. The first sentence following the original subhead (here omitted) entitled "A transition period," p. 6.

4. Several short subheads following this sentence have been leapfrogged for concision; these omissions include "The commission on country life," p. 7, through "Some contrasts of town folk and country folk," p. 14.

5. The first sentence following the original subhead (here omitted) "Comparisons of town and country affairs," p. 16. The extra return preceding the original subhead is here preserved as a section break.

may rise and fall, but the land still remains; and a man can remain on the land and subsist with it so long as he knows how to handle it properly. It is largely, therefore, a question of education as to how long any family can establish itself on a piece of land.

In the accelerating mobility of our civilization, it is increasingly important that we have many anchoring places; and these anchoring places are the farms.

These two phases of society produce marked results in ways of doing business. The great centers invite combinations, and, because society has not kept pace with guiding and correcting measures, immense abuses have arisen and the few have tended to fatten on the many. There are two general modes of correcting, or at least of modifying, these abuses, by doing what we can to make men personally honest and responsible, and by evening up society so that all men may have something like a natural opportunity.

There is a town mind and a country mind.[6] I do not pretend to know what may be the psychological processes, but it is clear that the mode of approach to the problem of life is very different as between the real urbanite and the real ruralite. This factor is not sufficiently taken into account by city men who would remove to real farms and make a living there. It is the cause of most of the failure of well-intentioned social workers to accomplish much for country people.

All this is singularly reflected in our literature, and most of all, perhaps, in guidebooks. These books—made to meet the demand—illustrate how completely the open country has been in eclipse. There is little rural country discoverable in these books, unless it is mere "sights" "or "places," nothing of the people, of the lands, of the products, of the markets, of the country dorfs, of the way of life; but there is surfeit of cathedrals, of history of cities, of seats of famous personages, of bridges and streets, of galleries and works of art. We begin to see evidences of travel out into the farming regions, part of it, no doubt, merely a desire for new experiences and diversion, and we shall now look for guidebooks that recognize the background on which the cities rest. But all this will call for a new intention in travel.

What future lies before the American farmer?[7] Will he hold something like a position of independence and individualism, or will he become submerged in the social order, and form only an underlying stratum? What ultimate hope is there for a farmer as a member of society?

6. The first sentence following the original subhead (here omitted) entitled "The two minds," p. 17.

7. The first sentence following the original subhead (here omitted) entitled "Will the American farmer hold his own?" p. 19.

VI. FARM

It is strange that the producer of the raw material has thus far in the history of the world taken a subordinate place to the trader in this material and to the fabricator of it. The trader and fabricator live in centers that we call cities. One type of mind assembles; the other type remains more or less scattered. So there have arisen in human society two divergent streams, the collective and cooperative, and the isolated and individualistic.

The fundamental weakness in our civilization is the fact that the city and the country represent antagonistic forces. Sympathetically, they have been and are opposed. The city lives on the country. It always tends to destroy its province.

The city sits like a parasite, running out its roots into the open country and draining it of its substance. The city takes everything to itself—materials, money, men—and gives back only what it does not want; it does not reconstruct or even maintain its contributory country. Many country places are already sucked dry.

The future state of the farmer, or real countryman, will depend directly on the kind of balance or relationship that exists between urban and rural forces; and in the end, the state of the city will rest on the same basis. Whatever the city does for the country, it does also for itself.

Mankind has not yet worked out this organic relation of town and country. City and country are gradually coming together fraternally, but this is due more to acquaintanceship than to any underlying cooperation between them as equal forces in society. Until such an organic relationship exists, civilization cannot be perfected or sustained, however high it may rise in its various parts.

Of course there are no two or even a dozen means that can bring about this fundamental adjustment, but the two most important means are at hand and can be immediately put into better operation.[8]

The first necessity is to place broadly trained persons in the open country, for all progress depends on the ability and the outlook of men and women.

The second necessity is that city folk and country folk work together on all great public questions. Look over the directories of big undertakings, the memberships of commissions and councils, the committees that lay plans for great enterprises affecting all the people, and note how few are the names that really represent the ideas and affairs of the open country. Note also how many are the names that represent financial interests, as if such interests should have the right of way and should exert the largest influence

8. The first sentence following the original subhead (here omitted) entitled "The first two remedies," p. 21.

in determining public policies. In all enterprises and movements in which social benefit is involved, the agricultural country should be as much represented as the city. There are men and women enough out in the open country who are qualified to serve on such commissions and directories; but even if there were not, it would now be our duty to raise them up by giving rural people a chance. Rural talent has not had adequate opportunity to express itself or to make its contribution to the welfare of the world.

I know it is said, in reply to these remarks, that many of the city persons on such organizations are country-born, but this does not change the point of my contention. Many country-born townsmen are widely out of knowledge of present rural conditions, even though their sympathies are still countryward. It is also said that many of them live in country villages, small cities, and in suburbs; but even so, their real relations may be with town rather than country, and they may have little of the farm-country mind; and the suburban mind is really a town mind.

Every broad public movement should have country people on its board of control. Both urban and rural forces must shape our civilization.

Some persons seem to think that the movement of city men out to the country offers a solution of country problems.[9] It usually offers only a solution of a city problem, how a city man may find the most enjoyment for his leisure hours and his vacations. Much of the rising interest in country life on the part of certain people is only a demand for a new form of entertainment. These people strike the high places in the country, but they may contribute little or nothing to real country welfare. This form of entertainment will lose its novelty, as the seashore loses it for the mountains and the horse loses it for the motor car or airplane. The farming of some city men is demoralizing to real country interests. I do not look for much permanent good to come to rural society from the moving out of some of the types of city men or from the farming in which they ordinarily engage.

I am glad of all movements to place persons on the land who ought to go there, and to direct country-minded immigrants away from the cities; but we must not expect too much from the process, and we must distinguish between the benefit that may accrue to these persons themselves and the need of reconstruction in the open country. It is one thing for a family to move to the land in order to raise its own supplies and to secure the benefits of country life; it is quite another thing to suppose that an exodus from city to country will relieve the economic situation or make any difference in the general cost of living, even assuming that the town folk would make good

9. The first sentence following the original subhead (here omitted) entitled "Movement from city to country as a remedy," p. 23.

farmers. And we must be very careful not to confuse suburbanism and gardening with country life.

To have any continuing effect on the course of rural development, a person or an agency must become a real part and parcel of the country life.

It is also proposed to send to the country the poor-to-do and the dissatisfied and the unemployed.[10] This is very doubtful policy. In the first place, the presumption is that a person who does not do well or is much dissatisfied in the town would not do well in the country. In the second place, the country does not need him. We may need more farm labor, as we need more of all kinds of labor, but in the long run this labor should be produced mostly in the country and kept there by a profitable and attractive rural life. The city should not be expected permanently to supply it. The labor that the city can supply with profit to country districts is the very labor that is good enough for the city to keep.

The relief of cities, if relief is to be secured, must lie in the evolution of the entire situation, and not merely in sending the surplus population into the country.

In my opinion, the present back-to-the-farm cry is for the most part unscientific and unsound, as a corrective of social ills. It rests largely on the assumption that one solution of city congestion is to send people away from itself to the open country, and on another assumption that "a little farm well tilled" will abundantly support a family. There is bound to be a strong reaction against much of the present agitation. We are to consider the welfare of the open country as well as that of the city itself. The open country needs more good farmers, whether they are country-bred or city-bred; but it cannot utilize or assimilate to any great extent the typical urban-minded man; and the farm is not a refuge.

IT seems to me that what is really needed is a back-to-the-village movement.[11] This should be more than a mere suburban movement. The suburban development enlarges the boundaries of the city. It is perfectly feasible, however, to establish manufacturing and other concentrated enterprises in villages in many parts of the country. Persons connected with these enterprises could own small pieces of land, and by working these areas could add something to their means of support, and also satisfy their desire for a nature connection. In many of the villages there are vacant houses and comparatively

---

10. The first sentence following the original subhead (here omitted) entitled "Sending surplus population to the country," p. 25.

11. The first sentence following the original subhead (here omitted) "Back-to-the-village," p. 26. The extra return preceding the original subheading is here preserved as a break.

unoccupied land in sufficient number and amount to house and establish many enterprises; and there would be room for growth. If the rural village, freed from urban influences, could then become a real integrating part of the open country surrounding it, all parties ought to be better served than now, and the social condition of both cities and country ought to be improved. We have overbuilt our cities at the expense of the hamlets and the towns. I look for a great development of the village and small community in the next generation; but this involves a re-study of freight rates.

Can a city man make a living on a farm?[12] Yes, if he is industrious and knows how. Many city persons have made good on the land, but they are the exceptions, unless they began young.

There is the most curious confusion of ideas on this question. We say that farming requires the highest kind of knowledge and at the same time think that any man may go on a farm, no matter how unsuccessful he may have been elsewhere. Even if he has been successful as a middleman or manufacturer or merchant, it does not at all follow that he would be successful as a farmer. Farming cannot be done at long range or by proxy any more than banking, or storekeeping, or railroading, and especially not by one who does not know how; and he cannot learn it out of books and bulletins. If a man can run a large factory without first learning the business, or a theater or a department store, then he might be able also to run a farm, although the running of a farm of equal investment would probably be the more difficult undertaking.

I am glad to see earnest city men go into farming when they are qualified to do so, but I warn my friends that many good people who go out from cities to farms with golden hopes will be sadly disappointed. Farming is a good business and it is getting better, but it is a business for farmers; and on the farmers as a group must rest the immediate responsibility of improving rural conditions in general.

The younger the man when he begins to consider being a farmer, the greater will be his chances of success; here the student has the great advantage.

City people must be on their guard against attractive land schemes. Now and then it is possible to pay for the land and make a living out of it at the same time, but these cases are so few that the intending purchaser would better not make his calculations on them. Farming is no longer a poor man's business. It requires capital to equip and run a farm as well as to buy it, the same as in other business. It is a common fault of land schemes to magnify the income, and to minimize both the risks and the amount of needed capital. Plans that read well may be wholly unsound or even impossible when

12. This question was the original subheading on p. 27 and has been run-in for context.

translated into plain business practice. The exploiting of exceptional results in reporter's English and with charming pictures is having a very dangerous effect on the public mind; and even some of these results may not stand business analysis.

It is not incumbent on cities, corporations, colleges, or other institutions to demonstrate, by going into general practical farming, that the farming business may be made to pay: thousands of farmers are demonstrating this every day.[13]

If the city ever saves the open country, it will be by working out a real economic and social coordination between city and country, not by the city going into farming.

We need to correct the abnormal urban domination in political power, in control of the agencies of trade, in discriminatory practices, and in artificial stimulation, and at the same time to protect the evolution of a new rural welfare. The agrarian situation in the world is not to be met alone by increasing the technical efficiency of farming.

13. The first sentence following the original subhead (here omitted) entitled "What the city may do," p. 30.

Women's Contribution to
the Country-life Movement

On the women depend to a greater degree than we realize the nature and extent of the movement for a better country life, wholly aside from their personal influence as members of families.[14] Farming is a copartnership business. It is a partnership between a man and a woman. There is no other great series of occupations in which such copartnership is so essential to success. The home is on the farm, and a part of it. The number of middle-aged unmarried men living on farms is very small. It is quite impossible to live on a farm and to run it advantageously without family relation.

It follows, then, that if the farming business is to contribute to the redirection of country life, the woman has responsibilities as well as the man. As the strength of a chain is determined by its weakest link, so will the progress of rural civilization be determined by the weakness of the farm as an economic unit, or by the weakness of the home as a domestic and social unit.

Now, the farmer himself cannot have great influence in redirecting the affairs of his community until he is first master of his own problem, that is, until he is a first-class farmer. In the same way, a woman cannot expect to have much influence in furthering the affairs of her rural community until she also is master of her own problem, and her problem is primarily the homemaking part of the farm. In the mastering of his or her own problem, the farmer or his wife may also contribute directly to the progress of the community. Every advance in the management of the household contributes to the general welfare: it sets new ideas underway.

If the farming business must in general be reorganized, so also must the householding part of it be reorganized. The solution of the farm labor problem, for example, lies not alone merely in securing more farm "hands," but in so directing and shaping the business that less farm hands will be needed

14. From *The Country-Life Movement in the United States* (New York: Macmillan, 1911), 85–96.

to secure a given economic result; so also the solution of the household labor problem is not merely the securing of more household help, but the simplification of householding itself.

So far as possible, the labor that is necessary to do the work of the open country, whether indoors or outdoors, should be resident labor. The labor difficulty increases with reduction in the size of the family. Families of moderate size develop responsibility, and cooperation is forced on all members of it, with marked effect on character. The single child is likely to develop selfishness rather than cooperation and sense of responsibility. To a large extent, the responsibility of the household should rest on the girls of the family; and all children, whether boys or girls, should be brought up in the home in habits of industry.

It is fairly possible by means of simplification of householding and by a cooperative industry amongst all members of the family, so to reduce the burden of the farm wife that she may have time and strength to give to the vital affairs of the community.

It is essential that we simplify our ideals in cooking, in ornament, in apparel, and in furnishing; that we construct more convenient and workable residences; that we employ labor-saving devices for the house as well as for the barns and the fields.[15]

We are so accustomed to the ordinary modes of living that we scarcely realize what amount of time and strength might be saved by a simplified table and by more thoughtful methods of preparing food. In respect to houses, it should be remembered that the present farm dwellings are getting old. A good part of the farm houses must soon be either rebuilt or remodeled. The first consideration is so to build or remodel them that steps may be saved to the housewife. We have not thought, in the past, that a woman's steps cost time and energy. Within twenty years all first-class farm houses will have running water, both into the house and out of the house.

It is rather strange that in our discussions of the farm labor problem, we do not realize that a gasoline engine or a water engine may save the labor of a man. Farmers are putting power into their barns. They should also put power into the house. This may be accomplished by means of a small movable engine that can be used either in the house or barn, or else by installing an engine in a small building betwixt the house and the barn, so that it can be connected either way. This can be used to lighten much household labor, as pumping of water, meat chopping, laundering, dishwashing, vacuum cleaning, and the like.

15. The first sentence following the original subhead (here omitted) entitled "The affairs of the household," p. 88.

Eventually, there must be some form of community cooperation in the country to save household labor. Already the care of milk has been taken from great numbers of farm homes by the neighborhood creamery, or at least by the building of a milk house in which the men by the use of machinery perform labor that was once done by the housewife. Whenever there is a cooperative creamery, there may also be other cooperative attachments, as a laundry, or other appliances. It will be more difficult to bring about cooperation in these regards in country districts than in the city, but with the coming of good roads, telephones, and better vehicles, it will be constantly more easy to accomplish.

I have said that it is important that the country woman have strength and time to engage in the vital affairs of the community.[16] I am thinking of the public sentiment that women can make on any question that they care to discuss thoroughly and collectively, whether this sentiment is for better orcharding, better fowls, better roads, extending of telephones, improving the schoolhouse or church or library. It is needful that women in the country come together to discuss woman's work, and also to form intelligent opinions on farming questions in general.

The tendency of all "sociables" in country and town is to bring persons together to eat, to gossip, and to be entertained. We need to redirect all these meetings, and to devote at least a part of every such meeting to some real and serious work which it is worthwhile for busy and intelligent persons to undertake.

Every organization of women should endeavor to extend its branches and its influence into the open country as well as into the cities and towns. Every public movement now has responsibility to country-life questions as well as to town questions.

I think it important that there be some means and reason for every farm woman going away from home at least once a week, and this wholly aside from going to town to trade. There should be some place where the women may come together on a different basis from that of the ordinary daily routine and the usual buying and selling. I do not know where this social center should develop, and in an atmosphere that is not conducive to gossip. In some neighborhoods it might focalize in the church parlor. The center should be permanent, if possible. It should be a place to which any woman in a community has a right to go. An ideal place for such a center would be the rural library, and I hope that such libraries may arise in every country community, not only that they may supply books but that they may help

16. The first sentence following the original subhead (here omitted) entitled "The affairs of the community," p. 88.

provide a meeting place on semi-social lines. I think that if I were a woman in charge of a rural library, I should never be satisfied with my work until I had got every woman in the community in the habit of coming to the library once every week.

The woman needs very much to have the opportunity to broaden her horizon.[17] The farmer has lived on his farm; he is now acquiring a world outlook. The woman has lived in her house; she also is acquiring a world outlook. As the house has been smaller and more confining than the farm, it has followed that woman's outlook has been smaller than man's.

I think it is necessary also that the woman of the farm, as well as the man, have a real anchor in her nature environment. It is as necessary to the woman as to the man that her mind be open to the facts, phenomena, and objects that are everywhere about her, as the winds and weather, the plants and birds, the fields and streams and woods. It is one of the best resources in life to be able to distinguish the songs and voices of the common fields, and it should be a part of the education of every person, and particularly of every country person, to have this respite. The making of a garden is much more than the growing of the radishes and strawberries and petunias. It is the experience in the out-of-doors, the contact with realities, the personal joy of seeing things germinate and grow and reproduce their kind.

If country women are to develop a conscious sense of responsibility in country-life betterment, education facilities must be afforded them.[18] The schools must recognize homemaking subjects equally with other subjects. What becomes a part of the school eventually becomes a part of the life of the people of the region.

The leadership in such subjects is now being taken by the colleges of agriculture. This is not because domestic subjects belong in a college of agriculture more than elsewhere, but only that these colleges see the problem, and most general colleges or universities have not seen it. The college of agriculture, if it is highly developed, represents a civilization rather than a series of subjects; and it cannot omit the homemaking phase if it meets its obligation to the society that it represents.

If the customary subjects in a college of agriculture are organized and designed to train a man for efficiency in country life and to develop his outlook, so also is a department of home economics to train a woman for efficiency and to develop her outlook to life.

17. The first sentence following the original subhead (here omitted) entitled "The woman's outlook," p. 92.

18. The first sentence following the original subhead (here omitted) entitled "The means of education," p. 93.

Home economics is not one "department" or subject, in the sense in which dairying or entomology or plant breeding is a department. It is not a single specialty. It stands for the whole round of woman's work and place. Many technical or educational departments will grow out of it as time goes on. That is, it will be broken up into its integral parts, and it will then cease to be an administrative department of an educational institution; and very likely we shall lose the terms "home economics," "household economics," "domestic science," and the rest.

I would not limit the entrance of women into any courses in a college of agriculture; on the contrary, I want all courses open to them freely and on equal terms with men; but the subjects that are arranged under the general head of home economics are her special field and sphere. On the other hand, I do not want to limit the attendance of men in courses of home economics; in fact, I think it will be found that an increasing number of men desire to take these subjects as the work develops, and this will be best for society in general.

Furthermore, I do not conceive it to be essential that all teachers in home economics subjects shall be women; nor, on the other hand, do I think it is essential that all teachers in the other series of departments shall be men. The person who is best qualified to teach the subject should be the one who teaches it, whether man or woman.

As rapidly as colleges and universities come to represent society and to develop in all students a philosophy of life, the homemaking units will of necessity take their place with other units.

One Hundred and Twenty-nine Farmers

To actual farmers I wrote in April 1926, as follows, choosing persons, as far as possible, who make their living from farming:[19]

> Now that the discouragements of agriculture are so much stressed, I am asking farmers in various parts of the country whether they really experience joy in farming and to indicate to me, if they will, what is the main satisfaction they find in the farmer's life.

I received reply from 129 persons, sometimes more than one letter, in thirty-three states and four Canadian provinces, fairly indicating the continent from Maine and New Brunswick to California and British Columbia; all the regions at present much distressed are represented, as well as all the New England states.

It has been a privilege to read these genuine letters. I have never before had such an interesting lot. I should like to publish many of them as they stand; but that I might have spontaneous expressions I promised that I would not quote any person by name. Some of the letters are expressed in literary skill. All of them go directly to the heart of the question. Practically all the respondents consider the return from farming inadequate; as one of them expresses it, who has a good two hundred-acre farm, "It is necessary for us to pay the old farm about $1000 a year for the honor of helping to grow the nation's food supply if we live just decently." Some of the writers, however, attest that they are even now making satisfactory profits, but these men are mostly engaged in growing special or high-class products. None of them asks for government aid, and most of them are afraid of attempts at special legislation for the farmer. The letters do not reflect the discouragements one would

19. From *The Harvest of the Year to the Tiller of the Soil* (New York: Macmillan, 1927), 196–207.

expect, from the current publicity of the situation. But as I did not ask for a discussion of this side of the question, I shall not dwell on it here.

I wanted chiefly to know whether the main satisfactions in the farmer's life were still to be expressed in the sentiments, or whether these old values have been smothered by the current commercial emphasis. I find these old sentiments still strong in these letters and probably better stated than in my youth and in the period of my active work with the farming people. I shall quote a good number of these expressions, being convinced that we need to be reassured by them.

The city man might not realize these satisfactions if he were to undertake farming; these joys are the rewards of those who have had long experience in the situations and have matured; none of these farmers would lure to the open country any person who by temperament and training is not adapted to the occupation.

To one not born to the situation, many of the satisfactions will seem unusual and perhaps of little moment; yet I know that my farm friends will appreciate such passing remarks as these, each from a different writer: "I breathe pure air and drink water not brought to me in pipes"; "I like to see the stock eat"; "I want to dig in the soil"; "I am never out of work"; "The city is a cage"; "Those people who are not happy unless they can see a movie every night would better stay in town"; "I would not trade my farm home for a city mansion"; "I like to have a job all my own"; "There is marked difference between staying on a farm and living on one"; "What is my 'main satisfaction'? Why not ask me which child I like best?"

In the letters from these 129 farmers, only one considers the money profit to be the main satisfaction in farming and the writer of it now represents a farm organization; but he adds that it is not so much for the profit itself as for the comforts and conveniences the profit enables one to obtain. About a dozen correspondents find conditions now so hard that they are discouraged; some of them are badly in debt and the load is heavy to carry at present.

Practically all writers recognize the satisfactions that inhere in the occupation in distinction from the amenities and accessories that may be purchased. My question was intended to uncover this aspect of the situation. The chief satisfactions, as revealed in the letters, are the independent way of life, healthfulness of the occupation, pleasure in productive labor, joy of the cooperative family living and the wholesome situation for the children, love of nature, close contact with living, growing objects and the response of these objects to the touch of the good farmer, the satisfactions of landscapes, innate love of the land, consolation in the ownership of real property. Even at the risk of some repetition, I now print extracts from a few of these letters as a current contribution to the subject. Long ago I made a somewhat similar inquiry and published the summary results (*The Training of Farmers*, 1909), but the present letters are especially notable as reflecting a background sentiment in a more or less troubled epoch. These are real assets.[20]

> Let me say that some years ago my only boy decided to stay on the farm and help me. Now my joy comes from helping the boy.

> The farmer is his own boss and paymaster, and his life can be as useful as any if not spent for selfish gain or aggrandizement.

> I like the smell of new soil as it rolls like an endless ribbon from the moldboard. Out here we have the enjoyment of irrigation. How the crops like water! I can just live in the fields in the irrigating season.

> I grew up here on this farm. Like Walt Whitman's child, I went forth every day and the things I saw became part of me.

> The main satisfaction is the abiding confidence that one is cooperating with the Creator in feeding and clothing the people.

> Freedom from overhead domination, from the petty jealousies of public positions, and the feeling that one is earning his own bread rather than obtaining it at public expense, mean much to me.

> A modern farm with reasonable improvements and facilities is a good place to live and especially to bring up children. Farming is an independent, interesting, healthful, hopeful life, in spite of, perhaps even partly because of, hard work and hard times.

> My answer is this: the opportunity for improved farm methods and application of discoveries, the friendliness of the dog and the horses, the strong sturdy boys and girls, the opportunity for recreation and study. (A farmer out of an agricultural college thirty-five years.)

> The chief satisfaction (joy) I get out of farming lies in overcoming the difficulties connected with operating a farm and disposing of the products to advantage. The raising of better cattle and crops than the average brings a sense of satisfaction difficult to duplicate. Further than this a close contact with cooperative buying and selling organizations which show enough progress to furnish the courage necessary to insure the continuance of this work is satisfying. We have long been looking for an easy solution of our problems. I believe that if the solution had been easy it would have been found before now.

> There is satisfaction in being at home with your family, working with your sons, cultivating the soil, watching the crops develop, handling the livestock. If farming was financially on a par with other business for equal brains and energy expended, everybody would be engaged in it.

20. Each of the following quotes represents a single, distinct letter from among the 129 letters Bailey received from farmers.

Compelling motives are the independence of living out-of-doors, work with growing plants under the varying seasons and climatic conditions, and the inherent desire to dig in the soil.

My main satisfaction in farming is that I own my home, and the farm furnishes the means by which I can support myself and family independently of anyone else. I enjoy seeing the crops develop under cultivation and care, and also the study and care of farm animals.

Every day this week I have worked in the fields. The odor of the freshly turned furrow has again become part and parcel of my blood and sinew. It signifies that winter frost has done its work and that there is in the ground fertility for the new crop. Its urge challenges my best effort. He who does not know this springtime fragrance of the soil with its promises of fruition does not fully know the joy of farming. To plant seeds in well prepared soil and by careful culture develop useful plants; to make of the wobbly colt or calf or pig an animal better than its sire—what could be greater?

Of course no one can continue to play a losing game and keep up enthusiasm; but in the thirty years I have been farming, few farms have proved to be unprofitable. I have always been attracted by puzzles; I know of no occupation that offers so many problems of the most intricate kind as agriculture. Experimenting, studying and solving these problems have given me much pleasure. The independence of the farmer's life has been a satisfaction to me. I also find pleasure in watching things grow. I have always felt that the profession of farming is useful, and that I am using what the Creator has put in my hands as he would have me use it.

I keenly enjoy all the farming experiences, as the smell of freshly cured hay, the quiet contentment of cows at milking-time, the cackle of a heavy-laying flock of hens, the sight of well-managed orchards, the fields of vigorous growing crops.

Every year the farmer lives in hope of better things to come, which gives him a greater love for the smell of the plowed soil, the songs of the birds, the beauty of the flowers, woodlands, hills and streams; and thus urged on by Nature herself, if backed by a reasonably happy family life, nothing but foreclosure shakes him from it. I must confess I am one of the majority and that the "mirage" lures me on.

I was raised on a farm and always liked farm work. It is a pleasure for me to breed, feed and develop good livestock. It is a pleasure to have a good growing crop of wheat, corn, oats, clover or alfalfa. You have heard of the song "Knee-deep in Daisies"; well, what looks better than a bunch of good Duroc-Jersey shoats knee-deep in clover? To me the farm is a manufacturing plant of the highest order. We have a variety of raw materials out of which we produce food for the country. We have more friction in our machinery than any other manufacturer, such as the weather, too dry or too wet, all the pests of livestock and grain. It is a pleasure for me to try to reduce this friction to the minimum, and with scientific help we can about master all but the weather. Then finally it is the best place to raise your babies. We have a boy, four, and a little girl two years of age, and they are waiting for me to finish this letter so they can go out with me to feed the pigs.

A happy comfortable farm home in my youth with no compulsion to stay there and my love of growing things and animals with opportunities for the best agricultural education of forty-five years ago are, I think, the reasons why I have kept close to the soil.

To work out the new problems and overcome the difficulties that the ever-changing conditions present to the farmer is a real satisfaction surpassed only by the joy of accomplishing the great transformation from the prairie wilderness to a real home through beautifying with shelter belt, hedge, lawn and flowers. (Alberta)

I am nearly seventy-four-years-old and have been a farmer all my life. There is satisfaction in working with nature. When I go to the city and talk with businessmen and learn of their discouragements and of some of the laboring men's hardships, I come home better satisfied with my life.

I think farmers genuinely experience joy in their occupation. No matter how depressing have been the results of the preceding year, in the spring time (to modify an old quotation) hope springs eternal in the farmer's breast. The changing colors of the trees and fields and the ever-shifting clouds continuously afford me satisfaction, increasing as the years go by. A farmer who avoids city associations which are more or less synonymous with high expenditure and display, may still lead a more or less joyous existence.

Freedom of action that once enjoyed could not suffer to be abridged. The spirit of creating, always hoping, always expecting, never on the dead level of monotony.

We find our biggest joy in owning this bit of earth, in working in the soil, the wind and rain in our faces, in the cool starry nights after the hot noon day, in growing our fine colts and pigs and lambs and calves, and especially in creating beauty in our flock of fowls; we love the wildflowers and birds; we take a healthy physical joy in the fine cream and eggs and vegetables we produce for our own use; we enjoy the community contacts and the local and State fairs and the folks down at our State College. We enjoy poverty on the farm much more than we would enjoy it in the city. (A farm wife.)

Love of the soil and the out-of-doors. It is in the blood. If I had my way I would have every boy and girl spend at least one full year on a real farm before the age of ten.

I am getting a lot of satisfaction out of farming. I presume the main reason is my love for the dairy cow. During the past few years she has consumed considerable amounts of rough feed and in turn delivered to me a finished product that had a market value.

The satisfaction of outdoor work, and seeing things grow and develop, as the results of my own efforts, is just as great to me as I always anticipated it would be, when I was a city boy, looking forward to owning and operating a farm of my own some time. Another factor which I had not thought so much about but which means more than anything else is the splendid partnership which this sort of life makes possible between a husband and wife. The average city man leaves home at seven-thirty in the morning and returns at six at night and his wife has had no chance to share in his joys or responsibilities. On the farm, the home life and business life are so closely interwoven that they cannot be separated. My wife is just as interested as I am in each undertaking that goes on, for she has helped make the decisions, and has seen the results of each years efforts added to the others. It is unnecessary to dwell on the advantages of a farm for bringing up a family, for they are so obvious. Our three healthy happy specimens are proof enough of that.

Perhaps the greatest satisfaction I experience as a farmer is the absolute liberty of thought, speech and action which belongs to the man on the farm. Close companionship within the family, opportunities to appreciate the bright and beautiful in nature, "adventures in friendship" of the genuine sort, and a fair return for thought and energy expended in the farm business are additional factors contributing to the joy I experience in farming.

Personally, I feel that at no time within my recollection has the farming business displayed more optimistic anticipation than now. Likewise I am firmly convinced that agriculture has never before offered such opportunities to a young man. I know of no job, however attractive, which could entirely disassociate me from the farm. I farm primarily because I like it better than any other business in which I might have engaged.

While I acknowledge there are many sorrows and disappointments in farming, yet I have kept at it for twenty-five years because there is no factory whistle to blow, no real labor trouble, and few troubles that there is not a joy in overcoming, such as weather, frost, snow, abortion and other things (I have never had T.B. [tuberculosis] in my cattle); and there is a great satisfaction in seeing livestock grow and thrive and in producing better stock or farm products than do others.

Farming is the job of an honest man, a patient man, and there is satisfaction in trying to work out justice to all on basic principles.

While the profits in farming are not large, there is the satisfaction that one has independence, freedom of action and speech and always a comfortable living. One is never out of work.

To the person not too heavily burdened with debt, farming still offers the freest and most independent life. The isolation of the farm has passed, the physical drudgery is passing with the advent of machinery, while the old advantages of wholesome and independent living still remain.

VI. FARM

Farming is more than a means of livelihood, a farm is much more than a manufactory for the production of raw material, a farm home is more than merely a domicile. If a farmer cannot count all his joy in securing financial return for his labor; if he does not delight in increasing soil fertility and producing perfect specimens of his various crops, if he does not derive pleasure in watching and making things grow, in making a ton litter of pigs, or in handling a high-grade calf, or making a particularly fine milk cow, he is in the wrong place by remaining on the farm. There is of course some satisfaction as also necessity in making farming profitable, but if the measuring rod of agriculture is to be the size of the check, then to my mind this is placing farming on too low a level, and means that eventually American agriculture will be in two classes to a great degree, the agricultural corporation and the peasant class.

The farm is a good place to work and a good place to get an appetite. After all, working and eating is the main thing in life. You do not get any fun unless you work and you do not have much fun unless you eat. A farmer ought to get lots of rest because he does not have anyone to bother him. When he goes to the city there is always something going on. We do not worry much about the farmer.

I love to see plants and livestock develop; watch a tree grow; and make a farmstead so beautiful that it will be the envy of passers-by. The fresh air, grass, fruits, vegetables, and freedom make country life so worthwhile that I pity any one who must live in town. Last year I had twenty-nine kinds of vegetables in my garden and on October 1st there were fifteen kinds ready for use.

I am living on the farm purchased by my grandfather for my father. I have had some share in paying off the mortgage, erecting the buildings and planting sixty-five acres of fruit trees. My main enjoyment is in the fruit part of the farm and the satisfaction of knowing that I have a foundation for a living that will continue. There is a certain independence on the farm, and time for thought. With my situation I cannot find words to express how much we love country life.

Yes, there is just as much joy in farming as ever but more grief in paying the bills. The main satisfaction is that one helps to clothe the poor and feed the hungry.

There is no profession like farming for those who make a study of it. If the farmer is unfortunate in being ill for a time, his dairy is bringing in a daily income; his crops are growing, as well also as when he sleeps at night.

The main joy or satisfaction to me in farming is the fact that the work is congenial, healthy and productive. The constant struggle to overcome unfavorable weather conditions, insect enemies and fungous diseases from the time of the blossoms to the harvest is a challenge to one's ability and resourcefulness. There is pleasure and satisfaction and generally a reward when you win out.

I enjoy living on the farm for the inspiration that comes from the growing things and for the fact that the country is the best place to raise a family. Eight months in school and four months in the manual training school of a farm with chores night and morning during school furnish the ideal place to make real men and women out of the children.

Yes, we experience joy in farming. The sense of cooperating with the vital forces that sprout the seed and bring the harvest gives a feeling of worthwhileness, interest and dignity that more than compensate for the sweat and toil and frequent financial discouragements. Then the beauty of hill and valley, of wood and meadow, is as much a part of our everyday life as the air we breathe.

For one thing I was born to my "job." By family tradition it seemed almost unthinkable that I could do anything else. Then I think I am "farm-minded" and that I find pleasure in growing things and in all the phenomena of nature and in the procession of the rolling years. Always there is the element of wondering as to just how things are going to turn out—will this be a fat year for corn? However, I think that for me the most satisfying fact of my business is that farming enjoys a continuity possessed by almost no other vocation. Finally we come to speak of things in terms of generations rather than years. It is true that to be a teacher is a wonderful privilege. The good teacher is immortal because he lives on in the life of his students. In the case of the professional man, I feel that very frequently his work dies with him; he cannot bequeath the things that he has made. But the farmer stands on the shoulders of those gone before. So I find myself saying, "Thus we did in grandfather's time"; "In such wise my father did his work." Today I carry on as I may and in days to come I trust my son will take up my work where I lay it down. Always I thrill to Whittier's lines—

> We tread the paths their feet have worn,
> We sit beneath their orchard trees,
> We hear, like them, the hum of bees
> And rustle of the bladed corn.

VII POETICS

He took me by the hand
And led me to my own hearthstone
We paused upon the wonted floor
And silent stood alone—
Till all the space was over-pent
With a magic wonderment;
And I found the Poet's store
On the threshold of my door.

—From "Poet," *Wind and Weather* (New York: Scribner, 1916)

Liberty Hyde Bailey displays his abundant gifts as literary and cultural critic in the three essays that follow, as he explores, broadly, the poetics of agrarianism and environmentalism. The first essay, "What Literature Can Do for Us" originated as one of four lectures Professor Bailey delivered in January 1905 at the Colonial Theatre in Boston as part of a university course. "What Literature Can Do for Us" is a remarkable piece of literary criticism from a man considered to be one of the foremost scientists of his day. In it, the author celebrates the new nature poet who will sing "small voices" of wood and field. This new poet will be both concrete and wildly imaginative, such that the young farm men and women Bailey taught could at once comprehend and be challenged by the poet's words. The verse of the day, Bailey insists, is too "bookish" and bears too much of what some have called "the odor of the lamp." In this remarkably contemporary statement of poetic necessity, the author declares, "The world never needed poetry so much as now." Walt Whitman is presented as an example of a writer who had "freed himself from the bondage of literary form." In the second essay, "The Threatened Literature," Bailey considers, and ultimately rejects, the then-fancied notion that science would make literature and religion obsolete; C. P. Snow, in *The Two Cultures,* would famously take up the same issue more than thirty years later. As a poetic scientist, Bailey notes points of intersection in disparate fields. Echoing contemporary surveys that document an unexpected religiosity in theoretical physicists, Bailey tells us that the best scientists do indeed possess poetical imaginations. All occupations well-pursued are in their own way divine, the author reiterates, and the writer or scientist expressing him- or herself is, in essence, enacting the poetic. The last essay in this grouping, "The Tones of Industry," is perhaps the most surprising of the great agriculturalist's oeuvre. In it, Bailey considers the untapped poetic, musical, and dramatic potential of the agrarian archenemy: industry.

What Literature Can Do for Us

Some of us do not enjoy nature because there is not enough sheer excitement in it.[1] It has not enough dash and go for this uneasy age; and this is the very reason why we need the solace and resource of nature so much. On looking over the lists of Christmas books, I was surprised to find how often the word "sensation" occurs. In the announcement of the forthcoming number of a magazine, I find twenty articles, of which at least nineteen are to be "tragic," "thrilling," "mystery-laden," or otherwise unusual. The twentieth one I hope to read. One would think that a piece of writing is valuable in proportion as it is racy, exciting, startling, astounding, striking, sensational. In these days of sensational sales, to have a book sell phenomenally well is almost a condemnation of it. An article or book that merely tells a plain story directly and well is too tame; so even when we write of nature we must pick out the unusual, then magnify and galvanize it. From this literature the reader goes out to nature and finds it slow and uninteresting; he must have a faster pace and a giddier whirl of events. He has little power to entertain himself; and, his eyes never having been trained to see what he looks at, he discovers nothing and the world is vacuous and void. He may find temporary relief in some entertainment provided for him out of hand, as the so-called news of the newspapers or some witless frippery on the stage. Yet, unless all poets and philosophers have misled us, the keenest and most resourceful delights that men have found have been the still small voices of the open fields.

There is another objection to much of the nature writing—the fact that it is unrepresentative of nature. It exploits the unusual and the exceptional, and therefore does not give the reader a truthful picture of common and average conditions. This has been true to some extent even of textbooks—they

1. The umbrella title for this excerpt is drawn from the subheading by the same name on p. 12 in Part I, "The Commonplace," from *Outlook to Nature* (New York: Macmillan, 1905). This passage includes pp. 12–15 and 22–25.

choose so-called "typical" forms and structures, forgetting that the typical examples exist only in books for purposes of definition. The best nature writing, as I conceive of it, is that which portrays the commonplace so truthfully and so clearly that the reader forthwith goes out to see for himself. Some day we shall care less for the marvelous beasts of some far-off country than for the mice and squirrels and woodchucks of our own fields. If I were a naturalist, I should go forthwith to study the mice and then write of them for all children; for, of all the untamed animals, what ones are known to greater number of children?—and yet do the children know except that they have been early taught by their elders to abhor these animals.

We need a new literature of nature and the open country, a literature that shall not be merely and plainly descriptive.[2] We need short, sharp, quick, direct, word-pictures that shall place the object before us as vividly as the painter would outline some strong figure with a few bold strokes of his brush. Every object and every common labor awaken some response beyond themselves, and this response can be set to words. The man employed at useful and spontaneous work is a poetic figure, full of prophecy and of hope. The cow in the field, the tree against the sky, the fields newly plowed, the crows flopping home at night, the man at his work, the woman at her work, the child at its play—these all are worth the stroke of the artist.

I saw a man walking across the fields, with spade on his shoulder and dog at his side; I saw his firm, long stride; I saw his left arm swing; I saw the weeds fall beneath his feet; I saw the broad straight path that he left in the grass. There were brown fields, and woods in the first tint of autumn. I saw birds; and in the distance was the rim of the sky. And beyond him, I saw the open ditch to which he was returning.

With the nature writers I like to include some of the authors who do not write specific natural history topics. If they write from the out-of-doors, with a keen love of it and a knowledge of what it comprises, adding to it touches of good human nature, then they lead men to the open as effectively as those to whom we customarily apply the term "nature writer." The landscape is as important as any object that it contains, and the human sentiment is more important than either. These writers invariably write the commonplace, and touch it into life and meaning. Of the greatest of these writers, to my thinking, is [Robert Louis] Stevenson—simple, direct, youthful, tender, and heartsome. His life was with nature; his work touches the cosmic and elemental.[3]

---

2. This sentence marks the beginning of the first full paragraph on p. 22. For concision, it leapfrogs from p. 15 to p. 22 after the sentence ending "to abhor these animals."

3. Bailey's twelve-line poetic ode to Robert Louis Stevenson has been excised here for concision.

I like to think that our nature poetry is also leading us natureward in a very practical way, since it is becoming more personal and definite, and brings us into closer touch with specific objects and demands greater knowledge of them.[4] It has been the progress of our attitude toward nature to add the concrete to the abstract; and this may be expected to proceed so far that every object of the environment and every detail of our lives will be touched with inspiration. If I cannot catch a note of inspiration from the plainest thing that I touch, then to that extent my life is empty and devoid of hope and outlook. The great voices appealed to the early Greeks—the thunder, the roaring wind, the roll of the waves, the noise of war; but we do not know that the shape of the leaf, and the call of the young bird, and the soft gray rain, appealed much to them. The Greek lyrics are mostly personal or personifying, and lack any intimate touch with the phases of natural phenomena. As men have come more and more to know the near-at-hand and the real in nature, this knowledge has been interpreted in the poetry; for poetry always reflects the spirit of the time. All English poetry illustrates this general tendency; but what we are in the habit of calling "nature poetry" is of comparatively recent growth. It is to be hoped that we shall never have less nature poetry that expresses the larger moods; but we must have more that is specific and concrete in natural history details, and which will still be poetry, for the race is coming nearer to the environment in which it lives. The individual seems sometimes to recapitulate the experience of the race; as each of us grows old and conventionalities lose their meaning and the small voices make a stronger appeal, we are conscious that we have had Wordsworth's experience [in "To the Daisy"]:

> In youth from rock to rock I went,
> From hill to hill in discontent
> Of pleasure high and turbulent,
> Most pleased when most uneasy;
> But now my own delights I make—
> My thirst from every rill can slake,
> And gladly Nature's love partake
> Of thee, sweet Daisy!

It is often said that as this is a practical age, with the industrialism developing everywhere, therefore poetry must die away. Nothing could be farther from the truth. It is true that industrialism is developing at great pace; this, in fact, is the glory of our time, for civilization has entered on a new epoch.

---

4. The first sentence following the original subhead (here omitted) entitled "Nature Poetry," p. 25.

219

Men's minds are concerned with things that never concerned them before; yet, the resources of the old earth have merely been touched here and there, and the wealth of mankind will increase. But all this does not mean that sentiment is to be crushed or that the horizon of imagination is to be contracted, but rather the reverse. The flights of science and of truth are, after all, greater than the flights of fancy. If sentiment is necessarily eliminated from business transactions, it is all the more important that it be added to the recreation and the leisure. The great constructive agencies of the time are essentially poetic; and the world never needed poetry so much as now. This thought is forcibly expressed in Charles Eliot Norton's advice, that has now been so effectively used by the press: "Whatever your occupation may be, and however crowded your hours with affairs, do not fail to secure at least a few minutes every day for refreshment of your inner life with a bit of poetry."

But this poetry of nature must be of the new kind. Perhaps the day of the formal "sustained" poem has passed—with its ambitious disquisitions, long periods, heavy rhetoric, labored metaphors. It is a question, also, whether even the sonnet, although highly artistic, is free and plastic enough to express the nature feeling of our time; for this feeling seems to be more and more impatient of historical limits and forms. The new nature poetry must be crystal clear, for we have no time for riddles, even though they are set in meter and rhyme. It must be definite, and it must apply. The best nature poetry will be hopeful, joyous, and modern. At least some of it must deal with objects, phenomena, and emotions that are common to common men: then it will become part of men's lives, not merely an accomplishment to be used with proper manners and on occasion. Perhaps this more vital song will relieve poetry writing of much that is too theoretical or fine-spun; and I hope that it may also divert the current from the weak and petty lovelorn type of verse-making which exploits personal love affairs that ought to be too private and sacred for publication and which in the end contributes nothing to the poetry of emotion.

This poetry, whether its flight is small or great, must be born of experience, and must be intrinsic; it must be the expression of a full heart, not the sentiment of a looker-on. No man whose heart is not full of the beauty and meaning of a leaf should write even a distich on a leaf. So, too, the nature poem of wide reach must be the poem of the man who is free. Such poetry must spring from the open air; perhaps it must be set to words there—at least outside the city. The city will have its great poems, but they will rise out of the city as Venus rose out of the sea. It seems to me that we have very little genuine nature poetry. Our poets, in spirit or in fact, now write largely from the city and the study outward, and their work is bookish. The product is the cultured poetry of the library and the study, and is under the influence of the schools. It continues to be burdened with outworn and useless metaphor, and it follows traditional forms of verse and line, as if verse and line were more than essence. Walt Whitman—poet of the commonplace—has most completely freed himself from the bondage of literary form; and he is only an earnest of what shall come. It is doubtful whether the great nature poet will be taught in the formal curricula of the schools. His spirit and his method will be as unconfined as the inaccessible mountains, the great plains, or the open sea. His poetry must be much more than pleasing and local: it must be rugged and continental.

It must be true that the appreciation of poetry is increasing; and poetry is prophecy. If it is not increasing, then our education is worse than most of us think; but if appreciation of poetry is increasing, then we are acquiring a stronger hold on aspirations that are simple and elemental and universal. I am constantly surprised at the poems that busy and practical men know; and also at the poetry that many busy men can write. There is reason to believe that there were never so many poets in the world as now. Poetry-making is not an occupation, but the incidental spark that strikes off from useful labor; it is the result of full and serious lives. The roll of machinery is rhythm and rhyme; the blowing of the wind is music.

It has been my good fortune to have had many years' experience in the teaching of farm boys. They are interesting boys—strong, virile, courageous. They have not been stuffed and pampered, and have not had too much schooling. They have had the tremendous advantage of having been let alone, and of having developed naturally. They hold their youth; their minds are capable of receiving new impressions with faith and enthusiasm. It is my habit to call these agricultural students together twice each month, and, amongst other exercises, to read them poetry. Usually at first they are surprised; they had not thought of it before; or they thought poetry is for girls: but they come again. They may hide it, but these farm boys are as full of sentiments as an egg of meat. There was one fellow [named Jenkins] who had to support himself and help members of his family. He was a good student, but the lines of his life had been hard. Whenever he called at my office it was to ask advice about money affairs or to tell me of difficulties that he feared he could not overcome. Apparently there was no sentiment in his life, and no room for it. One evening I read to the students Matthew Arnold's "Buried Life." The next day, Jenkins came to my office, entered hesitatingly as if requesting something that he might not have, and asked whether I would loan him the poem till he could learn it, for he could not afford to buy.

I believe, then, in the power of poetry—in its power to put a man at work with a song on his lips, and set the mind toward nature and naturalness.

VII. POETICS

I like the definite poem of a tree, or a stone, or a dog, or a garden, if only it tells the truth and stops when the truth is told. The old-time short nature poem was wont only to point a moral—usually dubious and far-fetched and factitious—having little vitality of its own. It really was not a nature poem, for the real nature poem is its own moral. The poems and stories of the Old Testament are always interesting to my students because they have something to say, they are direct, not surfeited with adjectives or burdened with rhetoric, and they are moral because they tell the truth and do not preach. We need to treasure the nature poem because it contains the elements of youth. So weary-old have we grown that we seem to be afraid to express our real selves; when now and then some person expresses himself in high places unconventionality and with native feeling, we hail him as a "strong man." It is only when we are with ourselves under the free open heaven that we seem to be able to feel things keenly and newly and freshly. When in the open I am hopeful and resilient; when in my study I am conventional and dull. I wrote this lecture in my study.

We need now and then to take ourselves away from men and the crowd and conventionalities, and go into silence, for the silence is the greatest of teachers. Walt Whitman expresses this well:

> When I heard the learn'd astronomer,
> When the proofs, the figures, were ranged in columns before me
> When I was shown the chart and diagrams, to add, divide, and measure
>   them,
> When I sitting heard the astronomer where he lectured with
>   much applause in the lecture-room,
> How soon unaccountable I became tired and sick,
> Till rising and gliding out I wander'd off by myself
> In the mystical and moist night-air, and from time to time,
> Look'd up in perfect silence at the stars.

The Threatened Literature

A fear seems to be abroad that the inquisitiveness and exactness of science will deprive literature of imagination and sympathy and will destroy artistic expression; and it is said that we are in danger of losing the devotional element in literature.[5] If these apprehensions are well founded, then do we have cause for alarm, seeing that literature is an immeasurable resource.

Great literature may be relatively independent of time and place, and this is beyond discussion here; but if the standards of interpretative literature are lowering it must be because the standards of life are lowering, for the attainment and the outlook of a people are bound to be displayed in its letters.

Perhaps our difficulty lies in a change in methods and standards rather than in essential qualities. We constantly acquire new material for literary use. The riches of life are vaster and deeper than ever before. It would be strange indeed if the new experience of the planet did not express itself in new literary form.

We are led astray by the fatal habit of making comparisons, contrasting one epoch with another. There may be inflexible souls among the investigators who see little or nothing beyond the set of facts in a little field, but surely the greater number of scientific men are persons of keen imagination and of broad interest in all conquests. Indeed, a lively imagination is indispensable in persons of the best attainments in science; it is necessary only that the imagination be regulated and trained. Never has it been so true that fact is stranger than fiction. Never have the flights of the poets been so evenly matched by the flights of science. All great engineers, chemists, physiologists, physicists work in the realm of imagination, of imagination that projects the unknown from the known. Almost do we think that the Roentgen ray, the wireless telegraphy, the analysis of the light of the stars, the serum control of disease are the product of what we might call pure fancy. The very utilities

5. From *The Holy Earth* (New York: Scribner, 1915), 124–129.

and conquests of modern society are the results of better imagination than the world has yet known. If it is true that the desire to measure and to analyze is now an established trait, equally is it true that it directs the mind into far and untried reaches; and if we have not yet found this range of inspiration in what is called artistic literature, it must be because literary criticism has not accepted the imagery of the modern world and is still looking for its art to the models of the past.

The models of the past are properly the standards for the performances of their time, but this does not constitute them the standards of all time or of the present time. Perhaps the writing of language for the sake of writing it is losing its hold; but a new, clear, and forceful literature appears. This new literature has its own criteria. It would be violence to judge it only by standards of criticism founded on Elizabethan writings. We do not descend into crude materialism because we describe the materials of the cosmos; we do not eliminate imagination because we desire that it shall have meaning; we do not strip literature of artistic quality because it is true to the facts and the outlook of our own time.

It may be admitted that present literature is inadequate, and that we are still obliged to go to the former compositions for our highest artistic expressions. Very good. Let us hope that we shall never cease to want these older literatures. Let us hope that we shall never be severed from our past. But perhaps the good judge in a coming generation, when the slow process of elimination has perfected its criticism, will discover something very noble and even very artistic in the abundant writing of our day. Certainly he will note the recovery from the first excess of reaction against the older orders, and he will be aware that at this epoch man began anew to express his social sense in a large way, as a result of all his painstaking studies in science. Even if he should not discover the highest forms of literary expression, he might find that here was the large promise of a new order. Possibly he would discover major compositions of the excellence of which we ourselves are not aware.

It is less than forty years since Darwin and less than fifty years since Agassiz. It is only twenty years since Pasteur. It is only a century and a quarter since Franklin, fifty years since Faraday, less than twenty-five since Tyndall. It is sixty years since Humboldt glorified the earth with the range of his imagination. It is not so very far even if we go back to Newton and to Kepler. Within the span of a century we count name after name of prophets who have set us on a new course. So complete has been the revolution that we lost our old bearings before we had found the new. We have not yet worked out the new relationships, nor put into practice their moral obligations, nor have we grasped the fullness of our privileges. We have not yet made the new knowledge consciously into a philosophy of life or incorporated it completely into working attitudes of social equity. Therefore, not even now are we ripe for the new literature.

We have gone far enough, however, to know that science is not unsympathetic and that it is not contemptuous of the unknown. By lens and prisms and balance and line we measure minutely whatever we can sense; then with bared heads we look out to the great unknown and we cast our lines beyond the stars. There are no realms beyond which the prophecy of science would not go. It resolves the atom and it weights the planets.

Among the science men I have found as many poetic souls as among the literary men, although they may not know so much poetry, and they are not equally trained in literary expression; being free of the restraint of conventional criticism, they are likely to have a peculiarly keen and sympathetic projection. Close dissection long continued may not lead to free artistic literary expression; this is as true of literary anatomy as of biological anatomy: but this does not destroy the freedom of other souls, and it may afford good material for the artist.

Two kinds of popular writing are confused in the public mind, for there are two classes that express the findings of scientific injury. The prevailing product is that which issues from establishments and institutions. This is supervised, edited, and made to conform; it is the product of our perfected organizations and has all the hardness of its origin. The other literature is of a different breed. It is the expressions of personality. The one is a useful and necessary public literature of record and advice; the other literature of outlook and inspiration. The latter is not to be expected from the institutions, for it is naturally the literature of freedom.

My reader now knows my line of approach to the charge that literature is in danger of losing its element of devotion, and hereby lies the main reason for introducing this discussion into my little book. We may be losing the old literary piety and the technical theology, because we are losing the old theocratic outlook on creation. We also know that the final control of human welfare will not be governmental or military, and we shall some day learn that it will not be economic as we now prevailingly use the word. We have long since forgotten that once it was patriarchal. We shall know the creator in the creation. We shall derive more of our solaces from the creation and in the consciousness of our right relations to it. We shall be more fully aware that righteousness inheres in honest occupation. We shall find some bold and free way in which the human spirit may express itself.

The Tones of Industry

One of the clearest notes of our time is the recognition of the holiness of industry and the attempt to formulate the morals of it.[6] We accept this fact indirectly by the modern endeavor to give the laboring man his due.

The handworker is more or less elemental, dealing directly with the materials. We begin to recognize these industries in literature, in sculpture, and in painting; but we do not yet very consciously or effectively translate them into music.

It is to be recognized, of course, that melody is emotional and dynamic not imitative, that its power lies in suggestion rather than in direct representation, and that its language is general; with all this I have nothing to do. [Georges] Meunier has done much with his chisel to interpret the spirit of constructive labor and to develop its higher significance. His art is indeed concrete and static, and sculpture and music are not to be compared; yet it raises the question whether there may be other bold extensions of art.

The primitive industries must have been mostly silent, when there were no iron tools, when fire felled the forest tree and hollowed the canoe, when the parts in construction were secured by thongs, and when the game was caught in silent traps or by the swift noiseless arrow and spear. Even at the Stone Age the rude implements and the materials must have been mostly devoid of resonance. But now industry has become universal and complex, and it has also become noisy, so noisy that we organize to protect ourselves from becoming distraught.

And yet a workshop, particularly if it works in metal, is replete with tones that are essentially musical. Workmen respond readily to unison. There are melodies that arise from certain kinds of labor. Much of our labor is rhythmic. In any factory driven by power there is a fundamental rhythm and motion, tying all things together. I have often thought, standing at the threshold

6. From *The Holy Earth* (New York: Scribner, 1915), 120–123.

of a mill, that it might be possible somewhere by careful forethought to eliminate the clatter and so to organize the work as to develop a better expression in labor. Very much do we need to make industry vocal.

It is worth considering, also, whether it is possible to take over into music any of these sounds of industry in a new way, that they may be given meanings they do not now possess.

In all events, the poetic element in industry is capable of great development and of progressive interpretation; and poetry is scarcely to be disassociated from sound. All good work well-done is essentially poetic to the sensitive mind; and when the work is the rhythm of many men acting in unison, the poetry has voice.

> The striking of the rivet
> The purr of a drill
> The crash of a steam shovel
> The plunge of a dredge
> The buzz of a saw
> The roll of belts and chains
> The whirl of spindles
> The hiss of steam
> The tip-tap of valves
> The undertone rumble of a mill
> The silent intent of men at work
> The talk of men going to their homes:
> These are all the notes of great symphonies.

Nor should I stop with the industries of commerce and manufacture. There are many possibilities in the sounds and voices that are known of fisherfolk and campers and foresters and farmers. Somehow we should be able to individualize these voices and to give them an artistic expression in some kind of human composition. There are rich suggestions in the voices of the farmyard, the calls of wild creatures, the tones of farm implements and machinery, the sound of the elements, and particularly in the relations of all these to the pauses, the silences, and the distances beyond.

Whether it is possible to utilize any of these tones and voices artistically is not for a layman to say; but the layman may express the need that he feels.

VIII APPRECIATIONS

Weather and wind and waning moon
Plain and hilltop under sky
Ev'ning, morning and blazing noon,
Brother of all the world am I.
The pine tree, linden, and the maize
The insect, squirrel, and the kine
All-natively they live their days—
As they live theirs, so I live mine.
I know not where, I know not what—
Believing none and doubting none
Whatso befalls it counteth not—
Nature and time and I are one.

—From "Brotherhood," *Wind and Weather*
(New York: Scribner, 1916)

This grouping of Liberty Hyde Bailey appreciations bubbles up from the emotive wellspring of soulful agrarianism: gratitude. To begin, "Apple Tree" offers fitting overture for a larger Bailey symphony of grace notes and blessings, as the apple was Bailey's most enduring botanical passion. The essay, sketched while Professor Bailey researched the palm and other tropical plants in the Caribbean, is infused with nostalgia, thanksgiving, and wonderment. Reminiscent of Robert Frost's desire to be a "swinger of birches," Bailey here reflects, "And often in my wanderings I promise myself that when I reach home I shall see the apple tree as I had never seen it before." The prose odes and elegies that follow "Apple Tree" suggest the particular pleasures and provocations of the farmer's holy life—wind, rain, weed, peach, horse, evening, morning. Notable among these benedictions, "Wind" equals John Muir's most transcendent writing in "Windstorm in the Forest" from *The Mountains of California,* and "Horse" captures the warm nostalgia of John Burroughs's "Phases of Farm Life" from *In the Catskills.* Throughout, Bailey draws on a vocabulary of praise as precise and moving as his lexicon of criticism. The author's wonder-filled frontier childhood also resurfaces again and again in these tales of halcyon days, suggesting the circumspection of a seasoned man coming full circle.

Apple Tree

The wind is snapping in the bamboos, knocking together the resonant canes and weaving the myriad flexile wreaths above them.[1] The palm heads rustle with a brisk crinkling music. Great ferns stand in the edge of the forest, and giant arums cling their arms about the trunks of trees and rear their dim jacks-in-the-pulpit far in the branches; and in the greater distance I know that green parrots are flying in twos from tree to tree. The plant forms are strange and various, making mosaic of contrasting range of leaf size and leaf shape, palm and grass and fern, epiphyte and liana and clumpy mistletoe, of grace and clumsiness and even misproportion, a tall thick landscape all mingled into a symmetry of disorder that charms the attention and fascinates the eye.

It is a soft and delicious air wherein I sit. A torrid drowse is in the receding landscape. The people move leisurely, as befits the world where there is no preparation for frost and no urgent need of laborious apparel. There are tardy bullock carts, unconscious donkeys, and men pushing vehicles. There are odd products and unaccustomed cakes and cookies on little stands by the roadside, where the turbaned vendor sits on the ground unconcernedly.

There are strange fruits in the carts, on the donkeys that move down the hillsides from distant plantations in the heart of the jungle, on the trees by winding road and thatched cottage, in the great crowded markets in the city. I recognize coconuts and mangoes, star apples and custard apples and cherimoyas, papayas, guavas, mamones, pomegranates, figs, christophines, and the varied range of citrus fruits. There are also great polished apples in the markets, coming from cooler regions, tied by their stems, good to look at but impossible to relish; and I understand how these people of the tropics

---

1. From *The Apple-Tree* (New York: Macmillan, 1922), 7–9. The original title of this essay was "Where There Is No Apple Tree." The title has been truncated here in keeping with the other one-word titles in this section of appreciations.

think the apple an inferior fruit, so successfully do the poor varieties stop the desire for more. There are vegetables I have never seen before.

I am conscious of a slowly moving landscape with people and birds and beasts of burden and windy vegetation, of prospects in which there are no broad, smooth farm fields with fences dividing them, of scenery full of herbage, in which every lineament and action incite me and stimulate my desire for more, of days that end suddenly in the blackness of night.

Yet, somehow, I look forward to the time when I may go to a more accustomed place. Either from long association with other scenes or because of some inexpressible deficiency in this tropic splendor, I am not satisfied even though I am exuberantly entertained. Something I miss. For weeks I wondered what single element I missed most. Out of the numberless associations of childhood and youth and eager manhood it is difficult to choose one that is missed more than another. Yet one day it came over me startlingly that I missed the apple tree—the apple tree, the sheep, and the milch cattle!

The farm home with its commodious house, its greensward, its great barn and soft fields and distant woods, and the apple tree by the woodshed; the good home at the end of the village with its sward and shrubbery, and apple roof-tree; the orchard, well kept, trim and apple-green, yielding its wagon-loads of fruits; the old tree on the hillside, in the pasture where generations of men have come and gone and where houses have fallen to decay; the odor of the apples in the cellar in the cold winter night; the feasts around the fireside—I think all these pictures conjure themselves in my mind to tantalize me of home. And often in my wanderings I promise myself that when I reach home I shall see the apple tree as I had never seen it before. Even its bark and its gnarly trunk will hold converse with me, and its first tiny leaves of the budding spring will herald me a welcome. Once again I shall be a youth with the apple tree, but feeling more than the turbulent affection of transient youth can understand. Life does not seem regular and established when there is no apple tree in the yard and about the buildings, no orchards blooming in the May and laden in the September, no baskets heaped with the crisp smooth fruits; without all these I am still a foreigner, sojourning in a strange land.

Wind

It is explained that wind is air in motion.[2] So be it; but this does not tell me why the wind brought me the scent of April or roared down my chimney when the storm drove over the hills.

The wind is taken out of the limbo of conjecture and is a subject for scientific study; it is so with all the phenomena of nature; yet in all this reassuring progress, not one whit of human interest has been lost. The mysteries are more rational, but they are mysteries still. To the accumulated legend and literature of the holy past we may add the noble prospect of scientific discovery. No longer are the "windows of heaven" taken literally, to be opened by angels and the storms let loose; for natural science is not literal and the imagination is stimulated, disciplined, and set free.

The fancy of the winds runs across human history. The winds were within the caprice of the gods and demons, held in leash for the good or the punishment of men, subject to favor and petition. They were amenable to conjuration, as testified by the selling of favorable winds to mariners in medieval times. Under the domination of the Prince of the Power of the Air, the weather had a theological explanation. Only within a century have we acknowledged the winds to be governed by the operation of law; and to this day there are those who will not understand and who look into the wind with superstitious fear.

No more does Aeolus hold the winds in his bag; the ancient explanations have lost their reality and are now poetic; even if we know how and whence the North wind comes we still may speak of it, on fitting occasions, as old Boreas in his great cloak and high boots sending chill into the hearts of men. With reverence for the past and with admiration for the beauty of personification, we may still contemplate the Tower of the Winds at Athens,

2. From *The Harvest of the Year to the Tiller of the Soil* (New York: Macmillan, 1927), 143–149.

and wonder at its water-clock contrivance. There is Boreas depicted; and also Kaikias, the Northeast wind, rattling his slingstones of snow and hail; Apheliotes, the East wind, with fruit and flowers in his mantle; Eurus the Southeast wind, bringing the dawn; Notus, the South wind, pouring his warm libation from his jar; Lips, the Southwest wind, who still brings the sailor home; Zephyrus, gentle, barefooted West wind, youthful and lightly clad, scattering flowers as he flees; Argestes or Sciron, the Northwest wind, with the pot of charcoals to conjure hot dry weather. Beauty still is in the mind's image of the wind, and poets still may weave its intangible substance into dreams.

The wind is the universal renovator of the earth. Imagine, if you can, a world of stationary atmosphere. It would not be a place for human life. No clouds would float across the sky; no breeze before the rain bring tidings of relief, in fact no rain; no panorama of the moving fields of grain; no roar across the landscape when winter hunts the shepherd home; no moving whisper of the dawn and no gentle balm of twilight; no sail on any sea, no freedom in the heat and cold. The wind is in every ear of corn, in the flowers on the plains, in the bounding life of herds. The calm indeed is pleasant when the temperature is agreeable, but only by contrast with the wind.

The air movement may be silent but the wind gives tone to everything it meets, although often inaudible to all but the attentive ear; it is the universal voice of nature. Trees become vocal; desert sands respond; lattices and eaves at night are wide awake; the seas and lakes become sonorous. The high wind lashes across the fields and the low wind breathes in the grass; the surface of the earth finds voice and expresses itself when the wind comes. Language is full of the voices of the winds; they blow and sigh and wail; they whistle and are shrill; they moan on the corners; they rustle in the leaves; they shriek over the housetops; they sing in the wires; in the quiet days they are gently astir in hanging boughs and whisper as they pass. And again the voices are majestic, and constitute the major intonations. In Alexander Smith's *Life Drama* the wind is a "grand old harper" who "smote his thunder-harp of pines."

Those who have ears may catch the sounds of the winds in every mood, and be comforted. Little do we recognize how much the wind is part of the circumstance of life. But if we bring together the words for the wind experiences, we realize at once how closely we have lived with winds. A good half hundred words are in the English. Aside from the names of the major kinds of winds themselves, we know in daily speech the little variants, the puff of wind, the gust, the whiff, the blast, the breeze, the zephyr, the squall and gale and storm and tempest; and we apply our own life process to it when we speak of a breath of air.

The farmer has the wind in his face. He meets it squarely. It is his by right of dominion. He does not avoid it, even if now and then he must seek protection. So much is it a part of him that he does not think of it, yet he would not be without it. He knows, even if only subconsciously, that it is the activating force of his situation. It enables him to make his crops. In olden time it ground his grain, and to this day it pumps his water although its place is taken more and more by oil and gasoline, but probably there would be no gasoline had there not been a motile atmosphere in the dim ages.

I visited a farmer who had harnessed his streams and piped his springs to buildings and had otherwise utilized his natural resources; his outstanding regret was the fact that he could find no useful work for the wind to do and it was going to waste as it passed over his farm, thus expressing the old innate conviction that the wind belonged to him for his use; but the wind was nevertheless aiding in pumping water into the cornstalks that he would soon cut and put into the silo.

The wind is the index of the changes in the weather, pointing the direction in twig and grass and drifting things and impressing it on the cheeks and the accent of the breath. Once it was supposed that winds have no directions of their own, but waft and wander without hindrance everywhere. This idea is reflected in the saying that inconstant and irresponsible folk are as fickle as the wind; and the vane is an emblem of all unsteadiness. A person may be a weathercock. Yet since Benjamin Franklin traced the circuitous storm, we know that winds have routes or at least have reasons; not even the winds are free from restraint; and some day, when the upper atmosphere is better known and sun relationship more closely understood, we shall probably have a new kind of prediction of wind and weather.

Yet the wind is the earth's rover. Whatever may be the physics of the air's motion, the wind as we imagine it sweeps far over the earth. We think of it, in the northern hemisphere, as bringing the cold from the North and the warmth from the South, the dust from the roads and plains; it drives the birds far out to sea, and fills the sails of big and little ships. It is a sensation when one finds oneself with the sun far to the northward, and the winds bring the cold from the South. But wherever we are, the winds provide the circulation on the planet. Deeper than the deepest ocean is the sea of air. At the bottom of this sea we live. We could not stand alone without its support. In the ocean are the different strata of life from the bottom to the surface. The swimming things do not live indiscriminately all through the deeps of the ocean, but each kind has its vertical range. There are currents and rivers in the ocean. So in the sea of air, the flying things have their vertical ranges. The songbirds and the sparrows and the insects are near the ground. The swallows and swifts fly higher up. Hawks and vultures may be higher

233

still. I was much impressed as a young boy with Sir S. W. Baker's account [*Ismailia*] of the vultures that he saw appearing first as black specks in the blue, as he lay on his back in the regions of the Nile tributaries beside a carcass of the hunt: how high had they been and how did they know? And rivers in the air are winds, with which vultures and other birds may wing and float, which brings us the warm soft rains of spring, the deluges of summer, the hails and snows of hoary winter, or the drenching downpours of the rainy season. Very wonderful are these rivers and minor currents that condition the life of vultures and of cattle and crops and men.

The winds we cannot control. In spite of all our cunning, they still will blow. Here man must have recourse to his powers of adaptation. He fits himself to them. In this way is he disciplined, and in this way likewise does he thrive. Some things we must accept. I like [James Russell] Lowell's statement in his "Democracy" that the only argument available with an east wind is to put on your overcoat. Indeed, "the wind bloweth where it listeth." In the presence of the wind, morning, noon, and blessed night, the man of the out-of-doors recognizes his kinship in nature. If you are of the open and fear not, make for yourself a poem of the winds. It should express the inner moods of your life.

Rain

This morning the boughs are heavy with rain.[3] The herbs are laden to the ground, some of them with their heads caught in the soil. The downpour began before midnight. We were aroused by the wind in the trees and the patter on the roof.

We lay awake to hear the drift in the leaves, until the roar was in the spouts; then sleep was sweet in the balm of the rain. At last the heat was broken. We were eager in the early morning to feel the freshness and to see the new earth. For still Elijah calls to Ahab: "Get thee up...; for there is the sound of abundance of rain." By eight o'clock the sun was out, and the bright fresh light glistened in every tree and bush. The grass was deep with hanging drops. The birds seemed unusually alert. The sky was clear and blue, washed clean of its dust. No work could be begun in garden or fields, although we were full of energy that the rain had brought. We were keen to be abroad and see the effects in ditches and tilled lands. Everything would be rinsed and fresh. Barefoot boys and girls were already in the pools, feeling the silt between their toes. But for us, grown old with conventionalities, it was either rubber boots or remain dry shod about the buildings. When would the grass be dry again?

By ten o'clock the boughs had resumed their normal position, the weight having been removed before our very eyes and yet we had not seen it go. No magic carpet or golden wand of the old fairy books could have wrought a more complete wizardry. Large drops were still hanging from the points of leaves, and little corpuscles still lay on leaves that were crumpled like cups. The herbs had begun to straighten by some force within them that we could not comprehend. The grass tops seemed dry but big drops would shake from them; the bottom still was full of wet.

3. From *The Harvest of the Year to the Tiller of the Soil* (New York: Macmillan, 1927), 150–156.

By noon the herbage was dry, except in deep and shady places. The heavy wet had vanished somewhere, and we could not recall it if we would. We knew it had gone into thin air, but if we had not been born to such experience, we should have stood dumb in wonder. The bare earth in the tilled fields was still wet and soft; unlike the leaves, the soil was soaked with free water and it would be giving up its moisture for a day or two, being wet on top as the water came up from below, a process that filled us all day with something like a new sensation. The crops looked their best. The herbage shone green, the wilt was gone, the corn leaves had unrolled.

There is tonic in the air today. The droning heats of midsummer have given way to the sweeping surge of the downpour. The rain barrels and tubs all are full. Crops are at work again. The livestock has its old-time animation. The ground exhales a challenge to new effort, and we know that the earth is young and that its power has not waned; it is renewed when the solvent comes. Now that the spell is broken we shall expect more rain. We shall make good crops of corn and late potatoes, and are sure the ground will be in condition to fit for winter wheat. The fall pastures will be good. The silos will be filled. Wells will have deep, sweet water. Little creeks that have been dry and weedy since May will run again.

Today is "growing weather," even though the season is late. The farmer knows what this weather is, but no man can define it or measure it. It is like a sensation, so indefinite is it and so elusive to describe and yet so real. The best things of life cannot be inventoried, and for the exalted moments we really have no symbols or names.

In all nature there is nothing so rejuvenating and so freshening as rain. It seems to arouse the very essence of all things inanimate and to awaken the souls of things that have being. There is life-giving vigor in it. So unlike is it to ground and rocks and grass and trees and animals and buildings, even to brooks and lakes, that it seems like a drift from another world or some other existence when the drops shuttle down between the leaves, strike on shingle and pane, burst on the rocks, and send up bubbling columns on the pools. All things look up to the sky and rejoice when the rain is past and when the sun shines again between broken, rapid clouds. The crops will drink it in. The animals will dry themselves and go far afield. I do not yet understand why there is such exuberance in mere wetness.

There are many kinds of rain, the "small rain" and "the great rain" as the King James version has it, the slow drifting rain that quietly and softly covers the earth, the mist of imperceptible drops that broods the landscape like a cloud and deposits itself as a soaking film on the garments, the windy rain that drives through the shutters and seeks every crevice, the roaring deluge that sweeps over the earth in fury and buries the land in torture and flood.

Out of the same sky it all comes, wrought by the same forces but in varying degrees of intensity; and if we were privileged to see the drops forming I fancy we should not catch the differences. It is a marvelous thing that clouds should hold so much water that they can discharge torrents on everything beneath them.

Birds and other animals partake of the rain more than we. I am always interested to watch their behavior in a shower. Human beings speak of being soaked, but they are thinking of clothes, as if raiment were part of them as are feathers or wool—do we not speak of being "wet to the skin" as if the deluge had gone clear into us? And do we not pell-mell to shelter when the rain comes? Who goes afield in the rain? And yet if you would know the fields and the woods and marshes, prepare yourself well and take a leisurely walk when rain is abroad.

Yet rain is not always a blessing to the farmer. It may prevent the plowing, the seeding, the tillage; weeds grow provokingly fast; the grain sprouts in the shock and the harvest is lost. These are indeed misfortunes. They are risks of the occupation that must be reckoned in advance. A varied husbandry suffers least because some of the effort is sure to be saved even in the worst times. In periods of long wet weather I am glad of meadows and pastures that are more or less perennial and do not require tillage, and of animals that grow and yield their milk in spite of rain. The farm has been ditched and shaped to take care of the runoff and to circumvent the ravages of erosion. The buildings, let us hope, are in good repair, the yards graded for drainage and with good walks to all essential points, the ditches and gutters free, the tools and food supplies well housed. The farmer is then conscious that he has done his best to adapt himself to his environment, and the rest is taken care of by an attitude of resignation and a calm acceptance of the natural hazards.

The hazards are in every occupation and business. They are in life, an integral part of it; otherwise we should live always without gratitude and thereby miss the great satisfactions. It is in the fact that most of the year is congenial to farming that the recompense lies.

The wild things also suffer from too much rain and too little rain, from burning heat and stinging cold, and for food in the bargain. They and we are parts in nature, partakers in the great adjustment. The earth was not made for man alone; we must give and take with the rest; but we hold the additional privilege to appreciate our situation and to be glad that we may know the rain. The naturalist stops not for fear of rain. I have never known a real farmer to quit the occupation because of the weather.

Through untraveled spaces the sun rays come. Water on the rolling earth becomes invisible and is lifted to the sky. Clouds form across the firmament.

VIII. APPRECIATIONS

Currents and countercurrents play an invisible pageantry. The drama breaks in lightning and rolls the welkin with thunder. The imperceptible water is condensed to liquid and drops upon the earth to enliven it. Again the water is vaporized and lifted; again the rain descends, and again the beans and the cotton and cattle and men are renewed. Here is the recurring miracle of the ages of the earth, from the first man until the last; no wonder there is the impulse to uncover the head when the shower comes!

Weed

They called it a weed, but it was only a thistle.[4] If thistles were more useful than wheat, we should call them a crop and the wheat would be a weed. Professor [Isaac Phillips] Roberts used to say that the worst weed in cornfields is corn, by which he meant that corn is customarily planted too thick. I sowed petunias in my garden; they made a glorious sight and my man was proud of them. Next year I planted onions on the place; the petunias came up again from self-sown seeds and he cursed them as weeds. If next year I plant petunias again and onions come up, then the onions will be weeds. Much time has been wasted in the effort to define a weed. We need no definition, but only a statement: a weed is a plant that is not wanted.

This statement I have made so many times that I have forgotten it, yet repetition may give it some standing. At all events, a weed is a plant. It surely is not wanted. In addition, most weeds have no direct uses to man, although we are fond of pigweed and dandelion greens, so much so that dandelions are cultivated for the purpose and they are no longer weeds until the area is needed for beans. Sweet clover, Johnson grass, and filaree are crops when wanted but nuisances when not wanted. Hemp becomes a rampant intruder. Celery and radish and fennel have run loose in California. The lantana we cultivate so carefully for its bloom in greenhouses and in the open in warm countries is a great pest in Hawaii. Cardoons have swept the pampas.

It is often said that a weed is a plant out of place, but this is not so. Nothing is more in place than a weed. There are "weedy plants," by which it is meant that they have good powers of persistence and propagation and are more or less unattractive and they have the companionable habit of following man in his travels; they are good colonizers; they make the most of

4. From *The Harvest of the Year to the Tiller of the Soil* (New York: Macmillan, 1927), 159–164.

opportunities; they are prompt, always on time, faithful in adversity, and have other commendable qualities. I admire the way they make use of all the corners and odd places that men neglect or overlook. I heard a man fulminating at the docks that grew back of the woodshed, but I did not see that it was the fault of the docks.

Weeds are quick advertisers of poor farming and of too-much-to-do and of neglect. They are great schoolmasters; this I have also said so many times that I have forgotten it. They enforce tillage at all inconvenient times. They have kept men going from the time men first began to till the earth, or until a man gave up and then they took possession and kept the ground in condition until another man came.

Some weeds are real invaders, conquerors of well-tilled fields. These must be met by outright effort, perhaps by a change in rotation or in the crop scheme. The first consideration is not how they came there but why they thrive so lustily. Some of them make use of poor land; but in general a great abundance of successful weeds is a compliment to a man's soil.

Weeds are the great commoners of the vegetable world. They are no respecters of persons. There is no aristocracy among them nor pride of breeding; yet I suspect that if the truth were known we should find good genetics to have been in operation; this is suggested in their success. Weeds must profit by the "unintentional culture" named by Darwin. What might they become if intentionally cultivated? Yet many of them are well-tilled, or at least they take advantage of the preparation and tilling; in the Corn Belt the pigweeds may be as good as the corn.

The earth would be bare and bald indeed were it not for the weeds. Man tills only a small part of the land he has cleared. He leaves much of it furrowed, scarred, and hard-featured. The weeds of one kind or another take up the task of recovering it. The gullying stops. Mold forms. All the biological processes of soil building go forward. The waste places about man's slovenly habitations are covered; we speak of ragweed and plantain as ugly plants, but this is because of their association with man's unkempt by-places and wastes.

Every weed means something. There is good reason why it grows there rather than elsewhere, why it prefers one region or soil or exposure. Sometimes its presence is indication that it has a life cycle similar to that of the plant with which it associates, as the cockle in the wheat, and the late annual weeds that take advantage of the cessation of tillage when the crop is "laid by." It is interesting to inquire why mulleins and evening primroses are partial to old, dry grasslands; why knotweed and broad-leaved plantain cover hard-tramped yards; why tarweed, mustard, and burdocks usurp vacant lots; why pusley is unknown in some places.

We allow no sentiment to attach to weeds, yet the essential interest is there. Let me tell you a story. It was in a Taoist temple far away in Honan [China]. Strange were the rites of the priests before the idols. Every utensil, every rude piece of furniture, the food wherewith to find sustenance for the tramps in the torturing heat and wet, the outlines of the clustered buildings, the speech and the conduct of the few people on this borderland, were all outlandish to an intruder from the occident. The nights came down like a pall of loneliness over the shaven hills, the doors were bolted, and the morning was far away. Even the plants, the birds, and the insects were strange. But there on the old stone temple wall grew the catnip, the same catnip that is under my window in America, the same that has greeted me in many wanderings in other lands. What memories it held, and what sweeps of the earth's surface were in its crenate leaves and its odor! Farmyards and castles, fields at evening, walks where every soul was a stranger, picturesque walls and ruins, lost days of youth with fragrant catnip tea, folklore, herbarium at home, the years that have crowded each other so fast and so fast—these were all in the catnip plants that grew in the chinks of the old wall of the temple in China.

Often am I impressed that travelers never see the weeds, and we know that other folk spurn them; and yet they are messengers sent around the world, the foreguard of comradeship, the perfect adaptation to all the conditions and needs of life, the tell-tales of old routes of trade. I have learned to love the weeds, so often have they been my companions on solitary journeys. Always do I look for them, as I look for old friends. Rank and raw, uncouth, broken and torn and ragged, often the bearers of heavy odors, asking no quarter, yielding no treasure, the weeds are the fellow rovers on the pathways of life.

Nor was the catnip the only old acquaintance back in China far from the thoroughfares of travel. In the yard of the temple were plantain, wild carrot, the sprawling mallow bearing the "cheeses" of childhood, and the black nightshade. Nearby were smartweeds and docks, foxtail grass, and peppergrass; and in one corner was a lusty plant of fennel, the same fennel that I found growing shoulder high in my garden when I came home. I was not so very far away, with so many good friends to meet me.

The weeds will not release their guardianship. Their hosts will contend with men wherever farmers break the earth. As the contests close, with the more careful use of land, the struggle of the opposing powers will become more intense. I have no fear of the outcome. I like to think of farmers, in the long conflicts, as conquering men.

Peach

Here I hold a peach.[5] It is a shapely oblong-spherical body nearly three inches in diameter, pleasant to clasp in the fingers, choice in its fragrance, captivating in its intergrade of tints. I do not know why it came here. I know that last winter a bare tree stood in yonder orchard, giving no sign of any intention but to be a bare tree. Then one day it shook itself loose in the glory of the resurrection we know as spring, and a sheet of pink brilliancy covered it.

The blossoms fell. Leaves came. A little object began to swell on a last year's twig, white-gray and fuzzy and solid. A brown, dry, papery ring fell from its end. The threadlike point withered and dropped away. The object gradually grew, we do not know why, it became as large as a marble and almost as hard, the white-gray fuzz turned to green, a groove showed along its side. Presently it took form, a blush was on the sunny side, and a passer-by exclaimed, "Oh, there is a peach."

A man from Mars, perhaps one no farther away than the depths of the great city yonder, seeing this savory fruit in my hand and the flexile tree in the orchard, would not connect one with the other.

Out of the tree, bare but a few months ago, this great peach has come, the birth of a twig no thicker than my pencil. Tree and twig and peach all came out of the soil and the air. This peach is oxygen, yet you never saw oxygen to recognize it as a separate substance; it is hydrogen, yet you have not seen hydrogen as an entity; it is carbon, the carbon you see in yonder smoke; it is nitrogen, that you have not perceived as such although you are always within it; it is calcium, magnesium, phosphorus, that you have seen only in their compounds; it is iron, the iron that is in the locomotive even now belching to start from the station over there; it is potassium, and other elements beside.

5. From *The Harvest of the Year to the Tiller of the Soil* (New York: Macmillan, 1927), 165–168. The first paragraph of "Peach" has been omitted for concision.

It is water—water delicately and deliciously flavored with many intricate compounds. Perhaps this peach is nearly ninety percent water, yet so nicely is the fluid held in fiber and cell that I revolve the fruit as I may and it does not spill.

This peach is sunshine. It is night, the twilight, and the dawn. It is dew and rain. It is noon, and wind, and weather. It is heat and cold. It is the sequence of the seasons, winter and spring, summer and autumn, and winter again, all of which have gone into the tree that gave it birth.

It is the linkage of the elements and the days, and the showers that freshen the earth. The peach is more, even, than all this: it is a living thing, vital with its own protoplasm, performing a thousand secrets hidden deep in its cells, containing its own energy to assimilate and to grow and to catch the tints of the rainbow and the fragrance of clean, fresh winds.

Here with light pressure I part the fruit in halves. The aroma is an elixir. The wrinkled pit or stone is in the center, surrounded by a darker luster like an aureole; for securely inside this stone lies the mysterious kernel, which is an embryo peach tree; and next year the embryo will not forget to grow, if buried in the ground, nor fail to make a peach tree; and in the years to come, when you and I shall not be here to see, it or its progeny will bear peaches still.

The continuity of the centuries is in the flat kernel within this stony pit. I do not know why a peach pit and not a plum pit is in this place; I do not know whence on the earth the peach came; I do not know how or why this fruit chose or elaborated its nutrients in such proportions as to make itself a peach and not an apricot. Had I before me unlabelled chemical analyses of a peach and an apricot I suppose I could not tell which was which, so nearly would they be alike; size, shape, color, texture of skin and flesh, season, most of the attributes that distinguish the two fruits to us, might not be shown. Yet here is the peach in my hand, perfect and complete; it is mine.

You have made the conditions right. You have chosen the land that the tree might thrive. You have tilled the soil. You have protected the tree from enemies. You have guarded it for several or many years. You have beheld the miracle.

Horse

Whatever may be the case in the present hour, in my youth every farm boy must have a colt of his own.[6] This colt was to be of the driving horse type; the boy would break him and train him and have visions of a red buggy with spindle spokes, and felloes with black lines and bowed thills with stripy ornaments. The harness would be of the lightest and simplest fashion, without breeching or collar or hames; only a breast collar would answer for the smart turnout that was in the boy's mind; and the horse of his fancy would be guided by his word, with the least possible attention to the reins. The animal would be groomed and polished and petted, the last thought before going to school and the first thought on coming home.

I suppose this youthful energy is now expended on an automobile. But the effect on the boy will be far different. In America, where every farm has had a horse and usually several of them (because of the large farms and long distances of travel and abundant, cheap feed), the breaking and training of the colts has had a marked influence in training the boys to self-reliance, deft handicraft, good judgment, and quick decision. The alertness of the farm boy has been due in no small degree to his handling of the horse. The boy has become a schoolmaster, a trainer of animals, almost before he entered his teens; for the horse is largely what his trainer makes him. Here is his first exercise of the dominion that belongs to a man. As a colt is more than a machine, and as he grows into horsehood gradually and as all the care is associated with processes of life, the boy comes into a variety of contacts that he meets in no other way. The care of a favorite horse when sick calls for sympathy and patience. I wonder whether the farm boys of the next generation will have missed a resource of high value.

6. From *The Harvest of the Year to the Tiller of the Soil* (New York: Macmillan, 1927), 171–179. For concision, this excerpt begins with the seventh paragraph of the original, p. 171.

To those of us who were first associated with oxen and logging and heavy, old lumbering wagons, the horse brought a quality of life that I fear is not recognized or appreciated by those of modern time. The quick movements, the high head, the spirited eye, the style of the horse, appealed to the imagination in those bucolic bovine days, and the whirl of the buggy wheels would go spinning through the head. What immense journeys we made when the horse came, what wonderful woods and gulches we saw, what strange peoples we hailed as we rolled over the roads! It comes back to me like a far-off magic, and I yet remember the sensations as we sped down the "hills" (which were only divides between contiguous ravines). These thrilling experiences must have addled the head of the youngster until he craved other excitement, for I remember that once in going over and down one of these declivities I said to my father that some day there would be carriages not drawn even by horses. Such things must have been talked about in those faraway days.

In the vast distances of America the horse has played an unimaginable part in the drama of the great conquest. I remember the prairie schooners headed for the limitless West, a thousand miles and more away. The drivers had the vision of the promised land, and the horse fulfilled it. Day by day, night after night, in heat and cold, on table lands and over mountains, in fevered swamps, by strange forests, over riverbeds where floods had been, in coulees and on long grassy plains, in sand and dust and mire, the horses plodded on. The wagons groaned and creaked. The ruts grew deep with every new load. Sometimes Indians watched and wild beasts were startled and bounded away. To all this the faithful horses were dumb. They had no part in the program, no reward in the victory, yielded no expression to the landscape: theirs was to pull and to obey. Yet the horse had the strength to break away, to lie down and go no farther, to kick the outfit into fragments. He was fearful in war in the early centuries, a new enginery to strike consternation into the enemy. "The glory of his snorting is terrible," as the New Version renders the rebuke in Job. "He goeth out to meet the armed men. He mocketh at fear and is not dismayed; neither turneth he back from the sword." Yet this is the animal that in later time obeyed the demands of peace and conquered a continent by plodding work on overlands and on uncounted short hauls everywhere, the faithful servant of the advancing hosts of men.

High-spirited by nature, accustomed to the romping freedom of wide-open spaces, yet the horse is the most faithful and effective of all the bonded slaves man has recruited in the animal world. Some strange element of docility must have been implanted by nature in the plexus of his brain; and centuries of accumulated precept and practice must have trained the man to be master of the horse.

VIII. APPRECIATIONS

In many important ways the horse was the center of the farm operations; in some cases this is true in the present day. His harness and other gear were the everyday equipment, with which the farm boy was familiar from his earliest years; they were his to handle and to tinker. He knew the burble in the nostrils when the barn doors were opened in the morning, the eager expectant ears, the impatient attitude for water and food. With the horses he was off to the fields for the day's work; their strong odor was part of him; the gait, the pull, the strain were in his muscles also; he was keen with them for the noon hour when, sweating under the collars and the backpad, they bubbled their noses into the water trough. He knew how tired they were at night when he stripped their heavy harnesses and they evidenced their relief. He heard their stamp in the night. Now and then when a spirited horse was turned loose and naked in pasture he saw the elevated head and flowing mane and heard the high whinny like an echo of ancestral plains and a challenge to the world.

Only a few years ago there was a caste system in the horse world. The aristocrats among them drew the magnates, the well-to-do, and all the persons of importance, perhaps with liveries and attendants in the bargain. Now prosperous men and women express their prosperity by the brand of machine they buy, as befits the mechanical and inventive age in which we live. Now, also, the horse, with us in the United States, is only one of the working class (forgetting for the moment the racecourses). He still carries much of the burden of the world, but mostly in the background and out of sight. He is essentially now a farm animal, for only eight percent of the horses in the United States are elsewhere than on farms. He is becoming a creature apart, characteristic of a great background population. These people he will still express, and the boy will delight to train a colt in all the years we can foresee.

I cannot forgo the memories of certain horses I knew, friends and companions of my younger days. They knew my voice, I knew their ways. We knew the roads and fields together. I rolled and stood upon their backs and somersaulted from them; they never told anybody. One fair horse, a gentle but a lively bay, Fred by right of name, was my special comrade until old age overtook him. Uncounted miles the bareback horse and the barefooted boy went alone in the wild new places. In those far-off days, before the woods and back lands were fenced, we hunted the cattle together day by day throughout the grazing seasons. Rangy and limber cattle they were, not carrying the cargo of milk of these later, tamer times, and they went miles away when turned loose in the early morning. But Fred and I knew the tip-tap of their bells, and whether they were grazing, or walking, or lying down chewing the cud.

Often the night overtook us. I remember once being hopelessly lost at nightfall in a great virgin forest. I had missed all the trails and marks I knew. The darkness was intense. Startling sounds came out of the depths. Night odors enveloped us. Cool gusts rushed out of mysterious places. I peered for strange shapes, and fears began to take form, although fear was not supposed to haunt boys brought up against the big woods. Once I heard a deep voice almost human and very close by. Then I dropped the reins on Fred's shoulders, threw myself on his neck with my arms about it, and asked him to take me home. There I clung as he went between great tree shafts, pushed through brush, jumped over logs, and plowed through bogs. As he was silent, so was I. After a long time he stopped, dead still. I straightened up, and saw ourselves dimly in a highway. I asked him to go; he well knew the way; near midnight we were at the barn.

Once we were caught beyond a raging forest fire, such as sweeps through miles of slashing and bark-peeling in dry times, with intense heat and fearful flying embers and belching sheets of flame. I had been in such fires before, but this time we seemed to be completely cut off from home, and we knew not where we would come out if we took to the back country. Several exits we tried in vain. Finally I chose an old timber road then roaring with fire, dropped the reins, threw my arms about Fred's neck, shut my eyes, and said, "Run for your life." Like the wind, I thought, we went through the fire that pressed us on all sides; then Fred stopped, and we were safe once more.

An old bell of a leader cow hangs over my table as I write. I have just rocked it with my pen. It emits tones that have been silent through the years. Once more the great woods stand mysterious and dark, the log roads run into them and are lost, I hear footfalls I do not know, and soon Fred and I will sight the cows browsing in a clearing and he will circle them, and then we shall all go home together.

In his later days poor Fred was foundered and became stiff in his fore quarters. He would often stumble and fall, but he always waited for me to get up. His easy gallop was great sport in the summer days, and he seemed to know that I enjoyed it. Once he stumbled and fell heavily. I went over his head in a great crash and must have been stunned, for I remember Fred trying to rouse me with his nose.

Old Fred, companion of a boy, is dead long years and years ago. He has no grave. No rites were said. For aught I know the elements that comprised his supple frame and gentle nature may have entered into other horses that boys have loved in later years. Perhaps they too have gone away together in twilight and at noon and have come to the Gates of Wonder.

Evening

Uncle Daniel quit when the sun did.[7] It was "blasphemous-like" to work in the field after the sun had finished. The sun was Uncle Daniel's timepiece. He was up with the sun, for that was the beginning of a Lord's day and one should not waste the Lord's time in bed. He worked till the sun went down, and as a consequence he frequently took a half or whole day off. Sun-to-sun made a natural day, for did not the Good Book speak of the evening and the morning of the sixth day when man was put at work? Sometimes when haying or harvest was on, the bay-and-gray team would still be in the field at sundown, but Uncle Daniel would always stop and wait for the sun to sink out of sight, as a fitting observance of the proprieties. To "lay abed" long after the sun is up and to spend half of the night "cuttin' up" by lamplight was perilously near blasphemy to Uncle Daniel. He was sure the sun was made for a purpose and it would not be shining in the early morning unless it ought to shine; the chickens and cows knew this. He was suspicious of those persons who had things to do that could not be done in daytime; they would bear watching. And the evening was made for rest and the night for sleep.

To Uncle Daniel the evening was a reality, not merely a time to change clothes or to go to a show. It was a time for reverential pause and for thinking over the good and evil, the work and the accomplishment, of the day. In this attitude there was real relaxation, and a good preparation for honest sleep. He would enjoy the sunrise.

Hush is on the fields when the sun sinks beyond the West. Soon the birds begin to drop one by one into trees and other shelter; they are in their accustomed places. In spring the robin curls his vesper deep into the gloaming. The dog is at home. A subdued sound is in the barnyard. The cows

---

7. From *The Harvest of the Year to the Tiller of the Soil* (New York: Macmillan, 1927), 180–183.

are waiting to be milked. Horses, cattle, and wild things afield will soon be lying down for the night. It is a natural halt in the activities of the day. The courses of events are in halves; evening and twilight are an ending and a beginning, although one event so softly slips into the other that we are not excited by such a stupendous change.

I like to think of the farmer as having his fieldwork so well in hand that he can enjoy the hallowed pause of evening, not too tired for appreciation, not disinclined to yield to its impressions. Isaac, the cattleman, "went out to meditate in the field at the eventide." It is the time often to walk alone over the fields, particularly in spring and summer, in temperate regions, when the twilight is long. It is a time to see pastures and meadows leisurely, relieved from strain of labor; to go to the back fields and note what is happening there; to sit on stone or log and let the farm come to one; to listen by the brook; to hold converse with the herds, when they are quiet; to enter the woodlot in the gloaming; to break through weeds and brush; to stop at nest and burrow; to see new shapes arise; to walk back to the house in the late cool twilight.

At twilight are the senses rested and alert, the passions subdued, and the mind ready for suggestions. It is then that the exigencies of the day may be allowed to drop away, and the native nobler impulses find expression. It is a time for consecration, to the countryman particularly. It should be so to all men, for as [Fitz-Greene] Halleck writes, "There is an evening twilight of the heart." In Eden "they heard the voice of the Lord God walking in the garden in the cool of the day," which to us visualizes the evening.

Few of us know the evening any more. All we know is flare of lights, a bit of reading under the lamp, an automobile ride, a show, some triviality to kill the time painlessly. Few of us are so placed that we can know it in the old and natural way. Few of us have a horizon line, or really see the stars come out or note the constellations, or feel the moonrise, or know the fore-winds of the night. We are covered by roofs and limited by conveniences and conventionalities. The welkin of the approaching night is only a subject for exclamation now and then; it is not a canopy to live under.

It is easy to spoil the twilight.

Morning

If few of us know evening, still fewer know the morning.[8] This is attested by the daylight-saving expedient whereby, by setting the clock ahead, we get ourselves up an hour earlier for a season without shocking our sensibilities.

The night has given us relief, if digestion is good, and courage returns with morning light; much of this courage is lost if we lie too long, dallying with the day. There is decision in prompt rising. If the first part of the night has not been spent in some time-killing occupation and if we have not contracted the easy indulgence of reading in bed, then recuperation should be complete by sunrise; prompt sleeping is a condition to prompt rising.

It is a good occupation that requires attention early in the morning. The person acquires the habit of living a natural day, and he is likely to bring a refreshing nativeness to the problems of life. He is disinclined to give first importance to arbitrary and artificial programs. Most of us seem to be "at odds with morning," to adapt the reply of Lady Macbeth. We are in a state of grievance for having had to get up and of rebellion in general. This is not a reassuring attitude for a day's satisfaction. Of all the hours of the twenty-four, the hour when the sun and we get up together should be the most exhilarating; the exhilaration of freshness is gone an hour or two later; we have missed the opportunity. We found the "secret of arcady" in Louise Chandler Moulton's phrase, "when the morning birds were mad with glee." One of the offices of morning in the scheme of nature is its regeneration or renewal of all things; in the Mosaic account even the sea returned to its strength when the morning appeared.

It is not necessary always to await the sunrise to partake in the universal awakening. Some of the best elements of it are in the dawn, which is the

8. From *The Harvest of the Year to the Tiller of the Soil* (New York: Macmillan, 1927), 184–190.

first eye-opening of the day; for then an indefinable charm of newness and change is on the landscape. If one is not circumscribed by the customs of genteel society, if the mind is open to suggestion, one may then partake in the creation—when the stars go out and the world emerges from Chaos, when perhaps the crescent moon is in the East with its points reversed, when the birds awake and cattle rise and stretch in cool pastures, when the breath of the dew begins to distill, and voices are awake on distant farmsteads. If one is a companion of the early morning, one feels a peculiar ownership in the total affairs of the day. For the joy of working afield in the early morning, in fact for the joy of working at all, I commend Thoreau's account of his beanfield at Walden. "All the morning, glad of your society," the brown-thrasher sings, and you prefer the song to "leached ashes or plaster. It was a cheap sort of top dressing in which I had entire faith."

Morning is a specially appropriate time for stirring the soil and pulling weeds. Vigor is in the arms. We go into the work with valor, even audacity. The combative instincts are strong. The day is still cool. A man will go lustily through a patch of weeds that he would hardly attack at two o'clock in the afternoon. Undoubtedly personal contact with the early morning makes for good health and cheerfulness. I suppose this is because habitual prompt rising is conditioned on regular habits, considerate eating, proper use of the night, and a mental attitude of readiness. The dissipater can have no real joy of morning; that time is to him an awkward experience.

But the impulsion to seasonable rising and to the enjoyment of the morning is for most early risers not the sentiment of welcome to a newborn day. It lies in the practical necessity of the pursuit to which one is committed, as I have suggested. If one's work is one's own, and if it progresses toward a steadfast permanent result, one is eager to be about it. Few of us, aside from the farmer, can look forward to anything like a permanent property or establishment. Undoubtedly it is partly to satisfy the desire for something enduring that persons of means erect monumental buildings and found institutions. We are wont to say in this country that hard roads and telephones and the rest are radically changing the open country; yet, comparatively, changes in the properties themselves come slowly. I know farms that have remained essentially the same for more than half a century, and probably they will not change greatly in another fifty years. The farmhouse in which my father was born more than one hundred years ago still stands and is occupied, and it was not then new. There is pride in old farm buildings, even though inconvenient, for memories cling to them tenaciously. It is good that some of the homes of men remain generation after generation, tying the years together. Even yet it is expected that the farm is to remain in the family. When I see the man at work in the early hours, I know that back of his labor is the feeling, perhaps unrecognized by himself, that he is working for his farm and for his natural successors, not for an employer. He has reason to expect that at least his land and its improvements will remain. It is worth-while to be up with the sun; the morning, like the evening, is a reality.

Hard against absorbing realities, the sun-riser is not only ready but is ardent. What will the morning be? What new satisfactions will it open? Are you eager to take hold of the new day? If not, inquire of yourself for the reasons. If there is to be enthusiasm for life, it should be manifest at least in the renewal of morning.

THIS morning the stars were fading out when I went afield. A uniform indistinct gray was over the sky and I could not make out whether the day would be fair. A delicious coolness enveloped me. Mists were diffused over the fields and hung heavily in the herbage. The dew was deep and water-gray, for no reflecting light had yet struck it; the grass and fences and corn tops were soaked with it. Over the tufts of grass were spread the funnel webs of agelena, as misty as the night.

When I first came out, the upper branches of the trees were astir but now a hush was on the landscape as if in preparation for a shifting of scenes. A bright light came on the treetops and descended to the lower growths. A few late sweet pinks glowed in the garden as I passed, still holding the memory of June. Thin recemes of the second bloom of a pale larkspur stood by the walk. The marble white of snowberries shone like candy balls on their slender spray. A clump of rugosa roses was wide awake with the glimmer on the thin fair bloom. The little, erect, green heads of bindweed were evident on the hedge. A robin quipped. There was the quirk of a nuthatch from a nearby bole. The phoebe call of the chickadee came down from the grove, and then its more familiar cadencing note. I heard grackles somewhere. A flappy crow cawed far overhead. A flock of blackbirds went over. A dawn-winged dragonfly zigzagged across my sight, and disappeared.

Now the light was strong on the eastward side of things, on houses with shiny windows, on furrowed trunks of trees, and indefinite shapeless shades, remnants of the night, stretched to northwestward. A faint violet flush appeared in the West. The darks were still under the bushes. On chimneys and upper stubs in dead trees single birds were perched, as if waiting. Hens were abroad and began to feed. The diffused noisy chatter of sparrows could be heard about the barns. A bunch of dogs awoke far away. Over the fence as I passed a pumpkin flower hung motionless three feet from the ground, in a festoon of young hops, having carried its gold through the night; a perfect object it was with its soft and crimply pointed curving lobes and deep bell in which the clumpy stigmas stood and the hollowed ovary ring in the bottom;

it was too good and rare to lose, so I set my camera for it and let it stand some minutes. A soft indefinite fragrance was in the air, apparently a compound of many odors I could not identify.

The violet light now faded from the West. A golden dazzlement overspread the East. Then on the rim of the farther field thin low clouds broke and parted, the edges resplendent, and the limb of lord sun came through. Suddenly the fields were awake with splendor. A sweep of young goldenrod on a distant slope caught the luster, and the glory went from treetops to roofs and high fences, the greensward took it up, and the water in the pond caught fire. For a few moments the brilliance and the wonder filled the air and earth. Then wagons began to move somewhere, a few hardy early risers emerged, smoke was in the chimneys, and the day became commonplace.

IX CODA, THE AGRARIAN WAY

Nay! There is no finality,
No dictum to obey
Nature is one vast infinity,
And the mind a small timidity
Feeling the way.

—From "Nay," *Wind and Weather*
(New York: Scribner, 1916)

T*he Seven Stars*—doubtless Liberty Hyde Bailey's most forgotten title from the Background Books series—is the source of this strange and wonderful essay-cum-allegory entitled "Journey's End." The final chapter in this fantastical volume finds the protagonist, Questor, arriving, as the chapter title "Journey's End" intimates, at the threshold of adulthood. As if a modern-day Arthurian knight, Questor is helped to epiphany by a leading lady, Winneth, who serves as both spiritual counsel and guiding muse. Questor is likely a semiautobiographical representation of Bailey as a young man as well as a composite figure of the many idealistic farmers' sons Bailey encountered as a lifelong teacher. Accordingly, Winneth bears some similarities to Annette Smith, the young woman who would become the real-life Mrs. Bailey. This comparison is further suggested by the tonal harmonies between "Journey's End" and the last poem, "Annette," in Bailey's Background Book of poems, *Wind and Weather,* which reads: "Tis many years since we were born / Tis many years since we were wed— / The winds have blown from night till morn / As they will blow when we are dead." "Journey's End" achieves resolution when Winneth provides young Questor a list of life principles—haunting statements of faith and caution that serve as an agrarian coda.

Journey's End

At last the letter comes, the more welcome because it is earnestly desired.[1] It is a letter of keen comment and suggestive advice. When he met her[2] in the early college days he was attracted by her wholesome, unaffected manner, by her familiarity with a few real books, by a certain athletic resilient habit, by her dislike of personal publicity, and by the readiness with which she lent herself to the affairs of the institution and associates.

The letter approves his pilgrimage in general. "It is well for you," it says, "to leave the usual places, to measure yourself against other situations. You are wandering indeed, but you appear to hold your determination to find a real rather than an expedient anchorage."

There is something in the letter that seems to hold her aloof until he finds that anchorage. This startles him. Again she says nothing directly about income and finances. Perhaps again she takes that for granted; and if she does, then certainly she had confidence in his ability to provide. Apparently she is waiting for a declaration of his purposes in life rather than any decision as to the gainful occupation in which he shall settle.

"It is not for me," she writes, "to find the mainspring of your life for you. If it is not real with you, then it will not last. In appraising any life, physical efficiency is assumed. Certain moral qualities likewise are assumed. But what is to be the motive? For what aim is one to live? The fact that most persons have no real aim beyond that of being 'successful' and comfortable, is no reason why the motive should not be discovered and put in the program early in life."

---

1. From *The Seven Stars* (New York: Macmillan, 1923), 158–165.
2. In keeping with Bailey's prose style elsewhere in this anthology, the impersonal pronoun "he" is used here and throughout in place of the character's allegoric name, "Questor," as is the pronoun "me," when it refers to Questor. "Her" has likewise been inserted in place of the original character name, "Winneth."

"What motive is to guide me, that plainly is the inference," says he, stopping midway in the letter. To make money, that is good but not sufficient. To live for applause is as empty as the noise of it. To be honest is surely not an aim, but a common decency: that is assumed to start with. To be religious is likewise not an aim: that is a man's responsibility and privilege; it guides and leads him where he would go. To be a good craftsman, whether the craft is making machines or crops or pictures or books or fabrics, is surely not the goal: we assume that one shall be competent in his craft, occupation, or profession. To be proficient is only to develop one's capabilities. He has known more than one person who had all these qualities and who yet went to seed as soon as he had secured a good job or a comfortable income. It is a sorry education that trains men only in knowledge and efficiency. To serve one's fellows is indeed a blessing to the servitor; and because it is a high form of action, then must one choose thoughtfully what particular kind of service one shall render. These and others like unto them were the kinds of sentiments that arose in the young man's mind before he was halfway through the letter. Then he continued the reading.

"I have followed your accounts and descriptions with some care. You have not put your desires into form. Let me suggest," she says:

"Do not be afraid of your enthusiasms."

"Stand by your ideals."

"Enter not the race for wealth. Do not take a job merely for the money there is in it, on the false assumption that when you have earned the money you will begin to live. It is a common fallacy—that a man will make his 'pile' and then begin to live; but he may then be too old and set to know how to begin to live."

"Begin to live now. Do not wait for retirement, or for old age, or for the sweet by-and-by, not even for tomorrow—tomorrow never comes."

"If possible, avoid a position in which you must subjugate your spirit to the routine; or a place or profession in which etiquette dominates the action."

"Do not live in a place or community where money sets the standard of merit or preferment."

"Do not enter into competition for social position. Such position will fail you in the end."

"Take part. Develop the quality of making steadfast friends, not merely admirers. Cultivate good fellowship."

"Fit yourself to love your work. Give service above that for which you are paid in the agreement. Serve for service sake."

"Be careful of publicity. You may advertise goods, but do not advertise yourself. Beware the glittering microbe of popularity."

"Prepare to travel far. The distance matters little. It may be around the world or around your premises."

"Live not in an atmosphere either of fear or of protest."

"Be active, but do not hurry. Have no vacant moments, even though your hands are folded."

"If you would be 'rich' desire it not quickly. The sensibilities should grow with the purse: this requires time. And be sure you know when you shall have accumulated enough."

"Perhaps these suggestions will help you to formulate your methods. Then you are to arrive at a philosophy of life. What is to be the nature of your satisfactions?"

As one stunned does he stand when he reads these admonitions. There is no conclusion in them, no statement of "philosophy" she would have him develop and declare. These are only "methods"—preparations, means to an end.

To a letter such as this he cannot reply at once. The night comes on. It is full of dreams and disconnected thoughts. Morning breaks. It brings a fresh, clean world. It is the morning of creation, with new hills, new trees, new skies, new labors. The cattle in the pasture are essential. The old man who milks is also essential; he is part of the scene. All persons are essential. Everything looks interesting. The harmonies are greater than the discords. Confusion revolves itself into concord; and concord is beauty.

"The meaning of life is its beauty," is the phrase that comes unawares to him, so suddenly and so comprehensively that it startles him. The obvious is likely to occur to us last. To find the beauty in labor, in objects, in actions, in sensations, in sentiments, in situations, to keep the earth clean, is a real quest, worthy and enduring, a prospect that widens as one looks, rises as one goes. This is the supreme manifestation of living. One must find the way to realize it. The highest beauty is the beauty of good personality.

The young man has read history enough to know that the problem, as he begins to analyze it, is not his alone. One must find the way to make one's products beautiful in the best sense, and to see that the same spirit is carried into actions and conduct. It then expresses itself in institutions, and in that complex of acceptable human actions known as civilization. The civic beauty undoubtedly culminated in the Greeks. There must have been much beauty of the common life to have found such noble expressions in architecture, sculpture, and literature. May not we, also, add beauty unto usefulness?

To every age its own dominating activity is the highest expression of human attainment. Involved in our vast commercial and political affairs, we forget the periods through which men have passed, and we are little concerned to foresee a larger epoch. After we have gratified ourselves in the exploitation of the earth, and race will be prepared to welcome another order. Assuredly we are not going back to the ancient, although we ought not to lose what it has bequeathed to us. Undoubtedly, we are in the most wonderful, as well as the most important, epoch in human history: we should be ready, then, for still more satisfying achievements.

We have not yet arrived at such a constitution of society as will make life mean even the half of which it is capable; but nevertheless and for all that, it is the privilege of each one of us to open the soul toward the sunrise.

Now the meditations swing back to the personal side. One does not need to look always for the highest salary or income, as if there were no other end in life, thinks he as he ponders. Some day we shall honor the person who declines to "make money" and to accept preferment, as an indication that he has other and better resources. The character of the work and the situation in which one finds oneself are real assets. One may take the offering or find the occupation that most nearly satisfies, or at least the one that does not violate the aspirations, offend the sensibilities, or shorten the vision. Therein may one work happily and loyally. Verily, one must have the creature comforts and some of the amenities; one must accumulate the little competence for safety and to protect the society against the burden of one's misfortune or support; but the great need, the excelling privilege, is to grow and keep buoyant.

All this he writes, and he is arrived at his declaration: "This granted, then *my aim is the artistic expression of life.*" "On this prospect are you ready?"

Promptly comes the answer, "Yes."

Index

Agassiz, Louis, xv, 15, 80, 121, 224
agrarians and agrarianism, xi, xiii, xiv, xv,
  1, 3, 4, 5–10, 17, 19, 21, 24–25, 28–29,
  32–33, 39, 77, 110, 135–36, 166, 188–89,
  202, 216, 228, 254
anthropomorphism, 6
Apple Tree, The, 4, 31
aristocracy, 137, 141, 144–45, 165, 240
automobile, 54, 150, 244, 249

Background books, 3, 28–30, 254
back-to-the-farm movement, 95, 135, 200
Bailey, Annette (Annette Smith), 9, 10, 13,
  34, 254
Bailey, Ethel Zoe, 13, 34
Bailey, Liberty Hyde: childhood and
  adolescence of, 7–8; college and university
  studies of, 9–12; Cornell University tenure
  of, 13–27; death of, 35; legacy of, 36–37;
  retirement of, 27–35
Bailey, Sara, 13, 33
Beal, William, 9, 10, 30
Berry, Wendell, xii, xiii, xiv, 1, 4, 6, 7, 10,
  24, 39
biocentrism, xi–xii, 6, 135, 137
Burroughs, John, 13–14, 27, 39, 228
business, xii, 43, 46–47, 58, 78–79, 95,
  107–9, 132, 138, 139, 140, 148–49, 155,
  158–61, 164, 174, 193, 197, 201–3, 210,
  213, 215, 220

city, xiv, 17, 23, 72, 94, 96, 98, 124, 126,
  128, 134, 139, 152–53, 155–57, 169,
  173–76, 188, 195–202, 205, 209, 212–14,
  220, 229
civilization, xiii, 58, 63, 82, 85, 95, 98,
  103–5, 107, 110, 114, 128, 133, 153,

155, 157, 164, 169, 172, 181, 188,
  195–99, 203, 206, 219, 257
community, xiii, 3, 7, 15, 58, 77, 89,
  93, 125, 135, 178, 201, 203–5, 206,
  212, 256
competition, 57, 75, 88, 107, 108, 129, 136,
  144, 148, 158, 161, 164, 256
conservation, xiv–xv, 2, 19, 25, 29, 32–33,
  78, 91, 98–100, 102, 103, 105
cookery, 67–69, 73
Cornell University, xiv, 2, 3, 5, 12 13, 15,
  17–20, 22, 24, 26–27, 30, 31, 33, 34,
  36–37
corporations, 102, 202, 214
Country Life Commission, The, xi, xiii, xv,
  1–2, 4, 18, 19, 20, 24–25, 77–78, 189
Country Life in America, 2, 16
Country Life movement, The, 3, 17, 20–21,
  99, 111, 188, 195
*Country-life Movement in the United States,
  The*, 4, 23, 78
curriculum, 26, 115, 117
Cyclopedia of American Agriculture, 16
Cyclopedia of American Horticulture, 16

Darwin and Darwinism, xiii, xv, 6, 77,
  87–88, 224, 240
Day, Edmund, 2, 37
democracy, xiii, 29–30, 45, 81, 85, 136,
  142, 155, 159, 162–65, 191–92, 194, 234
dominion, 77, 92–93, 95–97, 100, 138, 159,
  163, 165, 179, 182, 186, 233, 244

ecospiritualism, xii, 6
education, xiii, 3, 15, 19–20, 23–24, 26,
  46–47, 50, 74, 80–81, 97, 99, 110,
  114–15, 117–18, 123, 126–31, 139–42,

Index

education *(continued)*
  144, 151, 161–62, 165, 177, 188–89,
  193, 195, 197, 206–7, 212, 221, 256
Emerson, Ralph Waldo, 13, 27, 115, 188
enmity, 84, 87, 136, 158–60
experiment stations, 13, 18–19, 24–26, 54,
  111, 129, 152, 190
extension (agricultural), 11, 18, 20, 23–24,
  26, 117, 129, 191

family farms, xiii, 17, 19, 24, 148
farmer's wife, 18, 189, 203–5, 212–13
Field, Forest, and Garden Botany, 15
Field Notes on Apple Culture, 11
food, 28, 33, 39, 56, 59, 60–62, 64–70, 73,
  93–94, 103–5, 144, 154, 183–84, 204,
  208, 211, 237, 241
forest, 55, 61, 68, 79, 92–93, 100, 103, 105,
  149–50, 152, 166, 169, 170–76, 182,
  186, 226, 229, 245, 247
fruit, 10–11, 47, 68, 70–74, 94, 214,
  229–30, 242–43

gardens and gardening, 13–15, 17, 27, 33,
  36, 41, 60, 73, 77, 90, 93, 97, 122, 146,
  154, 157, 189, 200, 206, 214, 222, 235,
  239, 241, 249, 252
Gore, Al, xii–xiii
government, xii, xiii, 19, 24, 25–26, 28, 78,
  80–81, 95, 102, 107, 108–9, 129, 139,
  144, 148, 152, 158–65, 188, 190–94,
  208, 225
grandparents, xiv–xv, 1, 58, 133, 214–15
Gray, Asa, xv, 7, 9, 10, 15, 121
Green Man, xii, xiii

*Harvest of the Year to the Tiller of the Soil,
  The,* 2, 3, 57
hay and haying, xiv, 39, 50, 52–53, 59
Holy Earth, The, 1, 3–6, 29–30, 34, 78, 135
home economics, 18, 78, 128, 206–7
horse, 45, 54, 60, 62, 74–75, 170–71, 176,
  199, 210, 228, 244–47, 249
horticulture, 2, 5, 7, 9–12, 14–16, 20, 28,
  30, 31, 33, 35–36

individualism, 27, 82, 155, 162, 197
Integument-Man, 110, 112–14

Jefferson, Thomas, 6, 19, 25, 27–28

landscape, 8, 14–15, 61, 74, 89–90, 92–93,
  133, 168, 170, 209, 218, 229–30, 232,
  236, 245, 251–52

Leopold, Aldo, xii, xiv, 1
liberalism, xiii, 39
Liberty Hyde Bailey Hortorium, 22–23, 36
literature, 28, 89, 117, 169, 197, 216, 218,
  223–26, 231, 257
Lord, Russell, 32–34

machinery, 45, 89, 132, 155, 193, 205, 211,
  213, 221, 227
Manual of Cultivated Plants, 16, 35
Michigan Agricultural College (MAC), 9,
  11, 12
middleman, 78, 106–9, 201
mining, 92, 94–95, 105
morning, 41, 61, 65, 88, 148, 169, 171, 213,
  228, 234–35, 241, 246, 248, 250–53, 257
Muir, John, xii, 5, 6, 8, 13, 27, 77, 79, 228

nails, 49, 50, 51, 154
nationalism, 160, 165
nature study, xiii, 2, 3, 5, 12–15, 17, 18, 26,
  28, 33, 110, 112–17, 119, 120–26
Nature-Study Idea, The, 4, 15
naturist, 88, 97, 135, 143, 166, 178
New England, 8, 96, 119, 155, 173, 208
New York Times, The, 24–25, 31–32, 35

Old Testament, The, 140, 222
ornithology, 9, 14
Outlook to Nature, The, 4, 15, 32

palms, 31, 33, 34–36, 228–29
peace, xiii, 4, 25, 29, 77, 85, 88, 91, 111,
  159, 162, 185, 190, 245
peach, 228, 242–43
Pinchot, Gifford, 19, 29
planetary agrarianism, 6, 29
Plant Breeding, 13
pomology, 9, 11, 15, 31, 71
Progressivism, xiii, xv, 19, 23, 25–26

radio, xiv, 39, 54
rain, 42, 61, 63, 65, 96, 103–5, 124, 133,
  134, 140, 144, 169, 171, 174, 183, 212,
  219, 228, 232, 234, 235–38, 243
Report of the Country Life Commission,
  18, 22
Roberts, Isaac Phillips, 12, 15, 17, 37, 239
Roosevelt, Theodore, xi, xiii, 2, 9, 17, 19,
  20–23, 25–26, 29, 86

Sage Place, 16, 35
science, 2, 7, 10–13, 15, 19, 23, 27–28, 32,
  62, 79, 93, 110, 113–14, 116, 119, 120,

124, 126, 129–30, 141, 161, 180–82,
185, 207, 216, 220, 223–25, 231
Seven Stars, The, 3, 10
*Sketch of the Evolution of Our Native
Fruits,* 13
soil, xiv, 39, 56, 58, 60–63, 66, 73, 75, 78,
94, 96, 98–101, 121–22, 128, 130, 132,
138, 140, 152, 154, 157, 177, 183, 185,
209–12, 214, 235–36, 240, 242–43, 251
South Haven, Michigan, 7, 9, 13, 34
Speculum, The College, 8, 9, 11, 12
suburbanism, 14, 133, 135, 189, 199–200
sunrise, 169–70, 183, 248, 250, 258
Survival of the Unlike, 13

*Talks Afield: About Plants and the Science
of Plants,* 11
teachers and teaching, xii, xv, 11, 13, 27, 37,
80, 98, 110, 112–14, 119–23, 125–26,
130, 156, 207, 215, 222, 254
tenancy, 147–48
Thoreau, Henry David, xv, 27, 39, 135, 154,
166, 251
trade, 56, 65, 93, 107, 143, 149, 156,
159–61, 186, 202, 241

Turner, Frederick Jackson, 8, 166
Tusser, Thomas, 64–66

USDA, 19, 22–23, 190

Wagenen, Jared Van, Jr., 36–37, 53
Wallace, Henry A., xiii, xv, 1
Wallace, "Uncle Henry," xv, 1–2, 8–9, 19,
21, 30
Wallaces' Farmer, 2, 19, 21
war, xiii, 25, 28–31, 34, 40, 77, 84–86,
93, 103, 107, 117, 136, 145, 158–61,
163–65, 219, 245
weed, 41–42, 53, 60, 61, 122, 154, 218,
228, 236, 237, 239–41, 249, 251–52
What Is Democracy?, 2, 3, 28, 136, 162
Whitman, Walt, 210, 216, 221–22
wind, 65, 96, 105, 113, 118, 122, 124,
134, 140, 152, 154, 170, 172–73, 175,
183, 186, 206, 212, 219, 221, 228, 229,
231–34, 243, 249, 254
Wind and Weather, xv, 3, 254
Words Said About a Birthday, 3, 34, 37
workmanship, 17, 42, 51, 75
world wars, 29–30, 34, 164

About the Editor

ZACHARY MICHAEL JACK, fourth-generation Iowa farmer's son and great-grandson of the farm conservation writer Walter Thomas Jack, is the author or editor of many books, including several previous collections on rural life: *Love of the Land: Essential Farm and Conservation Readings from an American Golden Age, 1880–1920*; *Black Earth and Ivory Tower: New American Essays from Farm and Classroom*; and *The Furrow and Us: Essays on Soil and Sentiment*. Two of the books, *Black Earth and Ivory Tower* and *The Furrow and Us*, have been nominated for the Theodore Saloutos Award for the year's best book on agricultural history. Jack has presented his research on rural life and writing at the Agricultural History national conference and the Newberry Seminar for Rural History, among others. He has also served as a guest editor of the journal *Southern Rural Sociology*.

Zachary Michael Jack's love of nature originates in his family's one-hundred-and-fifty-year-old Iowa Heritage Farm and timber. He is the founding director of the agrarian School of Lost Arts for children, advisory board member for the Interversity Place Studies Listserv, and a consulting editor for the series Voices from the American Land edited by environmental journalist and policymaker Charles E. Little. The author of two place-based collections of poetry, *The Inanity of Music and Wings* and *Perfectly Against the Sun,* Jack is an assistant professor of English at North Central College, where he teaches courses in rural studies and serves as a member of the environmental studies faculty.